The Fool (Khenté)

«ԽԵՆԹԸ»

Raffi (Hakob Melik Hakobian)

CONTENTS

AUTHOR'S BIOGRAPHY

Hakob Melik Hakobian (Armenian: Յակոբ Մելիք-Յակոբեան), better known by his pen name Raffi (Armenian: Րաֆֆի), is a renowned Armenian author born in 1835 in Payajouk, an Armenian village situated in the Salmas province (presently in the north of Iran, near Lake Ourmia) in Persia. He died in 1888 in Tiflis (present-day Tbilisi). Raffi is a prominent figure of Armenian literature.

His father, a wealthy merchant and farmer, belonged to the local bourgeoisie. Thus, Raffi's financial situation, along with his being the eldest of a large family of 13 children, allowed him to benefit from a high quality education.

His education began at Ter Todik, his village's school, which was known for its strictness and punishment methods. Raffi described and denounced these methods in one of his novels, Kaytzer. At the age of 12, Raffi was sent by his father to continue his secondary education at a boarding school in Tiflis, away from his native land.

Tiflis, today known as Tbilisi, was at the time one of the largest Armenian intellectual centers. Alas, due to the degradation of his father's financial affairs, Raffi was forced to return to his native country. It was at this point that he began teaching Armenian language and history in the Aramian school in Tabriz, the Augoulis school in the Nakhitchevan region and, later on, in Tiflis.

Throughout his life, Raffi took many trips to the villages and provinces of Eastern and Western Armenia. Wherever he visited, he became aware of the daily misery experienced by the unarmed Armenian population, who lived in constant terror of the Turks and Kurds. Raffi, like other Armenian intellectuals, was convinced that it was not viable to continue living thus. He would thereafter seek to deeply transform Armenian society. In order to do so, it was necessary for him to make the people themselves aware of the tragic reality in which they lived.

Raffi was a prolific writer. His works were published in the magazines *Mshak* and *Ardzakank*. His main work, The Fool, first appeared in series in the magazine *Mshak*, (an Armenian journal founded by Grigor Artsruni in 1872) and was a great success. *Mshak* played an important role in awakening the Armenian people from the lethargy that had overcome the majority of them since the loss of Armenian independence at the end of the 14th century. Raffi's patriotic text was read by virtually all Armenian youth of the time. In his novels, Raffi depicted characters of national heroes and Armenian revolutionaries. In fact, there is a well-known Armenian phrase that goes: "there are no Armenian freedom fighters (Feddayines) that have not read Raffi."

Raffi considered that teaching the population the Armenian language was a fundamental and vital measure. He used various methods (the press, novels, teaching) to improve the education of the Armenian commoners.

Raffi passed away in 1888 in Tiflis (present-day Tbilisi), and his funeral attracted a huge crowd. He is buried in the Pantheon of Armenians at the Khodjivank cemetery in Tbilisi, where Hovhannes Tumanian, Gabriel Sundukian, Ghazaros Aghayan and Grigor Artsruni are also buried.

Presently, there is a school as well as a street named after Raffi in Yerevan, Armenia. His works were translated in several languages.

AN INTRODUCTION
By K. A. SARAFIAN

Head Department of Education, University of La Verne Visiting Prof. of Education. University of Southern California (USC), Summer Session.

I was delighted to receive the urgent request of the publishers, asking me to write an introduction to the English version of the "Khent" (The Fool) of Raffi, translated by Jane S. Wingate.

This request I accepted with pleasure. For the translation into English of a choice number of masterpieces of Armenian literature, ancient and modern, has been one of my fondest dreams. I believe that we, the Armenians of America. Owe a great debt of gratitude to this glorious country, the United States of America, under whose protective wings we have been enjoying peace, prosperity, happiness and unlimited opportunities for growth in culture, material wealth and creativeness. In fact, we are all refugees of political persecution. We have found here a haven of safety after having been tortured mentally, morally and, at almost regular intervals, physically, at the hands of our merciless rulers in Turkey. And some of us owe our very existence to the generous philanthropy of the American people who have come to our aid and snatched from the claws of death our half dead and buried bodies from the burning sands of the Arabian desert, where our age-long persecutors, the inexorable Turkish authorities had driven us during the dark days of the First World War with the flimsy excuse that we were in sympathy with the Allied cause.

We enjoy now in America, "The Land of Liberty and The Home of the Brave," a cultural democracy, the like of which is not found anywhere in the world on such a vast scale. To this cultural heritage every race has contributed something worthwhile from its precious spiritual resources. This fact explains why America is blessed more than any other country with an incomparably rich culture and a way of life which is a shining example of unity wrought in a framework of diversity and heterogeneity. This wonderful national unity and like-mindedness is not brought about by extraneous pressures but by a subtle spiritual force, embodied in

1

friendliness, brotherhood, cooperation, sharing and a free and unhampered interaction of mind upon mind, of culture upon culture in the pursuit of a better, nobler, richer way of life.

I am convinced that we, the Americans of Armenian origin, have made some worthy contributions to this contemporary life of the United States. I am sure, however, that we can make and we ought to make still greater contributions.

It is well known that as an ancient people with an excellent culture, the Armenians have a rich intellectual and spiritual heritage. In their literary possessions they have many hidden treasures which have not been tapped adequately. These must be brought to light. Great scholars of Europe and Armenia, such as Hubschmann, Meillet, Keltzer, Marr, and Atontz and a host of others have attempted in the past to unearth some of the precious spiritual possessions of our ancestors. But this has been only a beginning. It behooves us, the intellectual leaders of America, to cultivate the field further and deeper. Do many people know that numerous Hellenistic, philosophical, literary and religious works of great merit from the third, fourth, and fifth centuries exist in the Armenian language? And that they have been preserved for world-civilization in their Armenian versions, the original Greek copies having perished in the cataclysmic events of the past ages?

Who does not remember, as a student of history, the name of Eusebuis of Caesarea whose "Chronicles" were retranslated from the ancient Armenian into Latin, the original manuscript having been lost? Again, it was in the Armenian language that the major part of the writings of Philo of Judea were preserved. This famous professor of the University of Alexandria was well known for his great contributions in effecting the fusion of the Christian, Greek and Hebraic cultures during the first century of the Christian era. And the works of last but not least among the cluster of great writers, the Stoic philosopher Zeno of the third century, was also kept from oblivion and obliteration thanks to the fact that it was translated into the ancient Armenian language during the Golden Age of Armenian literature.

Besides these great masterpieces of the ancient Hellenic world, we can be proud of the works of our own Armenian historians of the Middle Ages and also of the subsequent periods, whose chronicles and histories, if brought to light, can shed new light upon the mysteries and problems surrounding the relationships of crusaders and the Eastern despots, and especially upon the history of the Middle East and the Near East. These works are chiefly buried in the Armenian language, and thus are not accessible to American and European scholars.

What about the many important liturgical, medical, mathematical, and

2

particularly exquisite poetic works of the Armenian authors, of ancient and modern times, which are hidden behind the curtain of language inaccessibility? Will it not be a great contribution to the civilization of the world in general and more particularly to the culture of the English speaking people of our adopted and beloved country if the best of these precious pieces of work could be rendered into English and brought to light thereby?

Now you understand why I greet with particular enthusiasm this noble labor of love, of Mrs. Wingate. Who has rendered into English, "Khent" (The Fool) one of the chief works of Raffi, the great novelist of Armenia, who was really the founder of the Armenian historical novel, and the novel of realistic portrayal of the life of a people, whose country, like ancient Gaul, was divided into three parts; one part suffering under the yoke of Turkey, the second part dragging its existence under the heels of the Czars of Russia, and the third part withering away under the oppressive rule of the Shahs of Persia.

The author of "Khent" whose real name was Hagop Hagopian, is well known by his pseudonym, Raffi. He was an Armenian hailing from that part of Armenia which was under the Mohammedan rule of the Shah of Persia. He made his debut as a writer in Tiflis, away from his native land, joining the literary school of "Mishag", which was an Armenian journal founded by Krikor Arzrouni in 1872. This publication under the wise leadership of its founder and editor, played a very striking role in kindling sparks of enlightenment and causing the awakening of the Armenian people from the deep lethargy in which the vast majority of the Armenians slumbered for centuries after they lost their political independence in 1393 A.D.

The editor of "Mishag" saw in the work of this bright young man the possibilities of a great writer and he encouraged him in his first faltering attempts at writing. Raffi, on his part, scrupulously attended the literary soirees given by the editor of "Mishag", and gradually attained refinement in his crude literary endeavors. He published in "Mishag" several short stories based upon his observation of the Armenians in Persia, Russia and the Caucasus. These were fine beginnings. Gradually his observations became keener, his literary style became more fluent, colorful, attractive and of fine quality, and his insight into the complicated mysteries of the life of the Armenian peasant especially became deeper, and his forecasts for the future became more prophetic.

In all his works he protested against injustices, great or small, he exposed human foibles, individual or collective, and scathingly assailed tyrannies, and fiendish atrocities, perpetrated by the Persians, Kurds and Turks. As a teacher in different localities, at different times, he had opportunities to study the life of the Armenians, and their educational conditions. Without

3

reserve, he ridiculed the tradition bound teachers in the imaginary person of Der Totig, and he censured the frivolities and laziness of the Armenian students attending the Russian Universities. On the other hand, he had words of commendation for the purposefulness and seriousness of the famous group of Armenian students of Germany. Some of these students became the champions of the movement for reawakening Armenian culture in Russia and the Caucasus.

Raffi himself was the protégé of one of these products of German education, Krikor Arzrouni, the editor of "Mishag". Having been steeped in the ideals of this intellectual nobility Raffi himself used the novels as an instrument of propagating these ideals of intellectual and political regeneration, and whipped public opinion into more promising and creative forms.

The novel for Raffi was not merely a literary genre the purpose of which was entertainment, but it was the most effective means of gaining the attention and interest of a vast multitude of readers imbuing them with his cherished ideals and dreams of a perfect society.

"The Fool" is one of these novels in which the author has a thesis to expound and a sermon to preach. The theme of the story is taken from the bloody events which followed as the aftermath of the war of 1877 between Turkey and Russia. Raffi in his travels had witnessed the deplorable conditions to which the Armenian people were subjected. These were chiefly peace loving peasants whose sole purpose in life was to till the soil and to produce good harvests in peaceful enjoyment of their quiet and serene life. He had witnessed how these industrious and extremely docile villagers were oppressed and subjected to all kinds of inequities on the part of the Turkish officials. He had observed with indignation how these innocent people were menaced continuously by the rapes, plunder and criminal attacks of the hordes of Kurdish bands, whose blood thirsty instincts were sharpened to a keener edge by the heated pressures brought upon them by the officials of the Sultans of Constantinople. In spite of the fact that their living conditions were unbearable, the Armenian peasants did not utter a word in protest, having been trained in docility by the clergy for centuries with the Biblical exhortation: "If they smite thee on the one cheek, turn the other also to them."

Raffi having seen the Armenian refugees who had escaped certain death at the hands of their pursuing enemies, the Turkish soldiers, in the province of Alashgerd during the Russo-Turkish War of 1877, set his imagination into motion and gave us a novel of great merit, weaving a succession of captivating episodes, gruesome events, and portraying the fascinating pictures of the Armenian peasant, first in the enjoyment of his life in the confines of his serene home and then his wanderings away from his home, tortured in the clutches of famine, pestilence and unscrupulous people.

4

This is a captivating story, which was read avidly by people of his time and which is read with the same consuming interest at the present moment by people who are remote in time and space from the scenes of events depicted in this novel.

Raffi has one obsession, which comes to the surface, time and time again, namely, he finds himself unable to comprehend how human beings can be so peace loving, so docile and servile that they will not dare lift a finger in protest against the perpetrator of atrocities which transcend human imagination by their extreme brutality. Referring to the scene of slaughter at Bayazid, Raffi puts in the mouth of the imaginary hero, Vartan, these words: "Look, look! In all the city you do not find a man who raises his hand against his slayer. What more can be done to a man to move him to passionate resistance? They have burned his house before his eyes; they have roasted his children; they have dragged away his wife and daughters; the man has seen all this yet he humbly bows his head to receive the stroke of the sword!" Again, Vartan makes this trenchant remark: "this people do not know how to die with honor."

The thesis of Raffi is that his people should be taught to defend their honor, their wealth and their lives, he longs to restore in the hearts of the docile Armenian peasants the heroic spirit of the Armenian national hero, Vartan, who won for the Armenians in the fifth century A.D. freedom of conscience by fighting with his small band of heroes against the multitudinous hordes of the Persian Zoroastrian fanatics.

Leaving to the reader the unique enjoyment of reading the fascinating and intriguing events related in the novel, let us turn now to a brief analysis of the artistic texture and structure of the novel.

Raffi was a writer endowed with a vivid imagination, keen observation and unbounded idealism. His novel is a mixture embodying all these qualities. He is almost incomparable in the portrayal of types and delineation of characters. Some of his depicted personages are real and charming, such as old man Khacho, the head of the village who represents the practical wisdom, the admirable industry, the harmonious and virtuous life prevailing in the peasant home. Khacho's household is a beautiful picture, inspiring at times, artistically portrayed by this great novelist, who excelled in the art of depicting domestic scenes. One loves to look at this painting of the simple life of the Armenian peasant with its serenity, quietude, its industry, its harmony and cooperative spirit. Another real character is Thomas Effendi, an Armenian who is employed by the Turkish authorities as the tax collector of the district. In him you will find everything that is corrupt, everything that is base, ignoble and unlovely. Der Marook, the village priest, in whom one sees the decadence of the splendid spirit of devotion and self-abnegation of the Armenian clergy of the bygone ages. In passing, I must point out that Raffi betrays, throughout the novel, a little

5

exaggerated anti-clerical spirit, so prevalent in his time, and perhaps justified. In this novel one finds oneself face to face, in the panorama of kaleidoscopic events, with the picture of the cruel and wily Kurdish chieftain, the rapacious and salacious Fattah Bey. In contrast with these, one also comes across the portraits of some unreal characters, the heroes of the story, created by the fertile imagination of the author. Vartan is the chief hero, who is in love with the comely daughter of this good man Khacho yet he is more in love with his ideal, namely an intense yearning to save his people from the shackles of slavery, ignorance, and turpitude. We meet other secondary heroes also, the inexperienced Tiutiukjian, the apostle of new ideas and ideals, and Melik-Mansoor, the astute and capable agent of this new imaginary state of affairs, which is beautifully depicted in the final chapter of the book, the dream of Vartan. The epitome of the entire philosophy of the author is condensed in this dream which Vartan sees at the tomb of his fiancee. He dreams that the peasant has been emancipated from the chains of tyranny. Everyone enjoys genuine freedom from fear and poverty. He dreams that the ideal of the inalienable rights of the individual for the pursuit of happiness has been realized and people live at last in peace side by side.

The excellent qualities of the novelist lie chiefly in his superior style of writing, which is lucid as the limpid waters of a mountain spring, colored with fascinating metaphors; a style pulsating with life, imagination, poetic rhythm, vividness, and warmth. If R. Abovian was the founder of the novel for the Eastern Armenians, with pioneering efforts, and crudities of his newly introduced (vulgar) vernacular language, Raffi was the founder of the Armenian novel, with a perfection of style, with an intriguing structure.

We must not forget that everything is not perfect in Raffi's works. He is weak at times, especially in the denouement of events and development of his characters. His delineation of characters and types is fascinating yet some are unnatural and artificial. However it may be, all his novels, and we have a host of them, are extremely interesting and captivating. They are readable and they have powerfully influenced all Armenians of succeeding generations, not only the common people but also intellectuals and writers as well.

The translation of the "Khent" (The Fool) by Mrs. Wingate, is therefore an effort worthy of our wholehearted commendation and applause. We are confident that not only Armenians of American origin, but Americans of diverse origins will appreciate this novel, and all the novels of Raffi, one of which "Samuel" was recently translated serially in an Armenian American publication.

Mrs. Jane S. Wingate is the daughter of Reverend John F. Smith, a missionary under the American Board of Commissioners for Foreign Missions, who was located at Marsovan (Merzifoun), Turkey. Knowing

Armenian from childhood she attended the Girl's Boarding School established there by the Mission. After her graduation she came to the United States for further study and was graduated from Monticello College at Alton, Illinois in 1885.

After a year or two of teaching in Wisconsin she was invited to return to Turkey to teach in her former school at Marsovan. Six Years later she married the Reverend Henry Knowles Wingate and went with him to Caesarea, Turkey, to build up a boys, school in that city, which later moved to a nearby suburb, Talas.

While living in a Turkish speaking community, she felt the need of preserving and improving her knowledge of Armenian and so she devoted herself to the study of Armenian literature, ancient and modern, and commenced translating folklore which she sent to the Folklore Society of England, of which she had become a member. Several of these translations were published in their magazine "Folklore" in 1911 and 1912. In 1930 they published her translation of the Scroll of Cyprian (Gibrianos). This scroll is in the possession of The Union Theological Seminary in New York City.

Because of her interest in Armenian literature she was shown many honors by the Armenian clergy of the region. Before leaving Turkey in 1917, she had translated a portion of the Armenian Church Liturgy and Raffi's "The Fool".

Some learned scholars from whom she received aid were Minas Tcheraz, Frederic Macler and Basmadjian; and in later years Rev. Manoug Norhadian; last but not least, Dr. K. H. Mallarian of Fargo, North Dakota, without whose assistance the translation of the twelfth century prayer poem "Jesus Son" written by Nerses Shnorhali would never have been completed. This was published by the Delphic Press several years ago.

More recently the women's division of the Armenian General Benevolent Union published in pamphlet form, the translation of H. Toumanian's epic poem "David of Sassoun." A more ambitious undertaking has been the translation of the saga of the entire race of Sassoun heroes, now ready for publication.

From time to time a number of translations appeared in the Mirror-Spectator but the greater number remain unpublished. In the same category is the translation of Basmadjian's "Coins of Armenia," lent by the Numismatic Society of New York City, in which all designs and legends in the brochure have been copied. Mrs. Wingate resides in New York City.

We take this opportunity to extend the heartfelt gratitude of the Armenian people to Mrs. Wingate for devoting her life to this noble task, to bring to

7

light some of the priceless jewels of Armenian literature by translating them into English for the benefit of a vastly greater reading public, for the connoisseurs of art in the English speaking world, who, I am confident, will deeply appreciate her fine translation of this thought-provoking novel by Raffi.

THE FOOL

Chapter 1

"The fool rolled a stone into a pit; a hundred wise men came to the rescue but they could not draw it out."

"While the prudent man is considering the fool is across the river and away."

"The replies of the fool become the proverbs of the people."

Bayazid was besieged.

Turks, Kurds, gypsies, vagabonds, and more than twenty thousand lawless freebooters, together with the regular Turkish army, surrounded the half ruined city. Its fires smoked like a wide spreading hearth. The houses of the Armenians seemed deserted. Some of the inhabitants had been put to the sword, and some had been taken captive. Only a small number had escaped, having been warned in time to enable them to flee across the frontier, into Persian territory, toward Macou.

The citadel of Bayazid remained impregnable.

A few Russian soldiers, together with the Turkish and Armenian militia were entrenched there and were awaiting their doom, with the fortitude of fatalists. The fort was encircled as if by a ring of iron which, as it contracted day by day, would inevitably strangle the hopeless prisoners. Communication with the outside world was entirely cut off.

The siege began on the sixth day of June, 1877, and had continued twenty-three days. It was at the time when the conquering sword of Russia was suddenly bereft of fortune in its course. The local Mohammedan populace, which had at first accepted Russian control with such willingness, now rebelled and sided with the army of Ismail Pasha.

General Lord Lucasoff, the commander of the division of Erivan, was then between Zeitekan and Tali-Baba, and he had fought gallantly against

Moukhtar Pasha, whose outnumbered his own, five to one. He seemed not to have heard what had occurred at Bayazid, which he had left under the protection of Commandant Ishdogvitch.

It was night. The horns of the crescent moon had just disappeared below the horizon, leaving dense darkness behind. Up to that moment it had betrayed the garrison with its silvery beams.

But even the darkness did not prevent the continuance of the firing. The citadel was dimly outlined upon the crest of the hill, and the guns were trained upon the spot, furiously attacking it.

Nearly a thousand Russian soldiers, and about an equal number of Armenian and Turkish volunteers were fighting against Ishmail Pasha's twenty thousand.

The replies from the fort were infrequent now, for the ammunition was nearly exhausted. Only an occasional shot was fired from one or two cannons toward the spot from which the enemy fired.

That same night in one of the shattered buildings of the fort which had served as barracks, and which the Turks had left in ruins after having conquered the Russians, a crowd of men lay on the ground, a worn and fainting multitude, who were driven to desperation by hunger and thirst.

"One drop of water, I beg of you!" I am dying of thirst!"— such were the cries on every side.

"Oh, for a bit of bread !" "I am dying of hunger!" cried others faintly. These poor wretches had scarcely eaten or drunk for nearly a week. The siege had begun so unexpectedly that they had not had time to bring up sufficient provisions, and now the besieged were obliged to fight against three powerful adversaries, against thirst and famine within, and the fire of the enemy without. On the eighth of the month the besieged had been deprived of hot food. They had killed and eaten the artillery horses and that of the commander. That left the barley for the soldiers, but that also was exhausted. At length provisions were so scarce that each man received only two ounces of hard-tack and a spoonful of water daily. And the heat of June was intense at that time. The condition of the sick was little better than that of the others.

There was no water in the fort. Outside the fort, about three hundred feet distant, there was a spring which the Turks had stopped up. Every night an attempt was made to go down after water, but often of the twenty or thirty who went down not one returned.

"Bread!" "Water!" Again were heard the despairing cries. But the roar of cannon drowned the cries of the wretched sufferers with its grim note of menace.

This was one of those moments when man loses his feeling of sympathy for his fellowman — loses it because he has nothing with which to help him. This is why no one paid heed to the cry of the hungry, and no one cared for the thirsty. Each was waiting for the final moment when the enemy should pour in upon them like a flood, sword in hand and each should bravely meet his fate.

Within the citadel, entrenched behind the ramparts, some soldiers were standing guard, and were watching the movements of the enemy from the loopholes. They did not dare to show their heads above the ramparts. From the heights above, the enemy shot at them unsparingly, and the bullets frequently flew near enough to these men to scorch and burn their faces.

From here could be seen the city, which presented a frightful spectacle. It looked as though it were illuminated also. The atrocious festival of man's inhumanity was being celebrated. It was a festival of wild beasts assembled by the Turks.

The homes of the Armenians were burning. Streams of fire poured from the doors and windows of each house, and mingling with the dense smoke rose high in the air spreader in every direction a steam of sparks. The conflagration steadily increased in violence, consuming the entire Armenian quarter. The burning timbers fell crashing into the courtyards, and buildings came tottering to earth, covering the inmates with a blanket of fire. These poor creatures having been surrounded by fire on all sides, had been unable to escape. The groans and cries of the wretched were mingled with the roar of the flames which writhed and twisted in the air like gigantic dragons, and spread a lurid glare of light in all directions.

In that illumination terrible pictures succeeded one another as in a mammoth panorama. The Mohammedans were massacring the Armenians; massacring those who escaped from the flames, sparing neither age nor sex. Young girls were being dragged away by the hair. From all sides were heard piteous cries and screams. But the tears of the doomed creatures did not avail to soften the hearts of these brutes.

Not only did the Kurds take an active part in these barbarities, but the soldiers of the regular Turkish army as well; and more dreadful to relate, the Kurdish women also. The latter, like furies, forgetting the love and pity which are woman's especial characteristics, snatched infants from the arms of their mothers and tossed them into the flames. The least resistance was punished with the sword.

11

A few Armenian volunteers were watching the scene from the fort, and wept as they saw such horrors. The massacre had continued three entire days and nights. "Oh, what butchery!" they groaned.

But one of their number shed no tears. His heart was filled with indignation, not against those who were burning and slaying, but against those who were letting themselves be slaughtered like sheep. "Look, look!", he exclaimed. "In all that city you do not see a man who raises his hand against his slayer. What more can be done to a man to move him to passionate resistance? They have burned his house before his eyes; they have roasted his children; they have dragged away his wife and his daughters; the man has seen all this but he humbly bows his head to receive the stroke of the sword! Curse you, fellow! You also are a man. Kill some of them yourself first and die fighting!"

"Vartan, you are always saying such heartless things," observed one of his companions.

Vartan turned away without deigning to reply. It was more than he could bear to look longer on that scene in which he saw presented the cowardly picture of his race. "This people do not know how to die with honor," he muttered.

A short distance from this spot, in a retired corner of the fort, among another group of Armenian soldiers, the following conversation was taking place: "If Bedros doesn't return, that means that we have lost five more men tonight."

"He is very late; I fear we shall not see him again."

"No, listen! That is his signal. Don't you hear the cawing of the raven?"

"It is he. Let down the rope ladder."

They lowered the ladder, and in a few moments a young man appeared at the top of the rampart bearing an enormous leather water bottle. His comrades helped him down and expressed their joy at his return. One of them embraced him but drew back affrighted, asking, "What makes your face so wet, Bedros?"

At that moment the flames of the burning city leapt up so high that they could see his stained face. "It is blood!" they exclaimed in horror.

"Oh, that's nothing," replied Bedros, with a laugh. "I hadn't washed my face for days. It got a good washing tonight."

Bedros related his story briefly: On reaching the spring he found a number of Kurds on guard, watching to prevent any from coming to get water. They attacked him, and by the time he "had stopped their mouths" as he expressed it, he had received a cut on the head.

"What became of Hanness, Thomas, Atam, and Nerso?" they asked.

"Devil take them," replied Bedros in his usual sarcastic manner. "One would think that those fellows had agreed together to betake themselves to their ancestors tonight. One fell beneath the wall of the fortress. He must have been hit by a bullet as he was climbing over. The next toppled over on the path; another lay like a log by the spring; while poor Thomas went a few steps further holding his hand against his side and cursing the Kurds; but I silenced them."

These four young Armenians of whom Bedros spoke, had been dispatched one after the other to fetch water, but had not returned. Such events occurred so often that death and murder had become common-place events and scarcely elicited remarks from his hearers. They did not even make any great haste to bind up Bedros' wounded head, nor did he pay it any attention.

"Devil take those Kurds!" he continued. "They seem to be able to see in the dark like the wolves, from which they get their name." (Kurds are koorts, i.e. wolves) "In whatever direction they hear a sound, there they send a bullet, and it seldom misses its mark."

Thus they talked on in the dark, till at length they bethought themselves to bandage Bedros' head; then taking up the bottle of water, upon which depended the lives of over a thousand men, they bent their steps towards the courtyard of the fort.

"Boys," said one of the fellows, "we will not give the Turks a drop. I am not joking. We have lost four comrades for this bottle of water and not one of them offered to go after it."

"No, that would not be right," replied Bedros. "We must share it with them, also."

"Why is it wrong?" retorted the first speaker. "They brought some water one day, but they hid it, and drank it all themselves."

"They were selfish, but we ought to show them what it means to be fellow-soldiers."

13

They now entered the courtyard of the barracks. "Water, water," rose the glad cry, and all began to crowd around the young men.

It is impossible to describe the soul felt joy, the frantic rejoicing with which that thirsty multitude pressed forward — water.

There was great confusion as each tried to be the first to obtain water.

"Bring a light, and don't trample upon us. You shall each receive a portion," said the young man who carried the bottle, as he set it down.

They lighted a torch, whose flickering light fell upon the faces of the motley crowd, beside itself with joy. One of the men took a small wine glass and began to dole out the water with it. It had a horrible stench, and its taste was exceedingly offensive. Several drank without noticing anything amiss. Then one exclaimed, "What is the color of that water?"

"Drink it, and never mind the color," commanded Bedros. "The Kurds have colored it like this for our sakes.

"How have they colored it, we would like to know," cried the men.

"They have colored it with our blood. May you never see how many bodies have fallen into the pool from which I took this water."

The men were horrified, but still they continued to drink the foul, reddish liquid into which the blood of so many of their fellows had been spilt, and in which their putrid bodies still lay.

One of the men attempted to treat it as a joke, and exclaimed: "How fine! The water is enriched, and so gives us more strength!"

The careless talk of the rejoicing men was soon interrupted by the whistling of a bomb over the fortress, and in another moment one fell into the enclosure and did deadly execution among them.

During this period, in one of the rooms of the fort, which the Ottoman commander had formerly occupied, the Russian commander, Ishdogvitch, was holding a council of war with his officers. The captains of the Armenian and Turkish volunteers took part in the deliberations. A lamp standing on a small table dimly lighted their sad and careworn countenances.

For several days past letters had been sent them in rapid succession by the enemy, calling upon them to surrender. The letters were written by

Lieutenant General Schamyl, the son of the famous Schamyl, who was now on the side of the enemy and had the honor of being the commander of the Sultan's troops. The last letter was full of threats and promises, and this was the occasion of this conclave. They were deliberating upon their reply.

"We will not surrender," cried the commander, "not as long as we are alive!"

"If the siege continues but a few days longer, it will be impossible for us to hold out," commented an officer.

"Our position is hopeless henceforth," added another. "We have neither bread to eat nor ammunition to use. I don't understand why the Kurds haven't fallen upon us before now. How can we help ourselves?"

"Yes, we have been very imprudent," said another officer.

"We are not able to correct the past; let us speak of the present," observed the commander, who presided over the council, and who according to military usage occupied the position of commander-in-chief during the siege, and was vested with full military powers. "We will not surrender as long as we live," he repeated.

"If help does not reach us from without, we are lost," responded a Khan, who was a captain of the Turkish volunteers.

"We have not strength enough to wait for assistance," said a Bey [chieftain]. "it is my opinion that we should throw open the gates of the fortress, break through the cordon of the enemy and make our escape as beat we can. Then we shall either succeed in becoming free or we shall fall into the hands of the enemy. "

"The latter is the more probable," remarked the captain of the Armenian volunteers, "but the consequences will be terrible. This fort now serves as a barrier for holding back the Ottoman army. When we lose it, then we open the way for Ismail Pasha's regular and disbanded soldiers, and in a few days they will take Erivan, Nakhitchevan, and many other places, unhindered. It is evident that the local Mohammedans were impatiently awaiting the arrival of those self-invited guests; but the Armenians are defenseless. A very insignificant number of soldiers was left to protect the country, for our principal force is now concentrated near Kars. Before they can reach us the Turks will have destroyed all before them."

The words of the Armenian officer aroused the anger of the Turkish Khan, and he exclaimed, "You express distrust of the Mohammedans!"

15

"My suspicions are not unfounded, for proofs are not wanting to confirm what I say. At this moment, among the besieging hosts, there are many from Zila who were Russian subjects before the war, but a crazy "molla" (priest) near Nakhitchevan dreamed that Islam was soon to rule over this land, and the people are ready to help bring it to pass."

The president of the council silenced the dispute, saying, "We must hold on and fight until our last breath. I hope aid will arrive soon. General Lord Lucasoff is not far from us. As soon as he learns of our condition he will hasten to save Bayazid. But he must be informed speedily.

"How?" several asked at once.

"By letter," he replied.

"Who will take it?"

"I think that among so many men there will be at least one brave soul."

"That may be; but how will he be able to reach him? We are surrounded by the enemy."

"He will make the attempt."

The council then decided to write a letter to General Lord Lucasoff, and after an hour, the commander, letter in hand, came out of the council chamber followed by the officers.

A muffled beat of the drum, assembled the men in the square in front of the officers' quarters. The commander addressed them confidently. "Men, our condition is evident to you all. Now our, hope rests upon God, and with His help, on aid from without. If help is delayed we are lost. Therefore, it is imperative that we make haste to give information of our condition in the necessary quarters. This letter must reach General Lord Lucasoff who is not far from us. As soon as he receives this letter he will hasten to our relief. Now which of you brave men will attempt to do this? Let him come forward and take the letter. I promise him a reward such as befits the magnitude of the undertaking. Speak up, men! Who will take the letter?"

Dead silence. Not a sound was to be heard.

"I repeat," continued the commander, in a more impressive manner, "that our salvation depends upon this letter. Who will win glory for himself, and become our deliverer?"

16

Again, not a sound was heard.

"Is there not one brave heart among you all," he cried with a tremor in his voice, 'who will attempt this daring deed?"

"I will," came the reply from one voice, and an Armenian youth drew near and took the letter.

This youth was Vartan.

Chapter 2

Early the following morning, when the first rays of the sun were lighting the heavens, a frightful scene was revealed, in and around Bayazid. Now the result of the massacre, which had been carried on by the barbarism for three days and three nights, was clearly to be seen. A deathly silence reigned over the city, broken only by the croaking of ravens who flew about in flocks to batten on carrion.

The streets of the unfortunate city presented a sad and mournful spectacle: houses had become reduced to heaps of ashes; here and there smoke arose from ruins; beside the ruins lay the charred remains of old and young, women and children. Half-famished dogs dragged forth the corpses, growling and snapping at the flocks of ravens which disputed the feast with them. From every quarter arose the stifling stench of putrid corpses.

Rising above this city of the dead, stood the citadel Of Bayazid, waiting for its melancholy fate.

The siege increased in rigor. Mountain, valley, hill, field and plain were covered with armed men besides a host of freebooters. The camps were separated into distinct groups, and each was the scene of great activity. Fanaticism and cruelty had made men become worse than the wild beasts, who put to death their fellowmen with unspeakable outrages. After having satiated their lust for blood, in some measure, they began to gratify their greed for plunder. The supposedly wealthy Armenians of the city were collected together in one spot, and were being put to torture to force them to reveal the hiding places of their money. The wretched men wept and groaned, protesting that they had delivered up all they possessed and nothing remained. They were not believed, so their children were butchered before their eyes, to force them to reveal their hiding place.

In another spot, the Kurds were dividing the heaps of plunder, and their wives were joyfully loading their individual shares to take to their homes.

A little further on they were loading their horses with Armenian slaves, and many were the fights among themselves over the more beautiful girls.

In another spot, some distance from the bustling multitude, wolves, wildcats, and birds of prey were breakfasting off the unburied corpses. And not very far from these, pious Moslems were zealously performing their morning devotions, and raising their bloody hands to heaven, giving thanks to the God of Islam for His blessings.

The smoke rising from the fires and hearths, clouded the horizon with a thick fog which prevented the sunlight from shining through.

The cannon still thundered; shot and shell poured down upon the fortress, but it stood firm, and seemed to deride the constant attacks of the enemy.

But in one part of the camp one individual attracted the attention of the whole camp. Leaping about and clapping his hands he proceeded to the middle of the camp, chanting as he went, a nonsensical Kurdish song:

"An old granddad became a frog,
Became a frog and went to sea;
Drew up some sand from out the sea;
The sand it turned to shining gold.
The gold he spent to buy a goat,
Oh, such a hobbling, scurvy goat:
Goat, goat, goat my love,
Bless you, goat my love:
Oh, tell me why, oh, tell me why,
You scurvy are, and hobble so?"

"A crazy man!" shouted the Kurds, and they flocked around him to have him repeat the song.

And truly, he seemed to be a crazy man. He was dressed like a clown or juggler's assistant who performs tricks between acts to amuse the audience.

He was a tall, wild-looking fellow. He wore a tall square-topped cap with bells attached to the four corners which jangled harshly at his every motion. He had smeared his face with shoe-blacking and streaks of red, yellow and blue paint. His clothing consisted of a single garment, a ragged military cloak fastened at the waist with a piece of rope. His feet were bare.

"Now bray like a donkey," they commanded.

The crazy fellow stuck his fingers in his ears, stooped, opened his mouth and began to bray with all his might. The crowd applauded his performance and threw him some copper coins. He picked up the coins and looked at them stupidly, then throwing them aside he said, "Give me bread." They gave him some. He snatched it from their hands and thrusting great chunks into his mouth swallowed them whole.

"Now let us see you dance like a bear," said they. The fellow then went through a number of grotesque motions, creeping on all fours, walking on his hands and various other tricks.

The fellow remained in the Kurdish camp all day, entertaining crowds of men. He spoke Kurdish like a Kurd; he swore; he cursed the Russians; he raved against the "giaours" (infidels) saying, "kill the giaours." His voice could be heard all over the camp till after midnight. But the next morning the "fool" had disappeared.

Chapter 3

The noonday sun shone with scorching heat upon the highway. It was the hour of day when travelers seek shelter from the heat. But at this hour a lone traveler was hastening along the road leading from Bayazid to Alashgerd. The road twisted and turned through the mountain pass, and was a succession of ups and downs. He walked rapidly, with never a stop and never a backward glance. Some urgent duty appeared to drive him on, and every moment was precious.

The traveler was young, and dressed like the crazy fellow of the night before. He wore the same ragged cloak, and a girdle of rope. He had discarded the cap and bells and the stains bad been washed from his face. His head was protected from the heat by a mat of freshly-woven rushes, such as mowers often weave for themselves. This rustic hat shaded his melancholy face — a face of deep despair. Even in his uncouth garb his was a figure to attract attention.

Presently he heard the whinny of a horse. He paused and looked about. The sound was repeated. He perceived that it came from a ravine near by. After a moment's thought he turned his steps thither. His first step was to climb a crag from which he might peer down into the ravine. There he saw a luxuriant growth of grass in which a saddled horse was grazing. That appeared to be all, but looking more closely he discovered near a clump of bushes the glittering point of a spear. "There is some one resting there, and he is alone, for there is only one horse in sight," he thought to himself. His further conclusions were that the man must be a Kurd, judging from his spear and from the trappings of the horse; also that he must be asleep since the horse's feet were fettered to prevent him from straying. Now he descended the hillside and reached the bed of a stream which flowed through the narrow valley, its bank, hidden by a thick growth of rushes. Then he began to creep silently toward the bushes near which he spear stood planted in the ground. A snake could not have slipped through the reeds as noiselessly as did this lithe and fearless creature.

At that moment a slight breeze bent the heads of the rushes and their murmur drowned the rustling caused by the foe if, perchance, he made a careful move. Everything promised success.

He had reached the bushes where the spear was planted. He paused within a few paces of it, and preserving his former attitude, he began to peer through the rushes. The sleeper's dress showed that he was a Kurd. The noonday sun had driven him here to rest. Was he asleep, or awake? It was hard to say for his head was turned away from the traveler. He was stretched full length upon the soft grass.

The traveler continued to observe the Kurd from his ambush. He was keenly interested to know whether the Kurd was awake or asleep. If his face were only turned toward him he would be able to know whether he was asleep or not. He was greatly disturbed and racked with anxiety. Unclothed and unarmed, he was about to attack a man accoutered with arms. But he must make an end of indecision. Time was flying. Every moment was precious. But how should he act? While he was in this dilemma he saw the Kurd raise his head and look about. He looked at his horse, and seeing that it had not strayed away, he settled his head again upon his saddle-bags in lieu of a pillow and lay still. So he was not asleep, or, if he had been asleep, he was awake now. The traveler was still undecided. His nostrils dilated and his lips quivered. Then he noticed that the spear was planted some distance from the sleeper and in line with his own hiding place. This circumstance relieved him somewhat. His muscles became less tense and something akin to joy shone in his eyes. A weapon! That was what he needed to carry out his intention.

Suddenly, like a tiger from its ambush, he sprang from among the rushes, snatched up the spear and stood over the outstretched Kurd.

"Give me your weapons," he cried.

The Kurd, seeing the outlandish figure in a tattered military cloak and ridiculous hat, looked at him contemptuously and without rising, raised his rifle and aiming it at the crazy fellow, said: "Take it; there it is!"

The rifle went off and the bullet grazed the man's side.

"Rascal, do you resist?" replied the fellow, thrusting the spear straight into the Kurd's throat. The hot blood gushed from the wound, and the man's head fell back on the ground.

The Kurd made an effort to rise once more and he drew his sword half-way out of its scabbard, but his hold weakened and the sword came no further.

"You dog, why have you killed me?" he cried in mortal agony.

"You have killed many of our people, and have carried away many; I learned from you how to kill and how to carry away. I am going on a long journey. You see I have neither clothing, weapons nor horse. I needed your clothing and weapons and your beautiful horse grazing yonder in the meadow. I knew that as long as you drew breath you would give me none of these; that is why I have relieved you of them. Perhaps I am depriving you of the spoil of Bayazid; no matter - Your brothers have been very busy there."

The Kurd heard nothing. His eyes were already closed and his lifeless body lay outstretched upon the ground.

All this had taken place in a very few moments. The traveler stripped his victim and dragging his body away, hid it among the bushes, covering it with his ragged cloak. Then arraying himself in the Kurd's clothing and girding on his weapons, he flew forward on his journey mounted on the beautiful steed.

Chapter 4

The day after these events occurred, a horseman, dressed like a Kurd and whistling like a lark, entered the camp of Gen. Lord Lucasoff. He said he had brought an important dispatch addressed to the General, so he was taken to the general's tent. He sent the letter in by the band of an officer while he remained without to care for his horse. After a few moments he was summoned to present himself to the general.

A martial figure of medium height and with a haughty leonine face was seated in the tent. This was Lord Lucasoff. His gray head was bent over the desk on which lay numerous letters just received. He picked up one of them and read it, smoking all the while. His expression indicated agitation and sympathy.

Turning toward the messenger he asked: "Are you an Armenian?"

"Not only an Armenian, but the son of a priest," was the reply.

The general, giving a searching glance at his bold face continued his questioning. "Was there any food in the fort?"

"If they wish to keep alive, they must soon begin to eat each other."

"Have they no water?"

"None. it has to be brought from outside. It is impossible to leave the fort by day, but at night ten or twenty men are let down from the ramparts to go after water. The Kurds know this well and fire upon them from a distance; often not one returns."

"How about the supply of firearms, powder and bullets?"

"It was exhausted, but an Armenian — give the Armenians credit for this —

found some which had been concealed by the Turks, and they are buying a reprieve with this,"

"How were you able to escape from the fort?"

"I climbed over the wall one morning before sunrise and walked right into the Kurdish camp. I entertained them for a whole day, singing and dancing and doing other foolish things. I went all through the camp, seeing everything. Then I said goodbye and came away."

The General looked at the young man in astonishment, "What are you saying?" he said: "Were you crazy?"

"Yes, sir," he replied quietly. "It is my fate always to play the role of the fool. It is not so bad. It has saved my life before. I pretended I was crazy and so entered the Kurdish camp." And he proceeded to describe his dress, the ridiculous garb in which he made his appearance in the Kurdish camp.

A faint smile appeared on the General's stony countenance, and he asked in a friendly fashion: "But where did you find this clothing?"

"God gave it to me. On the way here I found a Kurd. I took from him this clothing, these weapons and that beautiful horse that stands outside," replied the young man telling further how he killed the Kurd.

"You seem to be a fearless fellow," said the General. Then with his former look of anxiety, he resumed his interrogations.

"Are there many Kurds?"

"They say there are more than 20,000, but they are not all Kurds. There are Mohammedans of every tribe mingled with them. Whoever has a horse and a weapon or two has run to Bayazid, and so a great multitude has assembled. On my way here I saw many more groups hastening in that direction."

"Have they cannon?"

"They have."

"What is their intention?"

"They are trying to hasten the capture of the citadel of Bayazid; then to go to Erivan, and the next week to Tiflis, for the lovely Armenian and Georgian young women attract them greatly."

25

Again a faint smile appeared on the General's face, and he asked with a sneer, "Are they going to Tiflis with 20,000? Nonsense!"

"20,000 is not too few when there are not 1000 soldiers opposing them. Besides, Ismail Pasha's entire force will soon join them; while in our region the Mohammedans are waiting impatiently with open arms to receive their co-religionists."

A mist of sadness, like a dark cloud passed over the General's face and his heart, which the varying vicissitudes of fate had not been able to disturb, began to swell. He raised his hand to his forehead, rubbing it as though trying to dissipate the melancholy which oppressed it.

After a brief reflection, he raised his gray head and asked:

"Did you enter the city of Bayazid?"

"I did. There is not a soul left of the Armenian Christians. They have massacred old and young. They took captive all the young women, girls and boys. They burned the dwellings and plundered their possessions. Only about hundred families who were forewarned, escaped to the Persian town of Macou, before the arrival of the Kurds. But they left their possessions in the hands of their enemies. Oh, these Mohammedans, how cruelly and shamefully they have treated the Armenians."

"How?"

"At the beginning of the war, when the Russians approached Bayazid, the Mohammedans were in great fear. They thought the Russians would surely take away their goods as the Turks do. With this idea they concealed their possessions in the homes of their Armenian neighbors, saying, "You are Christians, the Russians will not touch you, so our goods will be safe in your houses." The Russians came, and naturally they took nothing. They treated Armenians and Mohammedans impartially. Seeing this, the Mohammedans were put at their ease, and proceeded to take back, without loss, the articles which they had put in the custody of the Armenians.

"And now, when it was rumored that the Kurds were coming, the Turks said: 'You did us kindness, so we wish to do something for you in return. The Kurds are coming and, will rob you — give us your goods and we will keep them for you.' "The Armenians believed them and gave all they had into their custody, and some hid themselves and their wives and daughters with their Turkish neighbors. But when the Kurds entered the city, the Turks said to the Armenians: 'Get out of our houses. If the Kurds learn that Armenians are hiding in our houses they will massacre us together with you.' And, thus they delivered the poor Armenians into the hands of their enemies, and possessed themselves of their riches. And when the massacre began the local Turks were the first to set their houses on fire — those Turks, General, who only six weeks ago swore in your presence to obey the Russian Government. They fired their guns in every direction. Even the Turkish women shot Armenians."

The General had listened in silence, and the young man continued:

"Oh, if you could only know, sir, how many fine young men perished in that conflict! We fought the Kurds stubbornly before yielding Bayazid to them. As you are aware, sir, there were very few Russian soldiers left to defend the citadel along with the Armenian and Turkish militia. Ishdogvitch, the hero of Bayazid, guarded the fort with his Russian soldiers, while the militia guarded the city. News had reached us of an immense host of Kurds under the leadership of Sheik Chellaladdin, and Sheik Abadoullah, advancing toward Bayazid. The Armenians at Van had sent us this information. We made haste and demanded that they fortify the citadel in time and send sufficient troops to enable us to withstand the enemy. But there were some who tried to make us believe that all those reports were false, and that no preparations were needed. Why those traitors tried to prevent us from being in readiness for the arrival of the enemy, I am unable to say. You, General, will surely learn the reason. But I can say this, that the Armenian is and will always be faithful."

There appeared to be points in the young man's narrative which it was difficult for him to make clear. The General interrupted him, saying, "Tell me what you did after the arrival of the Kurds?"

"When the Kurds came, after a few unsuccessful fights, Ishdogvitch hastened to entrench himself in the citadel, to defend it. Part of the militia remained outside, for there was neither room nor provisions for all in the fort. Some of our Turkish militiamen fled to Iktir, and some into Persia. But we Armenians determined to defend the city, or perish in the attempt. We were few in number but many of the Armenian inhabitants of the city were ready to join us. The poor creatures knew the fate that awaited them should the Turks take Bayazid once more. You are aware, general, with what rejoicing the Armenians had received the Russian conquering army on its arrival at the city. The Ottoman could not forgive this demonstration and wished to wreak vengeance on a people who preferred to bow to the Russian eagle rather than to the Ottoman crescent."

"You have strayed from my question, again" interrupted the General. "Tell us how the affair ended."

The young man tried to check his loquacity, which had been occasioned by the fullness of his heart, and continued. "Perhaps we might have succeeded in saving the city, with the help of all the Armenians of the place, if we had possessed sufficient weapons. But they could not obtain arms; still many did join us. To tell the truth, at first the fight was glorious. A small company was fighting against a vastly more numerous foe. A few hundred Turkish volunteers took part with us. But, suddenly, we saw our Mohammedan comrades fleeing. It was not pleasant for them to shoot their co-religionists. So, we Armenians remained alone and held out for a long time. This continued for several hours until our store of ammunition was exhausted. Then began hand to hand fights. Many fell; many were captured, and the remainder, seeing that their efforts were in vain, left and fled. Then the enemy took possession of the town."

"I understand," said the General, and rising he approached a small casket from which he took a cross which he pinned on the young man's breast, with his own hand, saying, "You deserve this, and I will recommend to those in command that they give you some office and a salary. Henceforth you must remain with us, I need brave men like you."

The young man bowed gratefully and replied, "This cross is sufficient, General. You will do me a great favor if you will allow me to go where I please now."

The General, surprised at the young man's lack of ambition, asked: "Where must you go?"

"To save the life of one who is very dear to me."

"I see you have a secret," said the General, kindly.

"Yes, it is my heart's secret."

"Then, accept this small gift," said the General, you may need it," handing him a roll of gold pieces wrapped in paper.

"I shall consider it a great favor if you dismiss me quickly," replied the young man, taking his leave.

"Go, and the Lord be with you," returned the General clasping his hand.

He bowed and went out.

Chapter 5

Let us turn back a few years.

In the province of Pakrevant, not far from the monastery of St. John (now called Iutch Kilisah) there was the Armenian village of o..... It was situated in a large valley where Nature had not spared any features that could enhance its beauty.

The valley extended between two mountain ranges whose slopes, rising one above the other held it in their bosom where it lay like a green lake, oval in shape. Through its midst the Euphrates river wound and twisted. This part of it was called Ak Soo (White Water) by the people of the region, and it was worthy of its name.

The uplands surrounding the valley were covered with rich meadows in which cattle grazed contentedly, while the whole extent of the lower stretches was devoted to the cultivation of wheat, barley, flax and various grains and legumes.

Here the industrious hand of the laborer left not an acre of ground uncultivated.

All along the valley were scattered small Armenian villages so hidden among the orchards and vineyards that from a distance they appeared like verdant forests which were especially noticeable because the remainder of the valley was treeless.

At the upper end of the valley, in a little hollow, lay the village of o..... The dwelling of landlord Khacho, or Khachadoor, was the largest in the village. Each morning a hundred cattle were driven out through its gate. His horses and cows, buffaloes and oxen were the finest in the place, besides which there were a thousand sheep being cared for by shepherds up on the mountains.

To this house belonged the village oil press, and a mill whose wheels were ever busy grinding grain for the villagers.

But the outstanding possessions of old Khacho were his seven sons. All were mature; the seven pillars of the house. Six were married and the house overflowed with their children and their children's children. So old Khacho had several generations growing up around him, all living together, working together, forming a little world by themselves. It had become a saying in the village: "old Khacho has as many children as he has cattle."

The youngest son of Khacho was unmarried, being a lad of sixteen, who was called Stephanie. He had not yet the maturity which is common in a land where youths mature early. His features were fresh and childlike, and he looked more like a woman than a man.

All of Khacho's older sons were occupied away from home, looking after their cattle or their farms. But Stephanie took very little share in their labors. He was Khacho's "Joseph, the beloved", whom the old patriarch did not wish out of his sight.

There were many similarities between Stephanie and Joseph. Not only was he beautiful, modest, quick-witted, attractive and sympathetic but his garments, like Joseph's were of the choicest He wore a striped tunic of Aleppo linen embroidered with colored thread; over this a jacket of crimson velvet embroidered with gold thread. His girdle was of fine Kirman wool, and his full trousers of broadcloth from Van. On his feet he wore red leather shoes made in Erzeroum, and on his head a red fez wound about with a dainty silk turban.

A profusion of auburn curls fell from under his fez to his shoulders. But in one regard he differed from Joseph in that while Joseph's brethren envied him, Stephanie's did not, but loved him dearly.

From a distance old Khacho's house looked like an ancient castle. It was built on a knoll and in form and location had all the advantages necessary to keep a dwelling safe from attack by enemies. This fortress was surrounded by walls on four sides enclosing quite an extensive tract in which stood several buildings.

From without all that could be seen were the four high towers at the four corners of the enclosure. Inside there were all the buildings and storehouses needed for a well-ordered domain.

Here was the sheep-fold, dug down into the earth, there the corrals for the horses, cows and water buffaloes. Here a shed where all the implements were kept; there the hayloft, the straw-crib, where the animal feed was kept. There were various bins and dugouts for storing the farm produce. Besides these there were the huts occupied by the servants and herdsmen and their families — these were Kurdish families. The wives acted as servants on the place while their menfolk were shepherds, herdsmen and plowmen. In a word, a small village dwelt within that fortress whose lord and master was old Khacho.

The dwellings assigned to the family were not as large and commodious as would be required in the Western World. They still preserved patriarchal simplicity as when a whole family lived in one tent, with only this difference that instead of a tent they lived in a house built of stone.

For his numerous sons, each of whom, together with his children, formed a large family, there were no separate rooms but all lived under one roof and in one room, and there was nothing there but the four walls crossed overhead by great beams. Here they built their fire, baked and cooked their food. Here they all ate, and here they all slept.

Here were to be seen new-born calves and young kids who skipped about with the children, running, jumping and filling the room with a lively racket. Often the hens entered and picked up crumbs from the floor or other things dropped from the hands of careless children. In a word, it was a Noah's Ark where all kinds of creatures were found.

A second building stood next to this one. It differed from the first only in this, that one side, overlooking the courtyard, was entirely open. This was called the kiosk, and was used as a summer living room. One door from the kiosk opened into the large room, serving it as a foyer. Next to these was a small room, called the "oda", or the guest room. It was used only when guests visited there and was always kept clean and neat.

Chapter 6

In spite of living in such plain and unpretentious surroundings those who lived there were happy and contented. Labor was unremitting but the blessings of God were shed upon it abundantly.

Old Khacho's barns were always full of grain and fodder, his store rooms with butter, oil and wine. He was blessed with some good in every season of the year, and plenty of work to fill each day.

It was spring. The snow was melting on the mountains; the fields were beginning to smile with their verdant green. The air was full of a warm, delightful fragrance, spreading fresh life in every direction. Rivulets ran through the valleys and through the meadows. The returning swallow invited the laborer at his work.

The sun had just risen, and the mountaintops were rosy in the morning light. The old man was returning home at this early hour wishing a "God have mercy" on everyone he met. His sons were going to bring the cattle out of the stables today, for the first time, after their winter confinement where they had had nothing to do but eat, rest, and grow fat in the dark, never seeing light of day. It gave great pleasure to the villagers to watch this sight, and many of them had gathered about old Khacho's gate to see the cattle driven out, and to observe how well they had been tended. "Light to your eyes, Khacho!" said a neighbor. "Aren't your boys going to bring out the buffaloes today?" "Yes, it is time," be replied. "I asked the priest how much longer we should keep them in, and he said they are coming out today."

From within, the tinkling of bells was heard, and the crowd drew back to make way. "That is Chora!" they cried, Chora was the name of a famous buffalo belonging to the landlord. It had a crescent-shaped mark on its forehead, and was famous for its strength and size. The gigantic creature leapt out snorting and bellowing. Stopping suddenly in the square before the gate, it raised its head and gazed about. At that moment the old landlord threw a raw egg at his head. As the shell broke the yellow yolk ran down his white forehead. This was done to keep off the Evil Eye. Chora was startled by this performance, and lowering his head, he gave a mighty roar and plunged toward the crowd gathered there. The old man's sons arriving at this moment, used clubs and poles trying to control the frantic animal. Human strength contended against animal strength. Coming out of the stable into the light of day Chora's eyes, unused to the light, saw nothing distinctly. He did not even recognize his masters who had cared for him all winter, and whose hands he had often licked. In frantic frenzy he charged first this way then that. It was impossible to control him. Old Khacho's six sons dealt blows upon him from every direction, but they had no more effect upon him than if the great clubs had been twigs. The old landlord watched the conflict from a distance, with as much delight as he might had it been a Roman circus. He saw before him two powerful forces; on the one hand his sons, and on the other the great bull. They were about equally prized by him. Upon these two forces all the labors of his management depended. The conflict grew fiercer. The chain which had fastened Chora's neck to a huge block of wood now broke. The villagers brought ropes with which to bind him, but at each rush of the ungovernable beast these, also, were broken, and as he plunged about, the crowd scattered like flies before him.

In this frightful commotion a deed of great daring was accomplished. One of the sons, named Abo, ran and seized Chora by the tail. The enraged beast, observing this indignity, tried to turn and punish the offender. He whirled around and around, but Abo circled with him, holding onto his tail firmly as he did so. This performance continued for several minutes. Cries of astonishment arose from every side. The furious beast bellowed and dug his hoofs into the ground, filling the air with clouds of dust. By this time Abo's brothers arrived with chains with which they finally bound the bull amid general rejoicing. Now the old man approached Abo, and, kissing him on the forehead, said, "May the Eye of God be upon you, my son. You have made my face become white!" (The opposite of blackening one's name), meaning that Abo had saved him from being disgraced before the people. He then approached Chora, as though he was another son, and patting its head, said "You rascal, why did you behave so badly?" By this time Chora was quiet, and could see clearly. He recognized his master and seemed sorry for his wicked behavior. A chain was fastened to his neck, and passing it between his forelegs, was attached to a great log which he must drag with him wherever he went. And finally he was driven down to the river for a swim, and a cooling bath in its waters.

The crowd of villagers still hung about old Khacho's gate to watch the rest of the buffaloes come out, for there were fierce ones among them but this time the old man's sons took greater care and no special difficulty arose. Then followed the fine, healthy sheep and well-fed cattle, any one of which was worthy to carry off a prize in a village fair.

The landlord broke an egg against the forehead of each to keep off the Evil Eye. Besides this he had had the priest write a charm for each one, and had it sewn in a triangular bit of blue leather, and hung it from the neck of each of the cattle. The villagers spoke words of praise for the care which the sons had bestowed upon the cattle, and the father's heart rejoiced at hearing them praised.

Each day the animals were brought out of their confinement for a little exercise until they became accustomed to the outdoor air and light and were ready to work and plow the fields.

Chapter 7

The April sun brought with it warmer and brighter days.

On the mountains red, yellow and white iris were already in bloom, and the Kurdish girls brought bunches of them to the Armenian villages to give in exchange for pieces of bread. Mushrooms and various kinds of wild herbs used for greens were so abundant that year that the Kurdish women would exchange a whole donkey-load of them for a few pounds of flour.

Old Khacho's sons had begun to plow their fields. Work had begun everywhere. There was not an idle man to be found in the entire village. All were busy with their farming.

It was morning. The hearth fires were lighted at old Khacho's. In one fireplace food was being cooked in pots and kettles. In another, bread was baking. The daughters-in-law and the maids were all busy around the fires. The house, filled with the smells of food, was one great kitchen, and one would think enough food was being cooked to feed an army. And, indeed besides the old man's large family, there were the shepherds and plowmen with their families who had to be provided for. There was a legion of them. Every day a great amount of food had to be prepared, and the old man's industrious daughters-in-law had not a moment's rest. They must care for all and please all.

Besides the cooking, there were other household tasks. One must milk the cows and sheep; another must heat the milk at a small fireplace and make the madzoun. A third must prepare the culture for cheese, and a fourth was churning butter.

A troop of Children were running about and playing with the young calves and lambs. Children and lambs grew up together—two forms of wealth which rejoice a villager and are his glory.

On the south side of the court, under a wall, was a row of beehives. The warm April sun shed its warmth here. While the women were busy at work on the other side of the wall, old Khacho opened the doors of the hives. The bees poured out gladly and fluttered around his gray head, humming and buzzing, making the air vibrate with sound. There were some bad ones among thorn, who gave the old man's face sharp stings. But he felt no pain, but drove them off, saying, "Go away, you devils. What harm has Khacho done you?"

In the meantime Stephanie stood a little distance away, watching his father with interest. "Go away, my child, the bees will sting you," he cried. "But why don't they sting you'!" asked his son. "They do, but it doesn't hurt me much." "Why doesn't it hurt you?" "Oh, I am used to it." "Let me become used to it, too," the lad replied smiling. The old man laughed kissed his son.

At that moment, the kizir (tax-recorder) appeared, having come to say that the Kurdish chief, Fattah Bey, had sent a messenger with word that he was coming to visit the landlord, and would arrive very soon for he was out hunting on the near mountains. A dark cloud seemed to pass over the old man's forehead, and his smiling face was darkened by sadness. But controlling his displeasure, he ordered the kizir to call some of his sons from the fields to wait on the guests, while he, himself, attended to providing fodder for the horses.

Fattah Bey's goings and comings were of such frequent occurrence at old Khacho's that the household knew beforehand what preparations were necessary for his entertainment. For this reason, as soon as the women heard the news, they had several lambs killed and cooked a great kettle of pilaf, knowing that he would have a retinue of at least twenty or thirty men with him.

Fattah Bey was the chief of a tube of Kurds whose sheep grazed on the mountains in the confines of the village o...

Not infrequently, quarrels arose between the Kurdish and Armenian shepherds, when the Kurds had, perhaps, stolen a sheep or had begun to graze their flocks in the pastures belonging to the Armenians. But these quarrels always ended without serious consequences, not only because the Kurdish chief was a good friend of landlord Khacho, but was also his "kirvan" (godfather). He had stood as godfather to some of the old man's grandchildren at their christening, and the old man had occupied a similar position during the circumcision of some of the Bey's sons. This brought the two into close relationship.

But why was the old man sad when he heard of the approaching visit?

36

Khacho was not a stingy man that he should be afraid of having to entertain the Bey with his troop of followers. Khacho's table, like Father Abraham's, was free to every man. Every day travelers and strangers ate of his bread. Khacho prided himself on being able to say that he never sat down to a meal without a guest. He would say, "God giveth the bread, therefore it belongs to Him, and His poor should eat of it."

But what caused him sadness when he heard that the Bey was coming? In silent meditation he stepped out of the house and stood at the gate to receive his guest. Seeing him there, some of the villagers joined him, and one of them remarked, "The Bey is coming. I wonder what belly-ache he has this time." "When the Kurd comes to the house of an Armenian," replied the landlord sadly, "he does not come without a belly-ache."

The points of lances appeared over the top of a hill, and in a few minutes a group of horsemen came in sight. "Here they come," said one of the villagers. The landlord couldn't see at that distance, but when another shouted, "It is they!" the landlord said, "Stand by and look after the horses until our boys arrive from the fields."

The Bey now drew near with his pack of hounds, and a troop of more than twenty horsemen, who were more or less related to him, and who surrounded him like a guard. Today he was mounted on a beautiful gray, an Arab courser, whose trappings were profusely ornamented with precious stones set in silver. The Bey was a man of forty years of age though he appeared much younger. He was large and well-proportioned and had a fine, manly face. He was dressed in fine linen, handsome broadcloth, beautifully embroidered, while his weapons were ornamented with gold and silver. On seeing him, the landlord stepped forward and stood beside the bridge which crossed the moat surrounding the house which the Bey must cross. But he, instead, dug his spurs into the steed's flanks, which then flew like a bird across the moat, and after prancing and curvetting gracefully, stood proudly before the landlord. "What do you think of that, old Khacho?" asked the Bey, patting the head of the magnificent creature. "You know horses. What do you think of this one?"

"May God keep off the Evil Eye. He is a beauty. Koroghlou himself hasn't a steed like that, and truly, he is worthy of you. Where did you find him? You didn't have him before."

"I received him as a gift from the Vali of Erzeroum," replied the Bey, much pleased. 'The Vali would rather lose his two eyes than this stallion but he gave it to me, his friend. It was given to him by the Sheik of Aleppo."

"He's a beauty," repeated the landlord.

37

The Bey, stirred by this praise, dug his spurs into the horse again showing off its fine points as it pranced about in the square in front of the gate, showing off his own skillful horsemanship at the same time. Then he dismounted and handing the bridle to one of his servants, ordered him to walk it about until it had cooled off.

Now the landlord, taking his guest by the hand, led him into the oda, which had been handsomely furnished in honor of the guest. Expensive Persian rugs were spread on the floor. Cushions were arranged against the wall, and a fine divan provided especially for the Bey.

Then the landlord, inviting his guest to be seated, said politely, "My house is your house. You own a place upon my head and in my eyes. I am your humble servant. My sons are your slaves, and my women your handmaids. You are welcome, a thousand times welcome. All that I have is at your disposal. Command me. Pray be seated."

The Bey expressed his thanks, and after one of Khacho's sons had removed his shoes from his feet he proceeded to seat himself in the seat of honor. Near him sat two of his cousins, and his other relatives. Some of his servants came into the oda, and stood, hands resting upon their pistols, ready to wait upon the Bey. Others had remained outside to care for the horses and hounds which were being fed from the old man's haylofts and storerooms. The Bey and his men were armed with rifles, pistols and spears, which they did not remove, although in the home of a friend. The Kurd does not lay aside his weapons whether at home or abroad, in time of peace or in time of war. His weapons are a part of his body. Khacho's sons, who had returned from their fields by this time, went out and continued to perform their father's commands; they carried no weapons.

They first offered the guests unsweetened coffee in small cups.

"Where is Stephanie? I don't see him," said the Bey. "Heretofore he has always served my coffee."

Concealing his displeasure, the landlord ordered Stephanie to come. Stephanie entered, his face beaming with pleasure. He went up to the Bey and kissed his hand. (Kurdish chiefs expect that act of courtesy). Then, stroking his silky head, the Bey said, "Do you know what I have brought you?"

"Yes, I know," replied Stephanie. "A beautiful fawn; I gave it grass but it would not eat."

"Just see, he has taken the gift already!" exclaimed the Bey.

38

"I knew it was for me," replied Stephanie, "so I took it."

"There, go now and play with your fawn," said the Bey. The lad bowed and withdrew.

"He is such a gentle lad," said the Bey, "he seems disappointed if he doesn't receive a gift from me every time I come here."

"It is not his fault. You have led him to expect one," replied the landlord, with a forced laugh.

"Oh, what fine mountains you have, friend Khacho," said the Bey, turning to another subject. "At every step you find game, wild goats, hinds, stags, and countless partridges and pigeons. This fawn, which Stephanie has, one of my hounds caught alive. You should see what fine hounds I lately received from the chief of the Zelantz tribe. I sent him a couple of mules in return. Just between ourselves, we had just seized the mules in a raid on some Persian pilgrims on their way to Mecca. But those hounds are wonderful. They run like the wind."

Dinner was served. The floor-cloth was spread, and upon it were set great trays containing lambs, roasted whole, and pilaf.

First of all sherbet was served in small cups, and then tann, made of yogurt, or madzoon, which was drunk out of ladles. There was no liquor. All then began to eat.

"Haven't you sent your sheep out to pasture yet?" asked the Bey.

"Not yet," replied the landlord. "We can't be sure of the weather yet. April is apt to be chilly. I am waiting till it's over."

"Heat and cold are in God's hands, friend Khacho. What is to happen will happen," replied the Bey. "Our sheep went to pasture a week ago. Do you know how quickly our feed was exhausted this year? Our shepherds have gone hungry the last few days."

The landlord understood the Bey's hint, and replied. "Isn't our bread yours? Command me, and I will send as much flour as is needed."

"May your house prosper and increase in wealth," said the Bey. "That is as it should be. Who shall distinguish between us? What is mine is yours, what is yours is mine. Isn't that so, friend Khacho?"

"God knows it is so. How much flour shall I send?"

"Ten donkey loads will be enough for the present. When that's gone, we'll take some more. Your granaries will not be emptied."

An unwilling smile crossed the landlord's face, and he nodded in assent.

After they had eaten, Stephanie brought water for them to wash their hands, and after that passed the coffee.

The Bey then ordered his servants who had remained standing throughout the meal, to go outside and eat with the others, where a separate table was set on carpets spread in the courtyard.

In the guestroom there remained only the Bey, a few of his relatives and old Khacho. Now the talk turned on the gift of the Vali of Erzeroum. The Bey told of the breed of his fine stallion. He said its records dated from the time of Antares, the most famous breed of all. "But this gift is going to cost me dear," he concluded.

"How so?" asked the landlord.

"Don't you understand? I must give the servant who brought it to me at least a hundred pounds."

Now the landlord understood what had given the Bey his "belly-ache," but he made haste to say, "What of it? Give it. A hundred liras is not too much for such a stallion."

"Who gives money to a Kurd?" retorted the Bey, angrily. "Only Armenians have plenty of silver."

The Bey's relatives, who had taken no part in the conversation until now, began saying: "What! Are you troubled about money?" "That's right," said another. "God knows it is so," and another added, "Goodman Khacho is so kind, there's no one like him .among all the Armenians."

Old Khacho saw that in spite of all he could say he was caught in a trap, and burdened with the debt, so, in order to prevent their suspicion, he replied, I wouldn't hurt the feelings of the Bey for a thousand liras."

"May you prosper," replied the Kurds.

The landlord arose and, leasing the oda, called his oldest son and told him to go secretly and bring hire a hundred pieces of gold from its hiding place in the hayloft.

40

"Why?" inquired the son.

"Don't you understand? These wicked men have come, eaten and drunk and now we must pay tooth-hire'," he replied sadly.

"Curses on them!" cried the son. "May God cut them off, root and branch!" He then proceeded to the barn as if to bring straw.

"Tooth-hire" means having to pay the Kurds for their kindness in coming to the home of an Armenian and eating there. The host must pay or be beaten unmercifully by his guests. Although this custom was not general, some form of payment was expected.

While the old man was out of the room, the Kurds were indulging in the following conversation. "If the old fellow doesn't bring the gold, I will order his house set on fire this instant," said the Bey, angrily.

"That won't be necessary" said another, trying to calm him. "Khacho is a good Armenian. We don't want to harm him. His door is always open to us, and we can have everything we wish from him. He's a good fellow. We must not forget his bread and salt."

Just then the old man returned, and laying a purse of gold before the Bey, he said, "God is my witness. I was keeping it for my soul's sake, to go on a pilgrimage to Jerusalem to become a "mahdesi" (hadji) but for love of you, I give it to you, Bey."

"Don't lie, Goodman Khacho, you have much more, very much," replied the Bey, taking up the purse and putting it in his bosom without counting it.

The day was well along. The Bey ordered his men to be ready to set out again. He came out of the oda and walked about with the landlord until the horses were ready. He saw Stephanie playing with the fawn, and spoke to him.

"Do you like it?" he asked.

"It is very pretty, but the dogs have wounded one of its feet, but I will cure it. Poor creature! It is in pain, and that is why it eats nothing," replied the lad, tying up the fawn's wound.

"I see you are fond of animals," returned the Bey. "I'll send you one of my young colts."

41

"I don't like horses."

"'What do you like, then?"

"I like goats, and deer, and partridges."

"Very well then, when I go hunting, I'll bring you all the creatures I take alive."

Then, as the servants brought word that the horses were ready, the Bey expressed his thanks to the landlord, and went out where his beautiful courser was standing before the door.

Old Khacho himself held the stirrup, and helped the Bey mount his horse. This act denotes that the host is at the service of his honored guest.

Mounted on his steed, the Bey put it through its paces again, after which he bade old Khacho farewell, and rode away.

The old man stood there motionless for a long time. He watched the Bey make the steed leap the moat once more, spurning the bridge, as though only the weak and feeble had need of that. He saw him swoop down on a rabbit that had chanced to cross the road and thrust his spear into its side. As he watched all this, he thought, "Why doth Heaven order thus? The Kurd has no bread to eat, but the Armenian sows and plows and prepares his provisions. The Kurd receives the gift of a fine steed, which causes the earth to tremble under its feet, but the Armenian pays for it—the Armenian who is not allowed to ride on any beast save an ass."

Chapter 8

That evening when all old Khacho's sons had returned from their labors, an oil light was burning in one corner of the room. The landlord and his sons were seated around the table. They were eating in silence. The fresh spring breeze brought refreshing coolness into the room. From outside came the bleating of sheep returning from pasture. In the bake-house the daughters-in-law were preparing food for the shepherds and plowmen. All must eat before the women could eat. The children, tired of play had gone to sleep without any supper. After eating, the sons went out. They had still much to do. They must look after the cattle, and water the fields, for this was the night when it was their turn to have the water of the stream turned onto their fields. And some one must go to the mill for flour. All sorts of jobs were waiting to be done.

The table was removed, but old Khacho and his oldest son, Hairabed, remained seated there. Hairabed prepared his father's pipe for him. Their silence continued. The spirit of sadness seemed to have spread its black wings over the hearts of that peaceful family.

"How much flour did the Kurds take?" asked the father, after taking a few puffs on his pipe. "Exactly twelve loads," answered his son, with displeasure, "and they were large sacks, filled to the brim. They had brought the sacks with them. They acted as though they had paid for it."

"Whose oxen drew the loads?"

"Ours, but, thank the Lord if they return the oxen. I fear they will eat the oxen along with the flour."

"The Bey wouldn't do such an ignoble deed," said the father.

"Who has given nobility to the Kurd? It won't be the first time they have swallowed the load and the beast at the same time. To tell the truth, I don't

43

care so much about the hundred pounds, nor the twelve loads of flour, but it vexes me that after giving them food freely, we have to give them flour besides, and send it to them with our own cattle. What an affliction this is! I don't know how long these Kurds are going to continue to plunder us. They come and they come. They carry away, and carry away. They ask and ask. They have neither conscience nor shame. God seems to have created us to feed them."

"Don't you know it is true?" replied the old man choking on his pipe as his gorge rose at the thought. "What can we do? If we don't give it with our own hands, they take it by force. We may be thankful they rob us in the name of friendship."

"We have taught them this way of robbing, ourselves," replied the son. "We might refuse, then the Kurd would be obliged to sow and reap and work for his bread. But we have taught him to be lazy and live off us."

"That is true," replied his father, sadly. "But it is hard for us to do other than the way we were taught by our fathers. We are reaping the bitter fruit of their folly. Now listen, my son. I can see that hatred has been stirred up in your heart, and that this slavery has wounded you sorely; but, again, I ask, what remedy is there? What can we do? If we don't give them what they demand, they will become our enemies and next you know they will carry off a whole flock of sheep. To whom can we complain? Who will hear our voice? Those who have been set over us to suppress wrong and to administer justice are all robbers, from Vali and Pasha down to the smallest Mudir and Kaimakam. They are brothers in robbery. You have seen with your own eyes how the Vali of Erzeroum, instead of sending chains with which to hang such a noted robber as Fattah Bey, sends him a fine horse as a gift; a gift to a criminal who has flooded our entire province with blood and tears. When the Vali, the governor of the province does this, who is left to whom we can make known our sufferings? Only God is left, but even God does not hear our voice. Our sins are many."

The son made no reply, so the father continued: "We are Armenians. God's curse is written upon our foreheads. We have torn down our dwelling with our own hands. Dissension, disagreement, envy, and enmity, and many other evils have nestled in our hearts, and we are suffering for our sins. The Kurd is not to blame. If we were agreed, if we were brave, the Kurd, the lazy, ignorant Kurd could not harm us."

He asked his son to light his pipe once more, and as he did so, his son said: "We are six brothers, Father. If you had given us a sign today, we six could have driven Fattah Bey and his horsemen from our home, and they would not have crossed our doorsill with such insolence."

44

"I know it, my son. But what would be the gain? You would have fought them; you might have killed one or two, or even many of them, but soon the whole tribe of Kurds would pour down upon us and would have laid us level with the dust. What Armenian would come to our aid? Not one. Many might rejoice. That is the way Armenians are. But the Kurds are not so. If you kill one, the whole tribe rises to avenge his blood. The blood of one member of a tribe is the blood of the whole tribe. They all seem to be children of one family. But is there such a unity among us? Each man bears his own burden; each man thinks only of himself, let come to others what may. What does he care as long as he is comfortable, and no one touches him. The fools don't understand that it must be one for all and all for one."

Old Khacho was not a man of learning, but life, experience and affairs had taught him much. His naturally vigorous intellect had developed under the storm and stress of life, and there sometimes appeared as much wisdom in his observations as in those of persons who devoted their lives to the study of human behavior. He continued to speak: "There is no remedy. We are obliged to work for and feed our enemy. We must keep the friendship of those who rob us. It is true, Fattah Bey has robbed us, but, still we cannot refuse his friendship, false as it is."

"Why?" asked his son.

"The reason is that by being friends with a great robber we escape from the hands of the lesser robbers. Now other tribes, knowing that Fattah Bey is on good terms with us, dare not touch our flocks and herds, or if they should steal anything, he will find it and return it to us."

"What is the good of that?" replied his son. "It all comes to the same thing. Fattah Bey gives us an egg but he gets a horse in exchange. He will not let another Kurd steal a sheep from us, but when he needs it he takes a hundred liras from us. We are his milk cows which he keeps and protects only in order that he may have our milk."

"That is true, my son," replied the father, "but we must remember that our ancestors, long years ago, taught the Armenian to keep his head on his shoulders in that way. I have read no books, but a bishop at the monastery at Iutch Kilisah once told me that every time enemies have attacked our land, the Armenians, instead of meeting them with sword and weapon, have met them with rich gifts — with trays full of gold. They taught us to bribe our enemies instead of fighting them. They taught us to give away our possessions to save our heads."

"But we need not continue to perform the mistakes of our ancestors forever," interrupted the son.

45

"It is very difficult to correct a wrong of longstanding. It has been repeated for thousands of years, and many more will be required to correct it. Go tell the people that we should deal differently with our enemies; that they are men like ourselves; that their bodies are not made of iron; that when they come armed to rob us, we shall use our own weapons against them. Preach to them continually. Do you think they will understand you? They will consider you a fool, and laugh at you."

The son made no reply. He saw a truth in his father's words, which was incontrovertible. But at the same time he wondered whether it was impossible to change the fixed beliefs of a people, so he asked:

"Suppose our fathers have walked in that path, should we not try to teach the people that they are on the wrong path?"

"It should be done, but who will do it? Those who have accepted the responsibility of educating, instructing and directing our people should be the ones to do it. Our priests and our bishops should do it, but they preach, 'If they smite thee on one cheek, turn the other also to them'. The school teachers should do it, but there is not one fit to do it in the entire province."

"I cannot agree with you, father," replied his son.

"Why does the Kurd who has neither priest nor bishop nor teacher, know how man should treat man? Who taught him that without weapons a man is like a blind hen that will give its head to whoever comes along?"

"The Kurd has no priest, bishop, or teacher, it is true," replied his father, "but he has a sheik, and the sheik, although he is his spiritual leader, bears arms himself, and goes to plunder unarmed people along with his people. He never preaches that these things are sins. But what do our priests teach?"

The son was silent. His father continued: "There is one comfort in all these misfortunes, that much as they carry away, our granaries remain full but the Kurd goes hungry."

"Do you know this proverb, Father? The thief can build no house for himself, but destroys the house of the house-owner. Although the Kurd does not plow nor reap, he has no bread in his house; he is always hungry, but snatching bread from the industrious Armenian, he leaves him hungry also. Do not quote us as an example to the contrary. Think how many Armenians have been impoverished by Kurds who lack food.

"That is true, my son. But there is another thing to notice. See how many

46

sheep are killed; how many are lost, but still they increase and multiply and become great flocks. While the wolf, although be destroys an devours the sheep, still is always hungry, and never multiplies. Do you ever see a large pack of wolves? The wolf is a wild beast. Today he seizes a sheep, eats and is filled, but he doesn't know where he shall find his next meal. He must always be on the hunt, but he doesn't find his prey every time. One who lives by hunting is full one day and empty the next. The Kurd is the wolf, while we are the sheep."

This was the old man's explanation of a bloodless combat.

"I think, Father," said his son, "that if the sheep had no shepherd or protectors, the wolves would not leave a sheep alive, and no flocks of sheep would be formed. It is true, we are sheep, but without shepherds. Since our condition is thus, there remains only one way for us to escape from the wolves. We must have teeth and claws like them."

Chapter 9

On the side of the highway leading from Erzeroum to Bayazid, which was the only caravan route from Trebizond to Persia, were pitched the tents of a detached Kurdish tribe. From the number of tents which covered the greater portion of a large, grassy plain, one could estimate the size of the tribe. Herds of horses, sheep, and cows scattered on the surrounding hills gave evidence that this pastoral tribe enjoyed wealth and prosperity.

On his return from the house of old Khacho, it was quite dark when Fattah Bey, who was the chief of his tribe, reached these tents with his followers.

In front of some of the tents the evening fires were still burning with food being cooked or milk heating and their flames threw a glow over the scene.

When the Bey's company approached, the dogs set up a loud barking and here and there were heard the subdued voices of the night-watchmen giving word to each other of the approach of horsemen. One of the Bey's followers spoke to the watchmen, telling them who they were.

The Bey rode up to the tent in which was lodged the guest who had brought him the gift from the Vali. He was a middle-aged Turkish officer, tried and tempered in all manner of deceit. He had at one time held the office of Mudir in the region of Van, but had been removed from the office because of taking excessive bribes.

"You have kept me waiting a long time," said the Mudir, rising as the Bey entered his tent. "I had intended to bid you farewell tonight."

"The head of the Sheik be my witness that you are a very impatient guest," answered the Bey with a laugh. "We have not seen enough of each other yet. Why do you hasten I hope you are not tired of my tent?"

"Not at all! Your hospitality is most agreeable to me. If I am ever taken to

48

Paradise (of which I haven't much hope) I wish it might be to your dwelling there! Nevertheless I must beg that you allow me to set out in the morning."

"Well, well! I have learned this much of the characteristics of the Osmanlis. They are accustomed to the smell of the cities, and to lying on soft couches from morning till evening. But what is there in this desert? It is my fault, I admit. I haven't entertained you as I ought. What could I do? You don't care to hunt; you don't care to ride; and there is no other amusement to offer in our hills."

The Mudir replied, again employing Turkish compliments. "The light of your countenance is above all other delights for me. I shall ever consider myself fortunate for having been privileged to become acquainted with you. But remember, Bey, that your servant is not an independent creature. His time is not at his own command. The Vali set ten days as the limit of my leave of absence."

"I will write to the Vali that I detained you. You know how highly he thinks of me."

"I know that the Vali would give up both his eyes rather than you. He treasures your words as if they were pearls. He said in the presence of all, that the Sultan has no chieftain so brave and faithful as Fattah Bey; and for this reason he has proposed your name as a recipient of the Majidieh of the First Order".

The Bey smiled disdainfully, and replied: "I don't care much for those things called decorations. They are mere ornaments for women."

"Then what do you like?"

"I like gold mejidiehs."

"You shall have those too, Bey. The Vali is most generous. Don't you observe that he has placed your name on the salary list, and that you will henceforth receive a salary from the Imperial Treasury for guarding the frontier and keeping the peace in this region? He accepted your request that no Mudir nor Kaimakam be placed here but that all the command shall be vested in yourself. He has done that and he will do anything else you desire."

"I thank the Vali."

While this conversation was going on, the servants of the Bey were sitting

49

on the ground outside the tent enjoying themselves in their own fashion. Each was relating the great deeds he had performed; how many women he had carried off, and so forth.

"Osman has stolen as many sheep as he has hairs an his head," said Omar. "You are no better yourself," retorted Osman. "You have carried off as many Armenian girls as I have sheep."

"Shapan doesn't like Armenian girls, they cry so easily," said another.

"That's so," returned Shapan. "The hearts of those creatures seem to be made of glass; if one touches them they are broken. But our women, God knows, have hearts of stone. Give them into the claws of a wolf and they won't whimper. I have no patience with women who cry."

"But there is this to be said," interrupted another Kurd who was the oldest of the number. "Those infidels never give up their cursed religion. I can't truly say that I seldom beat them, and you know I keep three. I always see them praying in secret. And there's another good thing about them, they can work like oxen and they are not such sleepyheads as our women are."

"Oh, but what lovely daughters-in-law landlord Khacho has!" exclaimed another young fellow." If their father-in-law were not our Bey's god-father, I would help myself to one of them."

This talk was interrupted by the barking of dogs and again the signals of the night watchmen were given. Several of the men took up their weapons and ran in the direction from which the sound was heard.

As they approached, they heard groans issuing from the darkness.

"For the love of God, take us to the Bey! We have a petition to present."

The dogs would have torn the poor fellows to pieces if the servants had not arrived in time to prevent them. It is impossible to approach the camp of the Kurds except at the risk of meeting these dogs, or the equally formidable sentries who, without warning, may thrust a spear into your side.

The strangers were a handful of men who threw themselves down on the ground outside the tent where the Bey was seated with his guest. The light of the lantern which hung in front of the tent showed them to be merchants and muleteers, one of whom had his head bandaged, another his arms, and others were wounded in other parts of their bodies, and blood was still flowing from their wounds.

The Bey, hearing the disturbance, called to one of his men, and asked to know what was the matter.

"Some merchants have come to make a complaint; they say their caravan has been robbed," was the reply.

An expression of displeasure crossed the face of the Bey, but concealing his inward uneasiness as well as he could, he commanded them to be brought in.

"This is a most astonishing occurrence," he said, turning to the Mudir; "such irregularities have never taken place on 'my land'." The Bey liked to call the territory occupied by his tribe 'his land', while really 'not a handful of that soil belonged to any Kurd whatsoever, for they shifted about from place to place like gypsies.

"How did it happen that their caravan was robbed?" he continued.

"Robbery occurs everywhere," replied the Mudir, tranquilly. "There is no land without robbers. Devils entered Heaven itself. There isn't a day when complaints are not brought to the Vali at Erzeroum."

The Bey, encouraged by the reassuring tone of the Mudir, resumed: "Believe me, Mudir, the head of the Sheik be my witness that I have kept these regions so well that even the birds of the air do not dare to cross 'my land'. I am amazed! What devil can it be who robbed these poor fellows?"

The wounded and bloodstained men now entered. One of them who was able to stand, advanced and addressed the Bey. "We have come to kiss the dust of your feet, Bey Effendi. We recognize only God above, and you below. For the love of the Prophet, help us! We are poor merchants, our caravan has been robbed; most of our company has been killed and you see the remainder here before your eyes. They are mortally wounded and cannot live long. The robbers have taken all we had; they left us nothing."

The wounded men, unable to remain on their feet, sat in front of the tent, those who were able to do so, stood.

"Where were you robbed?" asked the Bey.

"Here among the mountains not far away. The robbers led our caravan out of the highway, drove us into a lonely valley, and there they bound us hand and foot and threw us into a ditch. After that they began to rip up our bales and they took all that was of any value."

51

"What time of day was it?"

"About noon; we remained bound in that ditch until evening. God had mercy upon us. One of our number succeeded in untying his hands and then he released ours also. if it had not been for that we should have remained in that ditch to die of hunger and to be the prey for wild beasts."

"Where are you from? Where was the caravan from, and where was it going?" the Bey continued.

"Your servants are Persian merchants. The caravan was made up at Trebizond, being composed of goods brought by ship from Constantinople. We had passed through Erzeroum and as far as this place, in safety, and were going to continue our journey and go through Bayazid on to Persia, but here we were overtaken by misfortune. Our caravan was loaded with the most costly merchandise, but nothing was left. The robbers took away what they pleased and burned the remainder."

"The bead of the Sheik be my witness, this is the first time I ever heard of such cruelty," exclaimed the Bey, turning to the Mudir, who had been an attentive listener to the conversation, and who now began to question the men.

"Were you able to see the faces of the robbers?" he asked.

"How could we?" replied the spokesman. "Their faces were concealed, and only their eyes were visible, and when they seized us they bound our eyes; then they began to open our bales; but we saw this much that they were Kurds."

"How many of them were there?" asked the Mudir, once more.

"About fifty."

"In what direction did they go?"

"We could not see. As I said, they had bound our eyes, as well as our hands and feet and had thrown us into a ditch."

"That is enough," angrily interrupted the Bey, to stop the Mudir's questioning. "I understand." Then turning to the merchants, he said: "Now go and rest. If the robbers are from our region, I will try to find them, and you shall not lose a sliver of anything. But if they come from some other quarter, I can find that out also. Be at rest. I will not excuse injustice perpetrated on 'my land'."

The merchants bowed, and called down on the Bey a hundred blessings.

"Gurbo," called the Bey to one of his servants, "take these men to your tent and treat them well, as you would treat guests from Heaven. Call the physician quickly that he may cure their wounds. I commit them to you. If they complain of you, you shall not escape punishment."

The merchants blessed him once more, and bowed themselves out of his presence.

After they had taken their departure, the Bey turned to the Mudir, with these words: "See this now! Behold such events have taken place! Can you tell, my noble friend, what Evil One has taken their goods? I am confident that they cannot be the Kurds of our region. I am a terror to robbers. For fear of me no one dares to do such things, but they come from other places, often from Persia, and rob in our territory. Who can tell a Persian from a Kurd when they wear the same dress? That often happens and causes us much annoyance. Nevertheless I must try to find these robbers. Ahmeh!" he said, turning to his cousin who had been sitting there in silence all the time. "Go this moment taking with you twenty horsemen. First go to the spot where the caravan was robbed; observe the prints of the horses' feet, and question the shepherds you may meet; in a word use every means to discover the rascals. I will not forgive robbery committed on 'my land'; that touches my honor."

Ahmeh set out by night to perform the Bey's bidding.

"Ahmeh has a dog's keenness of scent," remarked the Bey. "If the robbers have not gone far he will surely find them."

"No doubt," replied the Mudir, significantly.

It was already late. The Bey ordered supper to be served. They ate and drank in comparative silence. After promising to start the Mudir on his journey in the morning, the Bey bade him goodnight and retired to his own tent.

The Mudir lay awake a long time, thinking of many things.

Chapter 10

The Bey's private tent consisted of two parts, one of which was allotted to his women, while the other was his sitting room. The material of which the tent was made was plain, like that usually used by pastoral Kurds. It was made of strips of black sacking, woven by his maid servants. The Bey entered and ordered the servant to secure the tent and then leave. Sitting there alone he seemed to be waiting for someone. The lantern suspended from the ridgepole gave only a dim, smoky light. No sound was heard from the women's side. They all appeared to be asleep.

Soon Gurbo appeared, the Kurd to whose care the Bey had committed the merchants who had been robbed.

"Are your guests comfortable?" asked the Bey, "with a meaningful look.

"Thanks to my lord's kindness, they are quite comfortable," replied the crafty Kurd. "They ate and drank, blessed you and went to sleep. Perhaps they will find their lost goods in their dreams."

"The dead do not return from Hades," added the Bey. "Well, where did you hide the goods?"

"Over in our village, in the house of lame Alo."

"Were they fine things?"

"God never gave such rich stuff into our hands before, Bey; gold, silver, velvets and cashmere; in short, everything you can wish."

"Didn't anyone see you enter the village?"

"Who should see us? There is no one left in the village. They have all gone

54

to the mountain pastures, and only a few Armenian families are left; and like blind hens they don't dare to step out of their huts after dark, but lock their doors, cover their heads, and go to sleep."

"Where did you hide the stuff?"

"In lame Alo's house, as I told you. There are a hundred holes in that old wolf's den. We piled the stuff into one of them and locked the doors. I have brought you the keys," he said, handing the Bey two keys.

"Alo is faithful to us; it is not the first time he has served us in this way," observed the Bey.

After telling what disposition he had made of the booty, Gurbo began to tell how they had pounced upon the caravan, how they had plundered it, what prowess they had shown, and so on.

"Well done, Gurbo! I have always had a high opinion of your bravery," said the Bey. "When we get rid of that scamp (meaning the Mudir) I will divide the booty and you shall each receive your proper share."

Gurbo bowed, but made no response.

"But one thing troubles me," continued the Bey, impressively. I didn't wish this business done while that man was here."

"You mean the Mudir?"

"Yes, the Mudir."

"That's no harm!" said Gurbo, laughing. "We will send the Mudir from here loaded with gifts and honors, so that he will carry away a good opinion of us. But we will send a couple of horsemen after him, and before he reaches Erzeroum they will cut off his head and bring back the gifts we gave. Then the Mudir will not be able to go and tell the Vali what he must suspect. Isn't that a good plan?"

The Bey did not reply immediately. He was meditating. "The murder must necessarily be done beyond the boundaries of our land, near Erzeroum," continued Gurbo. "Then the sin will be far from us, and no one can connect us with the occurrence."

"It is not necessary," said the Bey, after a few moments' reflection. "If he reports us to the Vali, I will find some other way to avoid punishment."

Then Gurbo, as if he had just thought of I, put his hand in his bosom, and drew out a casket wrapped in a handkerchief. The casket was of silver, richly ornamented. He gave the casket to the Bey, saying: "I didn't leave this in Alo's house. It was such a small object I was afraid it might get lost."

The Bey opened the casket. In it there were arranged in order various ornaments for women; rings and bracelets of gold enriched with precious stones.

"Their owner was a Jew, who had ordered those things made in Constantinople for a Persian prince who was to marry a Princess this winter," said Gurbo, adding with a sneer, "The poor bride is robbed of her jewels. The Jew begged that we let him keep the things. I gave him a blow that stopped his noise." With Gurbo this meant that he had killed him.

"You may go now," said the Bey. "Pay good attention to your guests. We will decide in the morning what must be done next."

The leader of the band of robbers bowed and took his departure.

After Gurbo departed the Bey sat for a long time examining the beautiful objects before him. He could not have explained why those bright jewels attracted him so greatly. "I will send this casket to the Vali at Erzeroum. I can find no gift more suitable than this," he meditated. Suddenly he changed his mind. He recollected a person dearer to him than any one else. "No, no, this lovely necklace must adorn her beautiful neck; those priceless bracelets are worthy only of her matchless arms, and those rings for her dainty fingers," he said with deep feeling.

His savage soul was under the spell of love; it was changed and became more tender. Wild beasts are rendered more fierce when they begin to love, but man is softened, and in so much the Bey differed from the beasts.

I must keep those ornaments for her, only for her." In his absorption he had forgotten himself, speaking these words aloud, and he was not aware that someone had raised the curtain of the women's quarters, and entering had silently stationed herself behind him. It was his wife Koorsit famed throughout the region for her beauty. But at this moment she towered over him like a pale and angry goddess, or an evil spirit about to destroy him. He looked up and was transfixed with terror.

For a few moments the two faced each other in silence like gladiators debating how to attack each other. The silver casket with its brilliant jewels still remained open before the Bey. The woman gave them a mere glance and crossed to the opposite side of the tent and seated herself upon a cushion. Those objects which would have excited the desire of most

56

women, especially Kurdish women who are like children in their fondness for shining things, seemed to be no more to her than bits of broken glass whose sharp points pierced the heart.

The Bey, regarding her anxiously, said: "Why are you angry? I will give you part of these also."

"I need nothing but a shroud; that is all I need," answered the woman, with a trembling voice.

The murky light of the lantern fell directly upon her pale face more beautiful in its anger, like that of an avenging angel.

"What is the matter, Koorsit?" asked the Bey gently. "I hope you have only had a bad dream."

"I do not dream. I have seen what has been going on with my own eyes."

The Bey knew very well that his crimes, and robberies, and bloodshed were not the occasion of his wife's agitation for he knew that Koorsit as well as every other Kurdish woman, would give her husband no peace if he should cease from stealing and plundering. Therefore there must be some other reason for her anger. Koorsit was the Bey's only wife, although according to Moslem law he was not forbidden to have several wives; but there were two reasons why he had not taken others. One, because the Kurds are few in number, and beautiful girls rare; and the other, that Koorsit was the daughter of the Kurdish Sheik, an influential man whose spiritual jurisdiction extended over all the tribes, and one word from him would be sufficient to remove the strongest chieftain from his position. And the Bey was beholden to him for his position. To add a second wife to his harem would be to offer an insult to the Sheik. The Bey thought of all this as he sat and studied his wife's sad countenance. The Bey saw the practical bearing of this reasoning, but made no account of its moral aspect. It would be impossible to displace his wife because she was a sheik's daughter, but when he turned his eyes towards the gaudy trinkets, again his fancy pictured the dainty creature for whom he coveted them.

He very well understood the reason of his wife's anger. Now the savage rage, which is found in wild beasts when they are smitten with love, filled his heart.

"Koorsit," he said menacingly, "what is it you demand?"

"I demand that our marriage vows be severed," she said firmly. I will not be your wife any longer. I will mount a horse and return to my father's house in the morning."

57

"Why?"

"I do not consent to have the wifehood of a sheik's daughter shared with a vile Armenian girl."

"I will keep her as your hand-maid."

"I have plenty of hand-maids."

"But I love this one."

"Love her as much as you please; but that love will cost you dear."

"What are you going to do?"

"I know."

"You threaten me, do you, you wretch! I will crush you under my feet like a potter's vessel."

"Don't you move from your place! Do you see this?" cried the woman - showing him the revolver she held in her hand. She had sprung to her feet.

The Bey was terrified. He had not anticipated such a bold step on the part of his wife. They stood confronting each other in a state of suspense, she with her revolver pointing at his breast, and he with his hand upon the hilt of his dagger.

At that moment the sound of an infant crying was heard from the other side of the partition. And the mother hastened toward the crying baby, saying only: "I will yet have my revenge."

Chapter 11

Goodman Khacho's wife had died upon giving birth to Stephanie. Khacho had not taken another wife, although it was not customary for men in his village to remain widowers. In the management of the household Sara, the wife of the oldest son, assumed control, and she was famed throughout the village for her wise management and good sense. She often went to the old man for advice, and all the household accepted her decisions.

One day, when all the family were busy with their usual occupations, a servant-maid, who had been to the fountain for water whispered to her, "A Kurdish girl is asking for you outside."

"Tell her to come here," said Sara, "You see I am busy."

"She will not come in. She says she has a very important message," replied the maid.

Sara went out. The girl was standing near the gate. She was a tall, slender girl with a dark skin, but not unattractive in appearance.

"Let us go away, over to that tree. No one will disturb us there," begged the girl, pointing to the spot.

Sara, noticing the girl's bright eyes began to feel suspicious of her. Why should this wild creature wish to take her to a distant tree where no one would be likely to pass? What business had she with her? "Come in," urged Sara, taking her by the hand. "We will go into the house. If you do not wish others to hear you, our house has many secret spots."

The stranger accepted the invitation of the mistress of the house without protest. Sara led her to a spot in the garden shaded by willows.

They sat down near each other on the grass.

59

"Now tell me, my dear," she continued, clasping the girl's hand in a friendly way. "What have you to tell me?"

"Koorsit Hanum sent Chavo to you," began the girl. "You surely know Koorsit, don't you? She is Chavo's mistress. She doesn't beat Chavo, and she always gives her her old clothes saying, 'You may have these, Chavo, you are a good girl.' But who would call them old clothes? They are quite new, don't you see? The mistress gave them all to me. She wore them one day, and the next day they were old for her." And indeed the Kurdish girl was dressed quite neatly.

But Sara could not imagine what all this irrelevant talk had to do with the message to her. The girl spoke in the third person. Sara understood so much, that the girl's name was Chavo, and that she was the hand-maid of Koorsit Hanum, whom she knew to be the wife of Fattah Bey, the friend of the family. But why had the lady sent this half-witted maid to her? This puzzled her not a little. Sara allowed her to make known the purpose of her visit in her own fashion.

"So your name is Chavo? What a pretty name!" she said.

"My mother named me Chavahir, (a corruption of Jevahir, or Jewel) but my mistress calls me Chavo. She says Chavahir is too long."

"I will call you as your mistress does. Chavo, my daughter, what did your mistress say when she sent you to me?"

The girl was not to be trapped into giving a direct answer. Her brain seemed to be confused with too many ideas, and she didn't know which to utter first.

She replied, "Chavo's mistress quarreled with the master last night. Don't look at me like that. Chavo isn't a child. She is very smart. When the mistress quarreled with the master, Chavo was hidden behind the curtains and heard it all. Oh, how angry the mistress was. She tore her hair and rent her clothes. Alas those clothes! Even Chavo can't wear them."

Noting that the light-minded girl was very fond of fine clothing, Sara said: "Surely Chavo knows how to sew. She will mend them and then wear them."

"Sew? Don't I sew? See these fingers!" and she exhibited the fingers of her right hand. "Just see! How many times Chavo's mother pricked these fingers saying, 'May you perish if you do not learn how to sew!'

"I see you are a very smart girl; now tell me why the master quarreled with the lady."

"The master said: 'I must have a new wife.' Isn't that a sin? Who is there like Koorsit? And what is the use of a new wife?"

Little by little Sara was getting hold of the facts. "There is no one to compare with Koorsit," she replied. "But tell me Chavo what new wife does the master wish?"

"Chavo's mistress will die if the master brings home a new wife, and then Chavo won't live long," said the girl, her eyes filling with tears.

"Foolish child!" exclaimed Sara impatiently. "Tell me who it is he is going to bring."

"Ask why the mistress sent Chavo to you, and then Chavo will tell you whom he will bring."

"Very well, why did she send you, then?"

"They quarreled last night, and in the morning the mistress said, 'Chavo, go to the house of our godfather Khacho. Take my salutations to Sara; ask her how she is, and say—' oh, I forgot to ask how you are!"

"No matter. What else did the mistress say?"

"The mistress said, 'You will call Sara to a secret place.' That is why I called you to go out under that tree."

"Here also no one can hear us. What did the mistress say?"

"The mistress said, 'You must send Stephanie away quickly. If there is no one who can take her away from here,' said the mistress, 'I will furnish men to take her wherever you wish.' It was not yet morning when the mistress spoke these words. She said, 'Swear, Chavo, that you will keep all this in mind, and that you will tell no one else.' Chavo swore."

Afterwards the girl told Sara that the mistress would kill Chavo if she should let anyone else know about this, and she added that she was very much afraid of the mistress for she might even kill her. She said she had seen her kill one of her servants, but why she had done so she did not say.

But poor Sara did not hear a word of all this. When she heard Stephanie's name spoken she was thunder-struck. She was terrified, and would have fallen to the ground unconscious if the girl's strong arm had not supported her. Although the simple girl could not understand the poor woman's agitation, still she felt that the news she had imparted was of a very serious nature, and she tried to comfort her.

"Sara must not worry. As long as Chavo's mistress lives she will not let the master carry off a girl from here,"

"What girl"" cried Sara, coming to herself. "We have no grownup girl in our house."

"The master knows that Stephanie is a girl."

Just at that moment Stephanie came into the garden to feed his fawn. The sunshine fell upon the lad's beautiful face, and outlined his fine form.

Sara pointed toward him saying; "See there! that is Stephanie, look well. Is he a girl? Who has told the master such a lie?"

"One of your Kurdish servants, the wife of the shepherd Hilo, told the master. The mistress says she will have the wretch killed."

"Hilo's wife has lied. She stole things, and we sent her away; so she tells lies about us."

Sara saw that although Chavo was a simple girl she was not a fool by any means, and seeing her fidelity to her mistress, which is not uncommon among half savage servants, she thought it safe to send a message by her in return. So she told Chavo to return her compliments to her mistress and ask how she was, and thank her for her message. And also inform her mistress that her thinking Stephanie was a girl was a mistake; still since she wished to have Stephanie sent out of the country, her request should be complied with. Then she added that she wished very much to see the mistress herself, that they might talk these things over together, and she begged that the mistress would plan some means by which they might meet secretly. Having said all this, she asked; "Now my smart Chavo, can you tell your mistress all this without forgetting any of it?"

"Chavo has a quick mind; Chavo will not forget," the girl replied, and she repeated all that Sara had said, making only a few slips. These Sara corrected, and Chavo repeated the lesson once more. "Now Chavo says it just the way Sara says it," said the girl to herself. "On the way back Chavo will say Sara's words over and over so that she may not forget them."

"Others might hear you," Sara remarked.

"Chavo isn't so stupid; Chavo will say it to herself."

The girl now looked at the sun, and seeing that the day was quite far advanced, she rose to go, for she had a long distance to travel.

"Wait, Chavo, my good girl, let me bring you something," Sara begged, and left her alone. Just then Stephanie, who was still occupied with his fawn, seeing the girl standing alone, approached her.

"Are you going?" he asked.

"Do you see how late it is growing?" she replied, pointing to the sun.

"You came to our house, but they have given you nothing to eat," said Stephanie.

"Oh, Chavo forgot she was hungry. Chavo has eaten nothing today."

"I will bring you something to eat."

The Kurdish girl, charmed with the lad's kindness of heart, threw her arms around him and kissed him.

Stephanie ran to the house and brought butter and honey wrapped in thin "lavash", (large, thin wafers which look like wrapping paper).

"Now sit down and eat," he commanded.

"Chavo will eat on the way home."

Then Sara returned bringing a pretty red silk kerchief such as Kurdish women greatly admire. When Chavo saw it she forgot her good manners, and snatching it from Sara's hands, like a child, began to tie it around her head; and then as though looking into a glass, she turned first to Sara and then to Stephanie, asking, "Is Chavo pretty now?"

"Very pretty," they both replied.

"Then kiss Chavo."

Sara embraced her affectionately.

"You also, Stephanie," she commanded. Stephanie obeyed also.

"And now Chavo bids you farewell," she said, and so set out on her return to the Kurdish camp.

Chapter 12

After sending Chavo away, Sara began to realize the full significance of the information imparted to her by the Kurdish girl. Stephanie was still standing near her and had no knowledge of the fate which threatened him. He laid his hand on Sara's shoulder and asked: "Why are Kurdish girls so foolish?"

"They are not foolish, my child," replied Sara, with motherly tenderness, "it is only because they are untaught, and have grown tip like the wild creatures upon the mountains."

"Like my fawn," added Stephanie, "for although I have cared for it all this time and have often taken it in my arms and petted it, still it does not love me, but runs away when I go near it."

While he was speaking Sara looked earnestly at the kind-hearted lad and her eyes filled with tears. She had never studied that delicate face before. She turned aside her head that the youth should not notice her tears.

But he was still curious about the Kurdish girl. "She said she was hungry, Sara, and had eaten nothing today. I gave her some wafers with butter and honey, and begged her to sit here and eat, but she took the food with her and went away eating as she went. Was she in great haste, Sara?"

"Yes, she was in haste; she has far to go."

"How far?"

"To the blue hills."

"How is she going to cross so many mountains, afoot, alone. with no companion? Isn't she afraid, Sara?"

"No, she is used to doing such things. What is a wolf's cub afraid of?"

Sara was called away and there was no more talk between them.

The poor woman passed the remainder of the day in great mental distress. She hardly knew what she was doing. Instead of taking up the article she wanted, she would take up another; instead of going where she intended, she found herself going somewhere else. She was constantly making mistakes. The hours passed in a fever of unrest.

When Stephanie's mother had died, Sara had taken the child and brought it up with her own. He was as dear to her as any of her own children. Now a sad fate threatened him. To whom and how should she reveal that the Kurdish servant had told her today? She was certain that if Stephanie's aged father should learn of the intention of the Bey he would be unable to bear the sorrow.

On the other hand Sara thought that concealment would be dangerous if not impossible. They must take measures in time to avert the threatened evil. But whom should she take into her confidence? These reflections disturbed her, and still she arrived at no decisive conclusion.

In the evening, on the return of her husband, Hairabed, he asked her what ailed her and whether she was ill.

"I have had a headache, but it is of no account," replied his wife, not wishing to startle him with a sudden announcement of the trouble.

"Put a little vinegar on your forehead," he suggested.

"I have tried everything."

Sara continued to try to lead up to the subject, little by little, when Hairabed gave her an opportunity to begin, by asking, "A Kurdish girl came here today, who was she?"

"She was the servant of Koorsit Hanum, Fattah Bey's wife."

"Every time that scoundrel or any of his people come here," exclaimed Hairabed, bitterly, "I always expect some evil to follow. Oh, when will the feet of those rascals cease to cross our threshold?"

"But we must consider all the harm they have done us so far as the blessing of God," replied Sara, with a significant look.

Hairabed turned pale at the idea these words conveyed, but before venturing to inquire further he tried to fortify himself by ejaculating piously: "All misfortunes are for the good of man; whatever sorrow God has sent must be borne in patience." Then he asked, "What is it? What has happened?"

Sara then told him what she had heard from the Kurdish girl.

On Hairabed's countenance were pictured every variety of emotion, horror, hatred, anger and grief, each in turn.

"I have been expecting this for a long time," he sighed, after hearing the whole story. "My poor father! He will die of grief when he hears it."

"That is what I have been thinking all day," returned Sara, "he will certainly die."

They sat in silence for a time. Each was thinking what to do.

"It will not be necessary to inform my father," Hairabed observed, finally.

But it will not be possible to keep it from your brothers," Sara replied.

"I will inform my brothers."

"Then in order to lose no time, inform them tonight," Sara urged. "Every moment is precious. Do quickly what must be done. Who knows what may happen."

Some of Hairabed's brothers were at home, but some had not yet returned from the fields. He rose and telling his wife not to mention the subject to anyone, went to consult his brothers.

Taking with him the brothers who were at home and going out to meet those who were just returning, he conducted them to a small grove near a mill where they would not easily be discovered or interrupted; for at home they might be disturbed, or their, father might come upon them in secret conclave.

When they were all seated on the ground, Hairabed informed them what his wife had heard. It is not difficult to imagine the impression which the news made upon the brothers. They seemed petrified with horror. It was as if a flock of sparrows, twittering and chirping in the branches of the trees, and filling the woods with their chatter, should see a hawk hovering near them, and suddenly every sound was hushed. This was how Fattah Bey's name and his wicked intentions affected the six brothers.

"Behold the worth of a Kurd's friendship!" exclaimed one of the brothers. "The Bey is our children's godfather, and yet he forgets that he has eaten our bread and our salt."

"What friendship can there be between the wolf and the lamb; or the fox and the hen?" cried Hairabed, passionately. "But we are worse off than sheep or hens. The sheep has horns, and sometimes fights against its foe; the hen uses beak and claw in self -defense; but we have nothing with which to protect ourselves. We are a disgrace to mankind; we are the scum of mankind; we should be purged away, destroyed, in order that mankind should not be contaminated by us." He spoke these words with such melancholy bitterness that his brothers were alarmed.

"What are we?" he continued in the same strain. "Industrious, hardworking plowmen, and we boast of it! But the ass, the ox, the horse and the buffalo are stronger than we and work harder. We are simply reasoning animals, and nothing more. We earn, they eat; we raise beautiful girls, they enjoy their love. Whatever is beautiful, whatever is good is not for us. Whatever is mean and worthless is left for us; we are not worthy of any good things!

"A few days ago I was talking with my father. He tried to persuade me that our condition is not as wretched as we think, and by way of proof he pointed to our visible wealth; but let a band of Kurds attack us and it will disappear in a twinkling of the eye.

"Now say to him, 'They are going to drag your dear child from your side; you shall see it with your own eyes, but you will not be able to utter a single protest!' Is this being well off ?

"Only an Armenian is able to be patient under such conditions—only the shameful, dishonorable Armenian! Come now, snatch a cub from the den of a tigress; she will tear you to pieces on the spot! The Kurd will do the same; but what do we do? Nothing!"

Hairabed's words so inflamed the hearts of some of his brothers that with one accord they resolved that they would resist; they would die rather than allow Stephanie to fall into the hands of the Kurds.

"There will be this comfort," said Abo, "that even though we do not save our sister we shall not see her disgraced but shall be at rest in our graves."

But some took a different view. "We shall all perish for the sake of a girl, and leave our children fatherless; what wisdom is there in doing that?" asked another brother, whose name was Ohan. "I wash my hands of this business. We have a sister, but if we had none it would be no great loss. Why should we lose our herds for her sake?"

Still another brother, regarding Stephanie's condition from a practical standpoint, began to defend Ohan's position saying: "I don't see any misfortune in this. In one respect it would be a good thing. When we have a brother-in-law line Fattah Bey, all the Armenians will be afraid to injure us. We have an example of this in neighbor Muggo. We don't dare to speak to him of our troubles, for he will report us to his Kurdish son-in-law, and some night the Kurds will come and kill us in our beds. Wouldn't it be fine to have such a brother-in-law?"

These words angered Abo. "Jesus Christ be my witness," he exclaimed, "you must be out of your head! What words you have spoken! An ass would not utter such foolishness. Are we to give our sister into the hands of a lawless unbeliever in order that Armenians should stand in awe of us? We want no such respect. They may pay us respect to our faces, but in his heart every Armenian will curse us. Who loves Muggo for having given his daughter to a Kurd? He is not loved; he is feared. But fear is another thing. Many are afraid of dogs and wolves."

One of the brothers, who had kept silent until now, began to oppose Abo, bringing forward his peculiar religious philosophy in defense. His arguments were that it is impossible to change God's plans; whatever is to be, will be; that God created the Kurd a Kurd, the Armenian an Armenian; He has given the Kurd weapons; the Armenian a spade; that neither can fill the place of the other; all these things are in God's hands; and he brought his arguments to a climax with the following example. The crow was desirous of having the plumage of the peacock; but who could give it to him ? God created the one in one way, and the other in another.

Abo answered: "You forget, brother, that the crow and the peacock are different birds; but the Kurd and the Armenian are both men. The Kurd was not born with weapons in his hand, but naked and weak, the same as the Armenian. Why should you throw all the responsibility upon God? Has He given weapons into the hands of the Kurd for the express purpose that he should come and massacre us; drag our daughters from their homes and carry them off? And has He made us the poor, cowardly wretches we are? God doesn't concern Himself with those things. He gives us minds that we may choose for ourselves. If you go and throw yourself into the river, God is not going to prevent you by main force; you simply destroy yourself."

69

Hairabed, the eldest brother, had listened to this dispute in silence. He felt grateful to Abo for the stand he took, but still he did not wish to offend his other brothers. "You see," he said ' earnestly, "here we are, six brethren, assembled, but we can come to no agreement. How much more difficult it is to unite a people or a nation! So long as we are as we are, so long will our condition remain as it is. They beat us; they snatch from our hands our wives, our daughters, our goods, our property, and we must needs submit to all these indignities and tortures, and like wretched beasts of burden we must work for enemies that they may live at their ease; while we give thanks to God that they at least spare our lives, and allow us to creep on the earth like the miserable worms we are!" Then Hairabed proposed that they remove Stephanie from home at least temporarily, to the monastery of St. John, until it should be possible to take her across the Russian frontier where she would be safe. But Ohan and Haggo did not agree to this even objecting that this also would be resisting the Bey's will. "By hiding our sister," said they, "we shall arouse the anger of the Bey, and he will revenge himself upon us." They approved only of letting things take their course, repeating that whatever God wills, will be; that man cannot obliterate the handwriting of God.

Some urged that their father be informed, that lie as the head of the family, decide what course to pursue. So the discussion dragged on, and still they arrived at no conclusions.

Suddenly, an owl hooted nearby. They shuddered. "Listen," said Ohan and Haggo. "The owl confirms our words. It will be bad for us to send Stephanie away from home."

Only Hairabed and Abo remained firm in their opinion. The conclave broke up in uncertainty.

Chapter 13

But what riddle was this? Stephanie first a boy, and then a girl! Let us explain the riddle. Its key is buried in a little tale.

In a quiet spot in Goodman Khacho's garden, sheltered on all sides by a cluster of trees, lies a lonely grave. No cross, no stone, no sign to mark it. It is a low mound slightly higher than the surrounding plot. Often in the stillness of the night the old man might be seen lying full-length beside the unpretentious mound, while he wept as though his heart would break. The other members of the family also would visit it occasionally and shed tears beside it.

Who lay buried there? Goodman Khacho once had a daughter named Sona. She strongly resembled Stephanie. When Sona reached her sixteenth year, many requests were made for her hand, not only because she was of a wealthy family, but especially because of her beauty. Her father found it very difficult to choose between the numerous suitors. But a sad event put an end to Sona's good prospects.

One day she went out into the fields to gather greens, but she never,, returned. Many inquiries were made concerning her. Some said she was drowned in the river; some that she had been devoured by wild beasts; some that the witches had stolen her; and some that the Kurds had carried her off.

They searched far and wide, and looked everywhere, but to no avail and they were unable to obtain any information whatever concerning the lost girl, even though her father promised a liberal reward to anyone who should bring proofs of her whereabouts.

Several weeks passed. Then one day a Kurd appeared at Khacho's gate leading a mule carrying a bier on its back. Sona's body lay in it. According to the story of the Kurd, the unfortunate girl had been snatched from the fields by a Kurdish chief, who was distinguished principally by his villainies. Sona finding no other way to escape from the hands of the monster, bribed an old Kurdish woman with some gold pieces which were sewn onto her headdress, to buy some poison for her. The woman did her bidding. Sona took the poison and died.

The Kurds would not allow the body to be buried in their burying ground, because she had affirmed till her last breath, "I am a Christian. I will not change my faith." So her body remained unburied.

One of the Kurds learning whose daughter she was, thought it might be worth his while to take the body to old Khacho, and claim a reward.

The Armenian clergy also would have nothing to do with the corpse. The reasons they gave were that she was a suicide, driven to death by a villain, and she had not confessed nor received absolution; therefore they could not allow her to be buried in the Armenian cemetery. This was why her grave was in her father's garden. Rejected by the church, she had found shelter in her home.

Naturally this misfortune brought great grief to the whole family, but this was not all. Sona's mother, Rhea, had given birth to Stephanie shortly before, and unable to bear the bitter pain caused by Sona's fate, grew weaker day by day and soon followed her daughter to the grave. That event influenced Stephanie's life. Stephanie was, indeed, a girl; but she was called by a boy's name, and dressed as a boy. Her baptismal name was Lila.

But why had they brought her up in this disguise?

Sona's death left her father so oppressed with grief that he had a foreboding that his other daughter would suffer the same fate. His anxiety was not without grounds, especially in his country, where he had known of many and many a young girl carried off by Turks or Kurds. Consequently he wished to have Lila grow up as a boy till she became of age. The mother concurred in this desire, but dying soon after was unable to bring up the child. The secret had been kept most scrupulously. Outside the family only three persons knew the fact: the village priest, and the godfather and godmother who were no longer living.

Lila, whom we may call by her proper name, was now sixteen. Few village girls remain at home after reaching that age. Her father thought it was time to think of settling her in a home of her own, but since Lila was supposed to be a boy naturally no one sought her in marriage. Besides, her father desired her to marry a man who would take her away from their village, in order that the deception he had practiced might not be known, although this was no uncommon course for people to pursue in his country. But where could he find a husband for Lila who would comply with these requirements?

Her father had set his heart on a man called Thomas Effendi, a talkative, tricky, short, smug man who was anything but a gentleman. It was not known where he was from. By his own report he was from Constantinople, and had rich relatives there. Lila's brothers hated the fellow heartily, not only because his face was repulsive, but because they knew him to be exceedingly profligate and cruel.

He kept quite aloof from the majority of Armenians, but kept company with Turks, and fawned upon Mudirs, Kaimakams and Kurdish Beys, He used their names to threaten Armenians, and he would boast of their friendship. Thomas Effendi was the Imperial Multezim, that is, the tax collector of the Imperial tolls and customs.

The Multezim is as much dreaded by the villagers as the destroying angel, or devil, and is a terror to the village. But what the peasant most fears, that he most respects. If the Satanic Majesty should appear in a village, the peasants would make haste to appease him with gifts and flattery. This is the way of mankind. In primitive ages men worshiped the good spirits and the evil impartially, offering sacrifices to both, and if anything, offering more to the evil ones. They may have explained this by saying: "The good are bound to do us good, but we must placate the evil lest they do us harm." With this idea in mind, it is easy to understand why Thomas Effendi was admitted into the home of Goodman Khacho as an honored guest.

Goodman Khacho, the largest landowner in the village, held a semi-official position, being the person with whom the officers had dealings concerning taxes, customs, and tithes of the products of the soil. For this reason the Multezim came to Khacho's house, and often he would remain there for weeks at a time, collecting the grain and other products due him as tax collector.

The "oda", or guest room of the chief landowner, is to all purposes the village inn. The Kaimakam, the Mudir, the Multezim, the bishop gathering "spiritual fruit", the mounted guardsmen and even the latest arrival from beggardom, all apply for entertainment there. There is little to choose between these various characters.

It was the morning after the council held by Goodman Khacho's sons in the woods, when Thomas Effendi appeared again in the village of o.... bringing with him two guards who were inseparable from him. He had come to set the figures of the tax on sheep and other animals, for it was late in the spring, and the villagers would soon be migrating with their flocks and herds to the "yailah" or mountain pastures, to graze, and to escape from the heat of summer.

After completing his day's work, Thomas Effendi made his way with Goodman Khacho to the home of the latter.

The Sultan would never parade the streets of Constantinople with such haughtiness on his visit on Fridays to pray in Aiya Sophia (St. Sophia) as that which this insignificant man assumed as he strutted through the streets of the village of O.... Swaggering along, with his nose in the air, he was constantly looking from side to side to see how many men were noticing him and paying him respect. He wore a kind of "muntir" or cloak, decorated with numerous buttons which he would have you believe that the Vizir had sent him. Upon entering the landlord's oda, he ordered coffee to be brought without delay, and proceeded to order what he wished for supper. Into whatever house the Imperial tax collector enters, he constitutes himself master forthwith. If the people of the house do not perform his bidding, he knows how to bring them around.

When they were seated, Goodman Khacho said to his guest: "Effendi, it was hardly fair to beat that poor peasant today."

"You are mistaken, landlord," replied the tax collector, with his purring voice. "The peasant needed to be beaten, and to be beaten well. The ass will not carry his load till he is beaten."

"But it was not the fault of the peasant."

"It is all the same whether it was or it wasn't. Perhaps he was not to blame today; another day he will be to blame. You have heard the fable of Nasreddin Khodja and his ass. When one of Nasreddin Khodja's asses broke its halter and ran away, instead of chasing the runaway ass and beating it, he began to beat his other ass which had not broken its halter but was standing quietly in its place. They asked him what the poor creature had done to deserve a beating. The Khodja answered: 'If this one should break his halter, you have no idea how he would run!"

"But I am certain that the man was not lying. I know that the Kurds carried off the greater part of his sheep," continued the old man, who was not convinced that it was necessary to beat the quiet, innocent ass in place of the runaway culprit.

"I know, myself, landlord, that the Kurds have stolen some of his sheep," replied the tax collector, impressively, "but if I should accept such accounts and every tale of how 'the floods came and the mill-race carried away', I should have to pay the Imperial taxes out of my own pocket half the time.

74

In last year's estimate that man was set down as owning one hundred sheep. I demand the tax on one hundred. But if the Kurds have stolen some fifty or sixty is that my fault? The Kurds rob every day. If these fellows are men let them prevent them."

"One ought to show some pity," still urged the landlord. "You have a right to require the tax on only as many sheep as he has in hand. He should not be obliged to pay taxes on the lost, the dead, and the stolen."

"How can I prove that they have really been stolen?" demanded the tax collector, angrily. "The peasants may hide their sheep, and tell me that they are lost, dead, or stolen, or they may make a thousand and one excuses."

The landlord made no reply.

"But you have not seen the new 'firman' (royal decree) which I have received from the Sultan," Thomas Effendi exclaimed. "If you knew what is written there, you would not be talking like this, landlord." So saying, he drew from his bosom a large packet, took out a number of papers, opening them one after another with great care, at last he unfolded an immense red sheet, printed in large, striking characters. "Take it and read!" he commanded.

The landlord gazed in astonishment at the imposing document. But if he had been able to read Turkish, he would have found that this great, red sheet was nothing but a theater poster or playbill advertising benefit performances for some actress.

Thomas Effendi looked at the old man reprovingly. "Landlord, the Sultan's 'firman' should not be treated with such little respect. When anyone takes it in his hands, he first kisses it and afterward proceeds to read." The old man did as he was bid, and humbly returned it.

"I have told the villagers a thousand times that this is the way the 'firman' stands now, and that the taxes have been increased, but still they don't comprehend; they still insist on the old way," said the tax collector, with rising anger. "I, too, am a man; my patience is exhausted and I begin to beat them. The stupid ass, though only an ass, if he once steps in the mire, won't step there again even if you cut off his head. But these peasants haven't as much sense as they." (It was Thomas Effendi's habit to draw all his illustrations and comparisons from donkey-life.)

"Listen, landlord Khacho, let me tell you of an experience of mine. You know that I have business in the villages around Alashgerd. Once a certain man had reaped and threshed his grain, and had it ready for inspection. He

75

sent for me to measure it and take the tithes. I demanded cash instead of the tithes. He replied that he was unable to pay the cash, and added, 'You have a right only to the grain, so take that which belongs to you.' (I can't tolerate having village asses talk about my 'rights'!) So, I said what I thought: 'Cursed be your father! I'll teach you what "rights" are!' I didn't measure his grain but went away and left it there. The rains came; the grain sprouted, was scorched, rotted and was destroyed. Then I went and said, 'I don't stand on my "rights" any longer, give me my grain!' But whence could he give it? The grain had become a moldy heap of dust. 'Then give me my money instead of the tithes!' I said. He had no money. I gave him a good beating; ordered his oxen to be sold and got my money! Now that fellow is so careful that he will carry a basket of eggs without breaking one! When he sees me he rises to his feet a verst away, and bows most humbly. That is the way to treat people."

"Is that mercy?" asked Goodman Khacho, in such a low tone that one would think he did not wish to be heard.

"What's that about 'mercy'?" sputtered the tax collector. "Government is one thing; mercy is another. Although you have been head of the village forty years, you haven't learned how to govern yet! You just heard the story about Nasreddin Khodja and his asses, now I'll give you another example. A Pasha is appointed to govern a certain Province. As soon as he enters upon office, he has a few men seized at random; he may have them imprisoned and even beheaded. It may be that those men are not guilty of any crime, but the Pasha must put a few men to death in order to inspire the people with a proper degree of respect for him. What does governing mean? It means keeping the people in constant terror. If I hadn't done as I did in regard to that villager's harvest, the others would have lost their respect for me, and I could no longer have done as I pleased there."

Thomas Effendi talked about his doings as frankly as a Kurd about his atrocities. What difference was there between this Armenian and Fattah Bey? Only this that the one was a low, crafty oppressor, while the other was a brave, spirited robber!

The fate of Lila was to be linked with one of these two persons. But no one asked which one she loved.

Chapter 14

Thomas Effendi was going to remain several days longer at the house of Goodman Khacho. He had still some further business in o....

Another guest was accustomed to visit Goodman Khacho's house two or three times a year. He was a young man from the region of Mt. Ararat, who would buy of Khacho sheep, oxen, wool, butter and cheese which he sold in Alexandropol, or in Erivan. In exchange for these commodities he would bring such merchandise as was not found in this region; various kinds of manufactured articles, such as calico, cotton, sugar, tea, coffee, and other articles. Such traders fill an important need in the villages like this one situated far from cities. The country-folk gave him what he needed, and received in exchange that which it would be difficult for them to go and obtain for themselves; especially in a country where there are no traveled roads for caravans, and where from fear robbers intercourse with the outside world is largely interrupted.

Every time this young man appeared there was great rejoicing in old Khacho's house. He had been there so often that they treated him as one of the family. On entering the village he would direct his caravan, consisting of a few pack horses, toward the old man's house; unload his animals, and take up his quarters there for weeks, until he should finish his trading, and be ready to return.

On the day following Thomas Effendi's arrival, this young man came again; and the two met at Khacho's gate as he was unloading his horses.

"Ah, you are here!" exclaimed the young man, crossing himself meanwhile and muttering "In the name of the Father, Son and... Alas, I have seen the face of a devil, and I shall have no luck this time!"

Thomas Effendi laughed heartily, and seizing the young man's hand said, "You are crazy, crazy! I have said a thousand times that you are crazy."

"Well say so! What evil have you brought me this time, I wonder! I have brought some poison for you to drink, so that the poor peasants may be rid of you!" he retorted, laughing in his turn.

Several men were standing near who had been helping unload the animals and carry in the bales. The Effendi thought that it was not fitting for him to be bantering with a fool in the presence of the villagers, so he turned away saying he had business in the village but that they should enjoy each other's company at supper.

"It would be a sin to eat with you!" retorted the young man.

"The tail of the ass grows neither longer nor shorter, and it is the same with your wits," responded the Effendi. "If you take an ass to Jerusalem, he is still an ass; he never becomes a Pilgrim," he added.

"Ah, when you bring your donkey tales, there is no end to them!" exclaimed the other. The Effendi quickly left.

Already every one from the oldest to the youngest in Khacho's house had heard of the arrival of Vartan, for such was the trader's name, and they were waiting with impatience for him to open his bales.

Nearly every one had entrusted him with some commission. He set his bales down in the hall and immediately the whole of Khacho's family swooped down upon him. One asked, "Did you bring the shoes I ordered?"; another "Did you bring my cap?" There was a clamor of voices on every side. Even the children tugged at his coat and asked for everything they could think of.

"I have brought them all!" he replied, "I have brought you each something."

"Then give them," they clamored.

"Away with you, you rascals!" he ordered jokingly. "Can't you let me rest a moment first? I will open the bales presently and give you what you wanted!"

'No, now, now!" they insisted.

They stood so little in awe of Vartan that they paid no attention to his objections, but began to open the packages themselves. As soon as the ropes were loosened there followed a scramble for the articles of which they were in search. The young man watched them with kindly amusement, and said, laughingly, "May your house have no evil befall it! But should the Kurds ever attack you, they wouldn't make worse havoc."

The only one who did not join the marauding horde was Stephanie, whom we may now call Lila. She stood apart smiling as she watched the excited scramble.

Vartan went near her and asked, "Why don't you take something?"

"What shall I take?" she inquired with a blush.

Truly, what could she take? She was weary of her disguise, but she did not dare touch trinkets such as other girls might enjoy.

Vartan understood the cause of her perplexity, and said in a low voice, "Never mind, I have brought you something you will like."

"What is it?" she asked in a whisper.

"I will give it to you later, but no one must see it."

Lila smiled her thanks and turned away.

Vartan was about twenty-five years old; he was a tall, powerfully-built fellow, with large features which could not be called handsome. His large roving black eyes might cause him to be taken for a robber. On his full lips he always wore a bitter, ironical smile. His carriage was free and bold; he had great skill in business.

Where he hailed from, or what his past had been, no one in this region knew. But there were many stories about him. They said he had broken his vows, for he had once been in a monastery, as deacon; he had also been a teacher. But no one knew why he had left either monastery or school. But what was well known was that in this region Vartan played the role of contrabandist. He had all the qualities needed for that profession: bravery, skill and quick wits. Constantly on guard against danger and accident, he combined firmness of purpose with fearless bravery.

There was this also, that not Thomas Effendi alone considered Vartan a fool, but both in the village of o.... and in the country around he was known as "crazy Vartan." In what respect was Vartan crazy? He was not a fool. He had studied much. He had acquired considerable knowledge. He understood and knew the conditions of life. In spite of his youth, he had been tried, and had suffered much.

Then how was he crazy? Simply because he did not know how to dissimulate (or did not think it worth his while to do so) and he tried to run counter to prejudice. He was very outspoken, and would say to anyone's face what he thought of him. He did not conceal his own faults, but would tell them all, and such persons are usually regarded singular characters. There are many who expect men to appear quite differently from what they actually are, and they can't understand straightforwardness. Many of the ancient philosophers and prophets and Nasreddin Khodja were considered "peculiar" although there was a kind of wisdom in their folly. But Vartan was not a philosopher and much less a prophet; still his observations, manner of speech and behavior seemed harsh and strange to most people.

When he promised Lila "a pretty thing he had brought her" and gave her to understand that he could give it to her only in secret, Vartan did not proceed with his accustomed directness. He seemed to prefer secrecy on this occasion. He soon attained his desire.

When describing Goodman Khacho's house the enclosed garden was not fully pictured. It was quite a large garden, and was so thick that one could disappear from sight by taking a few steps among the shrubbery.

After storing away his goods, Vartan stepped into the garden. He wished to rest in the shade of the trees. His heart was filled with a delicious tumult; his spirit was in turmoil. At such times, trees, flowers and the rustle of leaves speak most eloquently to the heart. Lying on the soft grass he gazed up at the blue sky through the interlacing branches, and was not consciously thinking of anything. He watched the flecks of white sailing across the sky, piling upon one another in great cloud banks. It presaged a storm. Vartan's heart resembled these. The indefinite and inchoate passions of his soul seemed to be uniting and taking shape into that tender sentiment called love.

Vartan had long known that Stephanie was a girl. He surmised, also, the reasons why her parents had been obliged to dress her as a boy and to have her grow up as a boy. It was these circumstances that had attracted the attention of the young man to the unfortunate girl, and filled him with a heroic desire to rescue her from her unnatural condition. But until this day these feelings had remained latent in the depths of his heart. Until this day no love passages had transpired between the two, nor had he let her know that he knew her secret. Stephanie had conversed with him freely, and the disguised girl bad not always been on her guard, but had shown the characteristics of her sex, such as a girl cannot conceal.

Vartan bad been lying in the garden a long time, and was becoming restless. Finally he heard a rustle in the grass, and turning, saw Stephanie standing near him. His heart beat more rapidly: that heart of iron, which was not easily agitated; Stephanie came a little nearer and said, "Supper is ready; my father has sent me to call you."

"Is the Effendi there?" asked Vartan rising, seating himself on a mound of earth shaded by climbing vines.

"Yes," replied Stephanie, making a crooked face, and adding, "May the Evil One carry him off!

"You don't like the Effendi either, do you Stephanie?"

"Who does?" she retorted.

Vartan thought he would use this opportunity to deliver the gift he had brought for Stephanie. So he begged her to wait a moment till he should bring it. He returned presently bringing a package. He stepped into the arbor and invited Stephanie to follow him.

"My father is waiting for you," she objected.

"We will not be long," he replied. "Sit beside me Stephanie, it is early yet. Now I will give you the thing I have brought you."

Stephanie obeyed, and Vartan proceeded to open the package. It proved to be a small ebony work-box, richly carved. Vartan took a key from his pocket and opened it. It was fitted out with scissors, thimble, needle-book, etc., all of silver. On one side was fastened a tiny mirror, and on another, a miniature music box. Vartan raised it from its place and it began to play. Stephanie gazed in astonishment at all these beautiful objects such as she had never seen before.

"Are you pleased with your gift?" asked Vartan. "Accept it from me."

Stephanie, who at first felt much pleased and delighted, suddenly grew grave. She appeared unwilling to accept the gift. She drew back and after a momentary indecision, replied: "What should I do with scissors, thimble and needle-case? They are for girls; you should not have brought them to me; you should have brought me something suitable for a boy," adding in a trembling voice, "I am not a girl," but she blushed as she said these words which seemed to burn her rosy lips.

Vartan had not thought that Stephanie would carry the concealment of her sex so far and be was accordingly much disturbed, and unable to control his agitation said, "But you are a girl, Lila."

81

"Oh, you know my name also!" cried the girl, as she fell upon his breast.

The young man clasped her in his arms, and Lila repeated in a low voice, choked with tears, "Yes, I am a girl, I am a girl."

This confession which she had kept with sealed lips for so many years, she now made for the first time to a strange young man, whom she loved and to whom until this day she had not dared make known her love.

The two were so absorbed in each other that they did not know that a pair of eyes had penetrated their retreat and had rejoiced at what they saw. It was Sara who had been attracted by the sounds from the music-box. "Now Lila is saved!" she said to herself, and slipped silently away.

Chapter 15

The evening meal was ready in Goodman Khacho's oda. The landlord and Thomas Effendi were waiting for Vartan. The tax collector's two gendarmes, furnished him by the government, were seated there also —two rascals who served the Effendi in all kinds of evil. There were no others in the oda for Khacho's sons would not think of venturing to sit at table with such exalted personages.

"He will come directly; he barks so loud that he will bring a curse upon our bread," said the Effendi, speaking of Vartan.

"Though he sometimes makes sharp retorts, he is not a bad-hearted fellow," observed the landlord.

"I know he is not bad at heart, landlord, but his mouth is full of venom. He should not be so disrespectful. When I cough even, men tremble. People should show Thomas Effendi proper respect. Don't you remember my showing you the Sultan's 'firman'? It is not every man who is armed with equal authority. And do you know this, that the Vali of Erzeroum always seats me next to himself; ask these men if you don't believe me," he said indicating the two gendarmes.

"They asked the fox for a witness—he showed his tail," the proverb says. These two witnesses were on a par with that.

"You may be sure I believe it," replied the landlord.

Thomas Effendi hated Vartan, not only because of their war of words that morning, but because on every occasion when they met, Vartan would hold the tax collector up to ridicule.

"If I wished to do so I could turn the world upside down in a moment," continued the tax collector, "and I'll show that good-for-nothing fellow

83

who Thomas Effendi is!"

"He is young and heedless," said the kind-hearted landlord. "You must give no weight to the talk of such a young man; but I repeat that he is not as bad as you think."

At that moment Vartan entered, pale and silent.

Thomas Effendi, who had been denouncing him, and "Pulling his tail" as they say, now addressed him in quite a different strain.

"Blessed one, how long you have kept me waiting! You know I would not think of touching a morsel until you were here to share it with me."

"I know it," replied the young man, taking his place without vouchsafing him a glance. Vartan scarcely uttered a word throughout the entire meal. He was moody and morose like the lowering sky above. Love, which begets joy in many, filling the heart with contentment, sweetening the bitterness of lives, love had saddened this man. He ate very little but drank much. He seemed to wish to quench the fire of his heart with draughts of wine.

Thomas Effendi talked incessantly, as was his custom. What did he not tell of his life and of his past? And in all his talk it appeared that Thomas Effendi was a great man. The Patriarch Nerses always called him his "son" it seemed; he didn't think much of Khirimian, for he was such a common man, and stooped to have dealings with porters of Van and Moush; Nubar Pasha in his letters always addressed him as "Honored Friend"; he had a palace on the shores of the Bosphorus, which he had rented to some English people; his grandparents had given a large sum to the Temple at Jerusalem, for which reason mass was said for all their family every day at the monastery of St. James; there was a coldness between Odian and himself because the former had offered to give him his daughter, but he hadn't cared to marry her, etc. etc.

Vartan gave no heed to his interminable chatter, but the simple-minded landlord listened in astonishment. "How fortunate my Lila would be," thought he to himself, "if she were to marry such a man: one who has refused the daughter of Odian, and who owns a palace on the Bosphorus."

Then he began to discuss the political situation.

This was at the time of the disturbances in the Balkan Peninsula, when the Slavs tried to obtain freedom at the cost of their blood. A conference had been held at Constantinople to ameliorate their condition, and Midhat, that famous diplomatist and juggler, had promulgated the Turkish constitution. Thomas Effendi, sitting in a village inn, was discoursing on

84

thrones and empires. He spoke first of the folly of the Slavs in attempting to revolt against the beneficent rule of the Turks, from which he proceeded to criticize the Armenians, saying: "There are such fools among the Armenians who think the Turkish yoke is heavy, and they are talking of freedom and independence." He declared that but for the Turk the Armenians would have become a lost people, and that Armenians are so constituted as to be incapable of governing themselves.

Then at last, Vartan was aroused, and he exclaimed, "To those like you who suck the blood of Armenians by reason of the irregularities of the Turkish Government, to tax collectors like you, the Turk and his misrule are always desirable. You catch fish in muddy water. You hate clearness and cleanliness. You love darkness, as all thieves do."

"Sir," interrupted the tax collector, "recollect that. Two gendarmes sit beside you."

"With these gendarmes you delude the poor, miserable peasants who are so ignorant that they believe that you have a palace on the Bosphorus, that you refused Odian's daughter and that mass is said for you every day in the church of St. James. As such you are worthy of nothing but curses. It is you who destroy the homes of the Armenians, all of your class; beginning with the insignificant village tax collector like you, up to the great lords in the Sublime Porte, who for their personal profit sell the rights of their nation!"

Thomas Effendi gives vent to his anger only when he is sure that his opponent is "a man for his teeth", as the Armenians say; that is, one whom he can tear to bits and maul and mangle as he pleases. But he knew Vartan of old, and for this reason he tried to turn it off as a joke.

"I see that the wine is too strong for you, blessed one. Why do you drink so much?"

Vartan gave him a withering glance in reply.

The landlord kept silence with difficulty. He felt the force of Vartan's words, but at the same time he did not approve of his boldness, thinking it highly unbecoming to speak in that manner to an official. He was very glad to have the meal over, but he did not anticipate the starting of a fresh feud.

Directly after the meal coffee was served. The Effendi had a standing order in the house that after he drank his coffee, Stephanie should fill his pipe for him, "because the pipe prepared by his hand tasted better," he said.

There was something strange about this. Fattah Bey wished his coffee to come from Stephanie's hand "because it tasted better," and Thomas

Effendi said the same about his pipe. The Kurdish Bey, however, had learned that Stephanie was a girl; but did the Armenian Effendi also know it, and did he also love her?

When Stephanie brought in the long Turkish pipe, intending to hand it to the Effendi, Vartan was filled with rage. He snatched the pipe from Stephanie's hand, and threw it out the window, and ordered her out of the room. She obeyed in surprise, and withdrew.

If the pipe had been thrown at the Effendi's head he would not have been more enraged. "I don't like such joking," he stormed. "You have disgraced me. This affects my honor."

"Such men as you have no claim to honor."

"I? I? The tax collector of this great province?" shouted the Effendi.

"Yes, you the robber of this whole province."

The tax collector made as if to rise.

"Don't you stir, or I will kill you like a dog," cried Vartan, laying his hand upon his sword.

One of the gendarmes tried to interfere. "You have no cause to be angry, sir," he said. "The Effendi has said nothing which should cause you offense." Vartan paid no attention to him, but turning to the Effendi again said, "Vile creature! You have learned to enter every house, to lick the table and guzzle the wine of the Armenians, and to demand degrading service of the young girls and boys. Vile creature that you are!"

The old landlord was too much astonished to speak, but from time to time he made the sign of the cross to avert the threatened evil. But the Effendi, in spite of his loud talk and bragging, was as timid as a fox. Seeing the furious passion of the Russian youth, he knew very well that he could not crush him as he had crushed the peasant at Alashgerd. This man carried a sword and was a Russian subject; so controlling himself as best he could, he said, in a very gentle tone, "God knows that I have no intention to degrade anyone, Vartan. You malign me for no cause."

"I malign you, do I? You, who go through the Mohammedan 'namaz' (forms of worship) with Turks, but have mass said in Armenian churches, to gain the good opinion of the peasantry; you, who in the company of Turks call Armenians 'giaours' (infidel dogs), but who curse the Turks when among Armenians; you, who have betrayed to the Turkish

86

Government every noble Armenian who worked for the good of his nation; you, who are a companion of thieves, and who give false witness in the courts, saying 'the Armenians have no cause to petition the Government to relieve them from oppression', you, who have been married in ten different places and have deserted your wives, and now wish to marry again here — don't you follow Turkish customs? But I say that the Turk is a thousand times more noble than an Armenian like you; for you are neither a true Armenian, nor a true Turk!"

His concluding charge that the Effendi had been married in ten places and now wished to take another wife here, fell like a clap of thunder upon the ears of old Khacho. Fool that he had been to think of giving his Lila to that man! Still was it not possible that Vartan had slandered him?

After Vartan had poured out all the gall in his heart, he left the room. Then, at last, the Effendi found his tongue. "I shall certainly write to the Sultan and to the Czar of Russia as well, and I shall have him sent to Siberia," he stormed. "It is impossible for me to overlook such behavior. Until you beat an ass he does not know his place," he concluded.

Thomas Effendi made very free use of the titles of the great when threatening his opponents, and would have it appear that he was in frequent communication with rulers and could obtain any favors for which he cared to ask. Old Khacho, though not a fool, having taken the Effendi at his own valuation, thought that he was indeed able to perform these mighty threats; so, believing that Vartan was as good as exiled to Siberia already, he threw himself down at the tax collector's feet and with tears in his eyes began to beseech, "For the love of God, don't exile him! Grant this favor, for the sake of my gray head. You know the young man is a 'fool'."

The Effendi meditated for awhile, and finally replied, "For the sake of the bread and the salt, which I have eaten at your table, I will grant your request."

Chapter 16

Troubles never come singly. When once they begin to cloud the prosperity of a peace-loving family, they thicken fast. Now from every direction misfortunes began to fall upon the house of Khacho. Vartan's quarrel with the Effendi was variously looked upon by the members of the family. Some ridiculed the Effendi's timidity, and admired Vartan's bravery, while others blamed Vartan, and called him a fool, for not being able to hold his tongue. Ohan and Haggo were particularly incensed against him, and said, "How can anyone speak so scandalously to an official?" An official had an importance in their eyes, not only in his official capacity, but in his private character as well, and it was a crime to oppose him.

The old man was not a little uneasy. Although be did not blame Vartan, but even though he was in the right, his behavior toward the Effendi was unfitting, be thought. Goodman Khacho understood the Effendi's mind perfectly; the old rascal would try to injure Vartan, and if he did not succeed in that he would pour his vengeance upon the old man's family. The tax collector had legal grounds for delivering the old man to the government, in that he had harbored such a well known contrabandist as Vartan. On the other hand Goodman Khacho had to give up a great hope. He was in a state of great perturbation. From the moment he had heard from Vartan that Thomas Effendi had been married again and again, and had left wives in a number of places, those hopes were battered. But how could he be sure that Vartan had spoken the truth? Every truth that comes out in a quarrel is regarded with suspicion. But what was there about this hateful and shameless tax collector that attracted Goodman Khacho, and made him wish to link the fate of his daughter with such a rascal?

The old man knew that he was a merciless, conscienceless, low oppressor, that nothing was sacred in his eyes; that he was ready to sacrifice everything for his personal gains, but in spite of all this, the old man forgot everything when he considered the attainment of power.

He had a superstitious reverence for the Mudir —the representative of the

Government. In his eyes the ignoble traits in the Imperial tax collector, this petty official representative, were condoned or neutralized by his office. The office excused infamy.

For this reason, having a man like the Effendi for a son-in-law was very attractive to Goodman Khacho; a son-in-law who was above the common crowd, before whom all must bow. Simple and upright as was the old man, he was somewhat vain. It was hard for him to condescend to give his daughter to a common villager, especially as he had had her grow up disguised as a boy. In choosing Thomas Effendi he had another practical purpose. For a landlord who had many dealings with the local government, the Effendi might be of considerable assistance should difficulties arise. But now his hopes were shattered. But if he had known what fate threatened his beloved Lila through the Kurdish chief, Fattah Bey, probably only the grave could have put an end to the old man's grief. But as yet, his sons had told him nothing. The agony of that secret gnawed and consumed them, especially Hairabed and Abo, who, since the unsuccessful consultation with their brothers, did not know what to do to save their sister. What would be the condition of Lila if the Kurdish Bey should carry her away from her father's house? Could she become the wife of a Mohammedan, or in the bitterness of her sorrow would she put an end to her life as her sister Sona had done?

All this anxiety, all this grief was on Lila's account, but she alone in her ignorance thought of herself as happy and free. After receiving her lover's gift, her disguise seemed to burn her body. She was a girl; she wished to dress as one—to become a wife. She could still feel Vartan's warm kisses upon her lips, and his sweet words still rang in her ears,. But beginning at the moment when she saw with her own eyes Vartan's victory over the Effendi — a man before whom the whole province trembled —Vartan's stature grew greater in the young woman's eyes. Vartan won Lila's devotion when he annihilated the supremacy of the proud tax collector whom she hated. Lila had often been obliged to endure the insolence of that shameless creature, and every time he came to her father's house she would try to escape and hide from him, but her father would send for her to fill the Effendi's pipe, because it would taste sweeter when filled by her hand. Lila went to her oldest brother, Hairabed, and told him all she had seen and heard in the oda and how Vartan had treated the Effendi.

"He did just right," said he. "He ought to kill the beast. He has learned how to torture the poor villagers, and he thinks we are like them."

Lila felt like embracing her brother, and wished to open her heart to him; to tell him that Vartan loved her and that she had loved him for a long time, but Hairabed hastily withdrew as though he had some very important work to do.

89

His wife Sara had had an appointment that day with Koorsit, the wife of Fattah Bey. The morning before, Chavo had come to her and told her that her mistress, on the pretext of fulfilling a vow, was coming to a shrine near the village of o... to offer a lamb in sacrifice to cure her child's cough, and she requested that Sara meet her there. Both Kurds and Armenians worshipped at the shrine.

Sara had rejoiced when she heard that Koorsit had planned this, for she had requested a meeting between them through Chavo.

Hairabeds haste to leave Lila was in order that he might learn the result of that visit. He went outside the village and waited impatiently for Sara. He went nearly half-way to meet her and waited in the shadow of a great rock overhanging the pathway. That spot afforded an interesting view of the mountain. He was at its foot and the slope above him was covered with broken rocks fallen from the crags above. He was surrounded by a thicket of bushes, with here and there a tree rising above them. His attention was attracted to an apple tree on which a parasite had grown, twisting itself around the trunk and branches even higher. It seemed to wish to press the tree down with its weight, to choke and strangle it, and devour the poor tree whose upper branches were already dry and leafless. There are moments when even the least learned turn philosophers. "Behold a good example," thought Hairabed. "Here is a wild plant, it toils not and labors not, neither has it roots in the soil, but seizing in its clutches a more cultivated plant feeds on it; greedily sucks its juice, and exhausting its life-giving powers, finally kills it. Is not that what the Kurd does to us? Is he not the parasite which lives off the Armenian?"

Hairabed was sensitive and had a good mind. How did he obtain that degree of intelligence? If he had not set his foot beyond the confines of his native land he would certainly have grown up with only the limited understanding and the superstitions of his fellow countrymen. While young he had had some disagreement with his father, and as often occurs in the provinces, he left home, to wander over the face of the earth. Fate led him to the chaos of Constantinople, where men of every country of Europe and Asia are gathered together. There, he gathered many ideas which are unknown to the ordinary villager.

The sun was setting and its last beams shed a beautiful glow over the tops of the surrounding mountains as he sat waiting for his wife. At last she appeared. He could see a bright look on her face from afar. "Is it a boy or a girl?" he called. "It is a boy," she replied and came and took a seat beside him. In village parlance, "a boy" signifies good tidings and a "girl" the opposite. So the question meant, "Is it good news or bad?"

As soon as she could recover her breath she proceeded to tell him all that she had learned that day. Koorsit had told her that the Bey was not thinking so much about Stephanie now as he was giving all his attention to some important affair which put her out of his thoughts for the present. The Vali of Erzeroum had ordered him to take a census of his tribe, and distribute arms and money, but what it was for she did not know. But Koorsit advised having Stephanie sent away or married quite soon, for she was sure that eventually the Bey would carry out his intention regarding the poor girl. "Although," she added, "I have spoken to my father about this, and he has assured me he will hold the Bey in check, but I don't believe in the Bey's promises, and I may be obliged to leave my husband and separate from him."

Hairabed listened to Sara's story with close attention, and when she had concluded he said, "For all that, the danger cannot be considered past. There is one cause for rejoicing in all this. The affair is delayed and we gain time to plan for Lila's safety."

"That is what I think," replied Sara. "There is no alternative. Lila must be married to some one."

"That will not solve the difficulty," Hairabed retorted. "The Bey is able to drag a married woman from the arms of her husband, and carry her off."

"She must marry some one who does not live here but will take her to some other part of the country," Sara replied.

"That is a very good idea, Sara," replied Hairabed, "but where will you find such a man? You know very well that not one of the men of our village would venture to marry her under such circumstances; for if one of them should carry Lila out of the country, the Bey would take his revenge by burning his house and slaying all his relatives. What man would make such a sacrifice?"

"The man is found," replied Sara, joyously.

"Who is he?"

"Vartan!"

Hairabed's troubled countenance brightened when Sara related what she had seen through the bushes the day before; how Vartan and Lila had embraced and kissed each other and sworn everlasting love.

"That's good," said Hairabed. "Vartan can save Lila."

The sun had set by the time the couple returned to the village. On the way home Hairabed was puzzling as to what the preparations of the Bey could mean. Was not this to prepare for some terrible project?

Chapter 17

When Hairabed and Sara reached home they learned that after the quarrel with Vartan, Thomas Effendi had left in great displeasure, and old Khacho was very uneasy lest the tax collector should set some evil afoot against them.

But Vartan, notwithstanding his irritable and inflamed nature, was not so thoughtless as to malign a person without grounds for it. He considered the Effendi a despicable person, a tool in the hands of the representatives of the Turkish Government, who oppressed his fellow countrymen. Besides that, he knew the tax collector's past history. That scoundrel had been through a large part of Armenia in his office as tax collector, and had actually married and then deserted several wives in some places and had ruined innocent girls in others. Now he had the same shameless intention regarding Lila, and taking advantage of her father's simple-mindedness, was planning to trick them. Naturally Vartan could not endure this, especially as it concerned the girl with whom he himself was in love.

But the quarrel with Vartan, and his disinclination to see his face again were not only the reasons why the Effendi left old Khacho's house so abruptly. The Effendi could bear his wounds patiently. He had learned of old to bear in silence worse revilings than these. But today he had received orders by special messenger to collect the Imperial tithes of wheat and barley in certain storehouses and not to sell any, as the Government had need of all of it. There must be some secret collection of grain afoot here and of weapons in Fattah Bey's camp.

When there were guests, old Khacho always used the oda; but Vartan was not considered a guest, he was one of the family. But after Thomas Effendi took his departure, another guest appeared. He was a pale, thin young man who looked like one who had spent many years in a schoolroom. What his profession or occupation was no one asked, but since he was from Constantinople and an Armenian, old Khacho thought it devolved upon him to show him hospitality. Except for his saddle bags, he had no other

93

luggage, and his well-worn European clothing showed that he was poor. The muleteer who had brought him left him at the village and he was looking for a lodging place when he met Vartan. They say there is a secret road between hearts. After a brief conversation the two young men seemed to become intimate friends, and like members of some secret organization, gave each other a brotherly handclasp, a though meeting now for the first time. Then Vartan led him to old Khacho's house

The new guest called himself Michael Tiutiukjian. As nearly all the surnames of Turkish subjects are taken from the trade of the father or grandfather, the father of this one was a maker of whistles such as children love. Certainly neither the name of the guest, which was hard to pronounce, nor his pale or sickly face, nor his restless eyes with their feverish brilliancy, nor his moody looks were agreeable to old Khacho. But Vartan whispered to the old man, "He's a good fellow. You will like him when you know him."

On entering the house, the guest asked Vartan: "Can you trust these people?"

"You can," replied Vartan.

When the lamp was lighted in the oda, the evening meal was served. This time all six of the sons were seated at table with their father, for Thomas Effendi was gone, so there was no guest of higher rank than they. Vartan was considered one of the family, and they regarded the new guest as one who ought to be thankful that he could eat a square meal.

The supper was eaten in silence except for a word or two between Vartan and the guest, or a remark by the father to one of the sons.

The hearts of those present were engrossed in their individual troubles. The old man was thinking of the tax collector's displeasure and his taking his departure in anger. Hairabed's mind was occupied with the affair of the Bey and Lila; he was thinking of all Sara had told him and wondering what should be done. The other sons were thinking of their plowing, and planning work for the morrow. Lila's pretty face danced in Vartan's mind and God only knows what was in the mind of the newcomer.

When the table was removed, Lila brought the basin and ewer and poured the water as they washed their hands, after which they returned thanks to God, as was their custom.

The old man began to smoke his long pipe, but Tiutiukjian drew from his breast pocket a fine cigar holder which was quite at variance with his well-worn clothing. Then taking out an expensive cigar, cut the end with his long fingernail and began to smoke. The room was filled with fragrance of Havana tobacco. The man must at some time have been able to enjoy the luxuries of life, but now was in reduced circumstances.

After supper Thomas Effendi was the subject of conversation. Tiutiukjian had heard about him from Vartan. Old Khacho, in a courteous manner, intimated to Vartan that his behavior toward the Effendi had been rash. "You know," he said "that I regard you as one of my seven sons." He was in the habit of speaking of them as seven, for he included Stephanie but he did not know that Vartan had long been aware that she was a girl.

"Let the sun of my seven sons be my witness if I lie," he said. "You also are my son, my house is your house; you may come and go, and stay as long as you please. My door is always open to you. But you should realize that this is not like other places; here men like Thomas Effendi are great men, very great men; they can do what they please. For this reason we must pay them respect, though unwillingly, and must sometimes keep silent about their words and deeds. What can we do? The proverb says: 'When in the hands of a villain, if you can't kill him, you must kiss him.' Possibly the Effendi will not be able to do you harm for you do not live here, but we shall have to pay for the insult he has received. You have heard the Turkish proverb, haven't you, 'He was afraid of the ass so he began to beat the saddle'?"

These words stirred up the young man's evil genius, and he said, "The Armenians of our region have a good proverb about the Turks. They say, 'Until you beat a Turk, he doesn't become your friend.' I do not consider Thomas Effendi any different from a Turk, and now I am sorry I didn't give him a good beating while I had the chance, although his friendship would not have been particularly welcome to me."

The old man frowned at this. The reply did not please him but Stephanie's face was illuminated with a bright smile which Vartan could not help but observe. She was still standing, for being the youngest she served the others. Vartan looked at her thinking, "She is the only member of the family who is in sympathy with me, for she is the only one who has experienced the man's evil insolence." Then he continued with increased vehemence, "You have allowed a low immoral, unjust man like this to lord it over you and you have closed your eyes to all his wickedness. For centuries the Turks and the Kurds have robbed, oppressed and killed the Armenians. This has become so much their habit that they can hardly live in any other way. But when an Armenian treats his fellow countrymen more barbarously than the Turk or the Kurd it is more than I can endure. I said these things to the Effendi's face and he replied not a word."

"I would have said worse things than those to him," said Hairabed, joining in the conversation, "but my father has always advised us to keep silence, to be careful, to be patient, for we shall be free some day. I don't know how long we should be patient."

"Until the coming of Jesus Christ," observed Vartan sarcastically, "but alas, by that time there won't be any Armenians left on the face of the earth; they will all have become either Turks or Kurds."

"Patience is life," said the old man in the tones of a preacher. "Our priests and bishops always preach this to us. Some day God will remember His lost sheep. We must have patience, my children, patience is life."

"Patience is death," spoke up Tiutiukjian, who had kept silent up to this time. His pale face was livid and his thin lips trembled. "Patience is death," he repeated. "Only in the tomb can man learn patience. Such Jewish patience as ours leads to everlasting destruction. The Jews were most patient, enduring all manner of persecution, waiting for the appearance of a Messiah who should rebuild the holy city of Jerusalem and restore the glory of Israel, and they wait until this day. I don't know what we are waiting for. Our priests and our bishops preach patience," he continued in a melancholy tone, "as a result our houses are destroyed and we have come to this desperate pass. If there is anything that can save an oppressed and downtrodden people, it is protest. Discontent, complaint, and a desire for a more favorable lot in life-these are the motives which may save us from our slavery; but in exercising patience these lofty motives are destroyed."

The old man made no reply, but Vartan and Hairabed gave him a friendly handclasp. The other sons understood nothing of all this, but said in their hearts, "Behold, another fool."

Then the old man ordered beds prepared for the guests while he and his sons withdrew. One of the daughters-in-law, her face covered, came and spread the bedding on the floor. The light burned for a long time in the oda as the guests lay awake in their beds. Tiutiukjian lighted his half-burned cigar once more and began to smoke. Vartan watched him for some time, and then said, "Friend, your language is not easy to understand. You will find it difficult to start work here. To talk with these people you must know hundreds of proverbs and anecdotes. Christ accomplished more with his parables than with the Sermon on the Mount."

"Yes I haven't learned the language of these people," answered Tiutiukjian, and retired in silent meditation.

Chapter 18

The oil lamp, diffusing a murky light, was still burning in the oda. Vartan lay awake for a long time. That night's talk had excited his brain. He was reflecting upon the coldness of the old man's sons toward the harmless newcomer. He was amazed at the suspicion with which they regarded that impassioned young man. Then, too, his heart was torn between two desires; one, love for the poor, oppressed villagers; the other love for Lila, who was also being persecuted. His companion was sleeping. The murky light of the lamp showed his pale face in whose sharp outlines his strength of character showed plainly. His sleep was restless. Occasionally his lips moved and broken words were heard in French or Armenian. "Peasants the hour has come, you must purchase it with your blood — your freedom. Present the future belong to us. Show forth — ye brave ones that the iron rod of the Turk has not entirely killed the life in you —and the love of freedom. In fire — and in sword you shall find your salvation. Forward, ye braves."

"Poor fellow," said Vartan, shaking his head. "He has read too many books. In the oda of a miserable Armenian village he is dreaming and declaiming about the barricades of Paris, poor fellow."

Just then the sound of someone singing softly reached Vartan's ears, and filled the night air with its sweet melancholy. He recognized the singer and went out of the room.

Yes, another individual in old Khacho's house was wakeful that night. She had turned and tossed in her bed. All about her men and women were sunk in deep sleep. The weary, toil-worn limbs of farmers are not roused easily at night. Only Lila was unable to rest. She dressed and stepped quietly out of the room. A cat could not have stepped more noiselessly than did the young girl as she went out of doors. The dog, seeing her from the distance, began to bark. "Hush!" she breathed, scarcely above a whisper. The dog quieted down.

It was a calm spring evening. The air was cool enough to make one shiver, but it seemed only to stimulate the young girl, and to fan her flushed face. She passed through the yard out into the garden and walked under the trees. Here the shadows were deeper; here no one would see her. She sat on the grass and rested her cheek on her hand, looking skyward. "The moon is out of sight, where is it?" thought the girl. "It must be asleep." Deep silence reigned about her. All was still; the wind which so often rocked the branches of the trees; the river, whose noisy roar she had always before heard on quiet nights; all was at rest; she only was restless; only she was awake. She remembered a song she had learned from her grandmother, and unconsciously began to sing a song:

The moon is asleep in the depths of the sky;
The bird is asleep in its soft downy nest;
The wind is asleep, not a leaf does it stir;
The stream is asleep, all its ripples at rest.

But I cannot sleep, tell me why? Mother mine.
I long to sleep now, but mine eyes will not close.
What keeps me awake? Tell me this, Mother mine.
My heart is on fire. Tell me whence this arose.

When she had ended the song, she dropped her head upon her knees, and, burying her burning face in her hands, began to weep bitterly. Why did she weep? She did not know why, herself. Was it because she thought of her mother, whom she had never seen, from whose lips she had never heard a word of love? What was it that had disturbed her innocent virgin heart?

Her tears eased her somewhat. She raised her head and looked about, and her eyes fell upon the grave beneath the four poplar trees, not far from where she sat. It was the grave of her sister Sona whom she had never seen, but she had heard the sad story of her death many a time. People around about considered her a martyr, and the sick were often brought to this grave. By her father's command an oil lamp was lighted and placed there every Saturday night. And tonight it was burning and lighted the white headstone. Lila looked at it in terror. Her sister's sad story became a reality to her as never before. Now she could see the black tent of a Kurd, and there sat Sona with a look of terrible despair. She was holding the cup of poison in her hand, raised it to her lips, and then drew back. For a long time she debated between life and death. See now! The Kurdish chief, Sona's abductor approaches the tent; now she makes the sign of the Cross and drinks. The scene changes. She sees Thomas Effendi with his sly, repulsive looks, and another, Fattah Bey, with his savage, cruel face. She trembles from head to foot. Does she know, does she realize the pit these two have dug for her? She knows nothing, but she feels that there is something sinister afoot.

She felt afraid of the grave. At that moment a hand was laid upon her shoulder, and a voice spoke her name. "Lila." She scarcely heard it.

"Lila," the voice repeated, "I will not let you go near Sona. I will save you." She turned, and there stood Vartan.

"Oh, yes, save me," she cried. "Take me to some other land. It is bad here, very bad."

The young man seated himself beside her. They were silent for a few minutes, finding no words to utter. Lila was still under the spell of the frightful vision that had passed before her eyes. Vartan wondered why the innocent young girl begged to be taken away from her fatherland, where she was so greatly loved by her family, why did she wish to leave it? So he asked:

"Why is this country bad?"

"It is very bad," she replied sadly. "Do you see that grave?" She pointed toward Sona's grave. "Do you know who lies buried there?"

"I know," he replied.

"I don't want to die like Sona, Vartan. I am afraid of poison. I am afraid of graves," and her eyes filled with tears.

"Why do you think you are going to suffer a fate like Sona's, Lila?" he asked, grasping her hand. "That was a sad thing, but it doesn't happen to every young girl. Why do you imagine you are going to suffer it?"

"I have always thought it. I have always expected it ever since I discovered why they dressed me as a boy. To be born a girl is a punishment from God, especially if one is a pretty girl. Listen, Vartan, I had a friend whom I loved dearly. She was a good girl and was a near neighbor. Every day her mother beat her because she was beautiful, and for growing lovelier every day. 'You will bring misfortune upon us,' she would say, and Narkiss, that was her name, used to cry every day. Her mother would not let her wash her face or comb her hair, and she always dressed in rags. But finally the Kurds carried her off. A few days ago I saw her. Oh! how ugly she had grown! and she said to me, 'Stephanie, being the wife of a Kurd is a very bad thing,' and she wept as she spoke."

99

Lila began to weep herself. When she became more tranquil, she asked, Vartan, won't you take me away from here?"

"I will," he answered. "Be assured of that."

"Take me quickly. Take me now! I will go with you wherever you wish."

"Wait a few days, Lila, till I talk with your father," he replied. They sat there talking in the darkness until the feeling of sadness was changed into the joy of loving.

Chapter 19

The next morning Vartan awoke very late for he, had passed the greater part of the night without sleep. A secret joy shone in his pale face, however. Tiutiukjian was not in the oda, but his saddle-bags stood in a corner of the room. Where had the man gone? Vartan knew that the man lacked experience and should be well looked after. All the members of the family were busy about their daily tasks. Some had gone to the fields to plow, and their father was watching their work. The daughters-in-law were occupied with their housework. Only Hairabed was at home. He thought it would be a good time to have a talk with Vartan about Lila. All the other brothers, except Abo, thought no more about her, and had probably forgotten the danger that threatened her from the Kurdish Bey. They had left Lila to her fate, repeating the fatalistic saying, "Whatever God wills, will be." He thought he should make some investigation into Thomas Effendi's past before letting him have Lila.

When Hairabed entered the oda, Vartan asked, "Where has my new friend gone?" Hairabed replied. "You mean Mr. Tiutiukjian? He is an odd fellow. He rose before sunrise and drawing on his boots, without washing or combing or eating breakfast, he went out of the house. We asked him where he was going, but he shook his head and made no reply."

"Where did he go?" asked Vartan, with increasing uneasiness.

"I don't know, but I saw him speak to a ragged barefoot girl who was bringing a pail of water from the river. He asked 'Why do you go about like that? It is a shame for a girl your age to dress like this.' The girl told him that they were very poor. Then he gave her a gold piece, which was very foolish of him. I believe it was the last piece he had."

"Very likely," said Vartan. "Where did he go next?"

"Then he approached a group of villagers standing by the church door.

They were discussing their taxes. He joined in the conversation and told them they had already paid more than they should. Then he told them they ought to have a school in the village for the boys and girls to attend. And he told them they should form a society for improving the condition of the people of these villages; and about a public loan; and about a savings bank from which they might borrow money at a low rate of interest when they needed money — Who knows what he didn't talk about?"

"What did the villagers say to him?" Vartan asked.

"They laughed and nudged one another, but answered nothing. One of them said to another, 'The fellow is a fool'.

"Praise the Lord! Then I am not the only fool," said Vartan laughing. "I thought they considered me the only fool hereabouts. Well, what next?"

"Next, one of the villagers invited him to come and have a drink at the cafe. He accepted. In there he found many who were drunk. He drank little himself but paid for the crowd. There, again, he began to talk about village improvement, and to explain why they were so wretched. He spoke in great excitement. I began to feel his power, but the others heard him with derision. One man asked him 'What office or rank do you occupy?' He replied that he was not employed by anyone. The villager then asked, insolently, 'Well, what else have you to give forth?' "

"Yes, to influence this community, one must be a mudir, a kaimakam, or a tax collector like Thomas Effendi," said Vartan, sadly. "Tell me, Hairabed, what next?"

Hairabed replied, "I took him by the hand and drew him out of the cafe by force. I was afraid that a disturbance might arise.

"Outside, he said to me, 'It is easier to understand people in such places. When they drink they speak their minds.' We continued our way through the village. He had a leather pouch hanging from his shoulder full of pamphlets. These he would pass out to whomever he met. Some refused them, saying they couldn't read, but some who were equally ignorant accepted them. I asked one man what he was going to do with it. He said, 'It's paper. I'll take it home where it will come in handy for wrapping up snuff for my mother.' "

Vartan was greatly troubled. "Have you one of those pamphlets?" he inquired. "Yes. I took a couple," Hairabed replied, and handed them to Vartan. Vartan glanced through them, and said, "Scattering such pamphlets among ignorant people is supreme folly. Where did he go next?"

"I went with him as far as the edge of the village, where he asked me to leave him alone. I did so, but saw him setting off toward another village. He walked so fast, you would think he had an appointment there."

Hairabed was beginning to lose interest in the stranger, and wished rather to speak with Vartan about his sister. But Vartan seemed to have forgotten about her. He started to leave the room.

"Where are you going?" asked Hairabed.

"I am going to follow Mr. Tiutiukjian," he replied. "You should not have let him go alone. He will get into trouble." They went to the stable. On the way they passed by Lila who was washing her face beside the stream; she, also, had slept late. Vartan called, "Good morning, Stephanie," and she replied with a meaningful smile.

His three horses were cared for by his attendants, Sado and Yegho. Ordering one of the horses saddled, he again in asked Hairabed in which direction Tiutiukjian had gone and set off in pursuit. His attendants had been told to see that everything was ready for a long, hard trip. This perplexed Hairabed greatly. Was he going away without doing anything about Lila, without settling her fate? Why was he so much concerned about Tiutiukjian? After Vartan had gone, he was returning to the house when he met his wife, who was bringing a pailful of milk from the sheepfold.

"Didn't Vartan say anything to you?" she asked.

"No, he didn't," Hairabed answered sadly. "He is very reserved."

"I know all about it," said Sara, happily. "Sit down and let me tell you." Husband and wife sat down on a log which lay in the yard.

Then Sara told him that Lila had confessed all to her; how, while the family slept, she and Vartan had met secretly in the garden. Lila gave her a full account of their conversation and that Vartan had said he would speak to her father, and that with or without her, father's permission he would take her away with him.

"That is why he ordered his horses made ready for a journey," said Hairabed.

"Why worry?" said Sara. "Let them escape; so much the better. If he doesn't carry her off, the Kurd will."

"I do not oppose it," replied Hairabed. "but..."

Poor people! Under other circumstances they would have been ready to kill her, having learned that she bad met a young man secretly, but now they were humbled by bitter circumstances.

Chapter 20

Vartan rode his horse all day and passed through several villages following Tiutiukjian's trail. In reply to his questioning, he was told that a young man had been seen who wore European dress, high boots, and a black, broad-brimmed hat, carrying a sackful of pamphlets slung over his shoulder. Everyone expressed the idea that the man was crazy.

Vartan returned to old Khacho's house without having found the wanderer. One of the shepherds reported having seen the young man in a Turkish village, where he was given a good beating. He recognized the man as his master's guest and was able to rescue him from the villagers.

"I expected that would happen," said Vartan, and turning to the shepherd, he asked, "Why did they do it?"

"I couldn't find out," replied the shepherd. "I offered to let him ride my ass and come back here, but he said he was able to walk."

This news grieved Vartan greatly. He knew Turkish beatings are no light strokes, especially when given to Armenians.

"Where did you last see him?" asked Vartan.

"He had come half way here."

Soon after the lights were lit in the oda, Tiutiukjian put in his appearance. He was weary and bedraggled. Vartan expected he would begin telling of the rough treatment he had received, but he didn't speak, only after throwing himself on a divan he asked for tobacco, saying he had none left. Vartan supplied him, regarding with deep sympathy this young man who seemed to him like a helpless moth, lured by the light of a candle, trying to extinguish its flame by its fluttering wings. He had tried to arouse the villagers only to be repulsed.

105

Just then old Khacho entered, followed shortly by his sons. They ate in haste as they must start work early next morning.

Tiutiukjian drank more than he ate, and his spirits seemed lifted, for he even sang snatches of an Armenian song. When the table was removed, he asked the old man to have the door locked as he bad something to tell them in private.

Old Khacho was astonished at this request, but had the door locked. They waited silently for him to speak. "Very soon war will be declared between Russia and Turkey," he declared. "Had you heard of it?" Vartan was the only one who had heard such a report.

This news fell like a thunderbolt on the old man. He had seen war between Russia and Turkey before and had not forgotten how the Armenians had suffered at that time.

Now Hairabed understood the meaning of the information given his wife by the Kurdish woman. Fattah Bey was getting his troops ready.

"Yes," said Vartan, "the horse and mule will fight each other, but only the ass, standing by, will be killed."

"That's so," said Hairabed. "The Armenians of this region will be annihilated during such a war." To which the old man gave sad assent.

"Listen," said Tiutiukjian. "This war is not like any other that has been waged between Turks and Russians. It has a different end in view. You do not read the newspapers so you do not know what is happening in another part of the world, called the Balkan Peninsula. There, there are Christian people who are Turkish subjects like us and who have suffered for centuries from the cruelty of the Turks. But they were not patient like the Armenians; they rebelled, and now, for more than a year they have been fighting to free themselves from the Turkish yoke. They overcame the Turks, but were reconquered; they suffered fearfully; finally Russia intervened, and appeared as the protector of Christianity.

"The representatives of the Great Powers convened at Constantinople and proposed to grant certain rights to those oppressed Christians, but were unable to agree, so the convention decided nothing. Then Russia determined to force Turkey to accept by power of the sword."

Although the story of these events had been spread to the most remote corners of the earth, it had never penetrated these parts. These peasants had heard nothing; therefore they listened to Tiutiukjian with astonishment. They had heard that Turkey was at war, but did not know

106

against whom she was fighting. They only knew that because of the heavier taxes which had been laid upon them, being told "there is a war on." "The present Turko-Russian war," said Tiutiukjian, "is for the purpose of freeing the Christian subjects of Turkey, and you, the most abused and oppressed of all the Christian subjects should know this. You have suffered every barbarity from the Turk, therefore it is time for you to do something on your own account."

"What can we do?" asked Khacho. "You say that Russia is fighting to free the Christians. God grant her success! She will come and save us, also."

"But remember the saying," Vartan interrupted, "'Until the child cries, the mother does not nurse him.' The Armenians by their silence, only waiting hopefully, will obtain nothing. The Armenians must raise their voice in protest against the Turk."

"Yes, they must protest," echoed Tiutiukjian, and that protest must make itself felt in the same manner as was done by the Christians of the Balkan states."

"You mean that the Armenians must fight, also," spoke up the old man.

"Yes, that is what I mean. That is the order of things at present, and it has always been so. He who does not know how to handle weapons, who is not able to kill his enemies has no right to enjoy freedom. Hence, if the Armenians wish to be free, they must show that they do not lack bravery, and that they know how to kill. That time has come."

A bitter smile appeared upon the old man's face, as he replied, "Bless you! How can they show that they have bravery when the Turks haven't left them so much as a knife with which to cut off the head of a hen."

Tiutiukjian found it difficult to reply, but Vartan said, "I will bring you all the weapons you want, if you will only fight. You know my trade. I am a contrabandist. I know all the passes, all the hidden paths through which to smuggle weapons."

"Weapons alone are not sufficient," said the prudent old man. "Are you able to give the Armenians here the spirit and the courage which fill the hearts of the other Christian races who are fighting for their freedom? What can weapons accomplish in the hands of a slavish people?"

"It is unkind to pronounce such a judgment upon a people, landlord Khacho," said Tiutiukjian. "Our people have not entirely lost the spirit and the courage nor the desire for freedom. They should be aroused, and now is the time. The Russians are going to fight against the Turks, let the

107

Armenians side with them. I believe that Russia will give us every assistance."

The sons of old Khacho had kept silence until now. Then Haggo, the son who had expressed the opinion that by giving their sister to the powerful Kurdish Bey they would benefit by being under his protection, now said to the stranger, "Brother, you smell of blood. We wish you neither good nor evil. Early in the morning pick up your things and leave this house for unless you do you will bring misfortune upon our heads."

Old Khacho reproved his son, telling him to be quiet, and said to Tiutiukjian, "Don't be vexed with my son. He doesn't know what he is saying. Listen to me. I have neither read nor heard what the people of other countries are doing. But as a farmer I know one thing. Until we plow and harrow the ground, we villagers do not sow the seed for we know that the seed will not take root and grow; it will only sprout and dry up. Jesus Christ said this, also, in the Holy Bible. Now, my son, the soil is not prepared. It should have been made ready. I mean the people are not ready. The soil should have been prepared thirty or forty years ago. When these preparatory steps have been taken then your seed will fall upon fruitful soil. It will flourish and ripen and yield fifty or a hundredfold. Nothing is accomplished in a day. We know that several seasons must follow the seed time; some warm, some cold, before harvest time. The seed lies patiently under the various tests brought by each season: sometimes storms beat it, sometimes hail, and sometimes snow chills it; but again the life-giving beams of the sun warm it. In a word, the seed must pass through various experiences before it can crown the hopes of the laborer."

"That is a very beautiful example," replied Tiutiukjian. "I agree with you entirely. But there is another thing we must consider, also. Now I shall speak to you as a farmer and a breeder of cattle, so that you may understand better. If you leave your seed which you have sown without destroying the weeds, you will find the weeds choking the grain until it is destroyed. It is a fight in which the stronger destroys the weaker. That struggle is seen between all plants; the fight in which the one tries to destroy the other in order to preserve its existence, and the one that is not able to fight and struggle loses its life. Nature itself, teaches self-preservation. Nature has given all forms of life the ability to fight for their existence; to some more, to some less. Trees, plants, animals and men, all have that ability. Only stones, wood, and lifeless objects remain unmoved and cannot protect themselves, because they have no life. But where there is life, there is also this natural struggle. It is the struggle for life in which every being tries not only to maintain its existence, but tries also to destroy its enemies in order that its growth may continue safely and without obstruction. Now I think you understand my meaning. That which is done by nature in the life of plants and animals is necessary also in the life of man. There is the same struggle here, but a fiercer one and it takes various forms. According to the education and the ability of each nation its weapons vary. In saying weapons I do not mean simply swords and muskets; the arts and sciences are weapons by which people carry on warfare with other people. Among uncivilized and savage people, warfare is carried on simply by physical strength—the sword. The Turks and the Kurds have used those weapons against us. The law of self-preservation demands that we accept the challenge and reply with the same weapon with which he threatens us. It would be folly on my part to demand that for which the people have no training. I do not say that we must take up the sword in order to destroy the Turks and the Kurds in order that we alone may live on the land. But I do say we must learn self-preservation in order that the Turks and the Kurds may not annihilate us. There is a great difference between the two ideas."

Goodman Khacho interrupted the monologue, saying, "I understand, I understand all you say; but I must repeat what I said a few moments ago; such a great change cannot be accomplished in a day, so that by some miracle we people lose our servility and take up self-preservation. You people in Constantinople should have begun this work long ago. If you had taught us self-preservation years ago, then when other nations began fighting for self-preservation, we could have joined in the fight. You did not give us your preparatory lessons. All this time you have been sitting silently in Constantinople, but today you come and say, 'Protect yourselves; take up your swords against the Turks and the Kurds.' We cannot understand how that can be done."

"You are right in saying that we in Constantinople have been idle and careless," replied Tiutiukjian, in an undisturbed manner. "It is true we did not prepare you; but I am not referring to what the Armenians here have lost, that is, their lofty and noble instincts, qualities which require a certain amount of education and development, and which it was our duty to supply; I speak of self-preservation; for that no great wisdom or learning is needed. The spirit of self-protection is so natural that it is found in all animals and savages. Is the Armenian lower than an animal? Is he as dead as wood or stone and has no feeling?"

109

Chapter 21

After old Khacho and his sons retired Vartan and Tiutiukjian remained in the oda alone. "It is true that the soil is not ready," observed Vartan looking sadly at the pale, mournful face of the man from Constantinople.

"Whose fault is it?" asked Tiutiukjian. "The old man is peace-loving; not like scribblers like us. He spoke the truth saying that we of Constantinople should have prepared the people. But what did we do? Nothing. We took no pains to learn the actual conditions in the interior. Present day Armenia with its frightful misery did not interest us. We were dazzled with its past glory. We had read of its ancient writers, and imagined a land filled with Dikrans, Arams, Vahans and Nerseses. In imagination we saw populous cities in which commerce and art flourished; we saw it, — villages surrounded by fertile fields whose yield filled the storehouses of the Armenian with abundant harvests. We believed that the majority of the Armenian population consisted of Armenians who lived on their hereditary lands enjoying peace and prosperity. But we did not know that the Armenian provinces were being stripped of Armenians, either because they were threatened by destitution, or because they were forced to accept Mohammedanism. We did not know that instead of finding living Armenians we should find only skeletons walking about, or extensive graveyards. We did not know that religion, which we considered the main prop of our national existence, was extinct, and there remained only the ruins of once splendid churches and monasteries. We did not know that our language, the sacred inheritance of the nation, had been lost, and that today only Turkish or Kurdish is spoken. We did not know that many of the present day brave Kurds who have become the rod and scourge of God for us and Armenians, were our brothers fifty or a hundred years ago, who once spoke our language and worshipped in our churches. In a word, we knew nothing.

"We had a very indistinct knowledge of modern Armenia. We had not learned that, owing to debasing conditions, and under the heavy yoke of slavery, Armenians had lost their finest characteristics, and had acquired meanness, littleness, timidity and deceitfulness."

Vartan was listening intently as Tiutiukjian continued. "The great powers held their meetings where we were. We might have done noteworthy deeds. The Patriarch resided there, he the head of the people, but who never took into consideration the body, his people. We had a National Representative Council, but it was occupied with intrigues and insignificant questions. We bad there the well-educated youth of the country who made the shores of the Bosphorus echo with Armenian songs on their national feast-days, who had no idea that at that very moment, blood and tears were being shed in Armenia. We had the press, which ignored the plight of the Armenians in the interior, but occupied itself with the doings of foreigners. We had schools, but they gave no useful teachers to Armenia. We had the theater which did not once portray the wretchedness of Armenia, but served its audience with the kitchen filth of France. We had the leaders of people who by flattering the arbitrators of the Sublime Porte gained glory for themselves. We had the material strength — money —used only to bedeck the palaces of the wealthy, while not a single 'para' was spent on improving Armenia. In a word, we held the tiller of national prosperity in our hands, but only in order, it would seem, to lead it to destruction. As for me," he continued, "my views and those of a few sympathizers are considered quixotic. What can we wait for? Shall we sit idle in Constantinople forever and not examine the conditions in Armenia, do nothing about education, do not become acquainted with the needs and demands of the people; do not prepare them for a better future, but suddenly appear there, give out arms to enable them to fight in self-defense? That is unreasonable. Nevertheless I do not despair; my faith is not lacking. Perchance I and all my companions will fall, but our, fall will make a path for others to follow; they may be able to pass over our dead bodies."

On hearing these words Vartan was unable to control his feelings; he embraced Tiutiukjian and said: "Such work demands sacrifice, it is true; praise and honor to whomsoever becomes the first victim."

It was past midnight. The beds had been spread in the oda long since, but the two young men remained awake still longer. Tiutiukjian was critical and merciless in his denunciation of the youths of Constantinople; of the clergy, and said that if a tenth of the churches and monasteries of the country should be converted into schools Armenia might yet be saved.

Suddenly someone knocked guardedly at the door of the oda, Vartan went and opened it. Hairabed and Abo appeared, the two sons of Khacho who differed from the others. "We came at such an unusual hour that no one should see us," said Hairabed, as he and his brother seated themselves. "I fear we disturb you."

111

"Not at all," replied Vartan, "We were unable to sleep and were still talking. It appears that all the rest are asleep."

"All but my father," replied Abo. "He coughs continually and cannot sleep. He is worried."

Vartan and Tiutiukjian well understood that the visit of the two brothers at this hour was not without significance, and they waited for them to make known their errand.

"We were not able to say anything in the presence of our father and our brothers," said Hairabed, finally, and went on to say, "We wished you to know that we sympathize with you entirely, and are willing to serve your purposes in any manner you consider best."

A look of gladness shone on the face of Mr. Tiutiukjian. It was like the happiness of the missionary when he gains two converts and thinks that now he has a flock, and that these two will be followed by thousands.

"It is quite wrong," said Hairabed, "to think that the Armenians here are dead in spirit and have no lofty aspirations. But there is one thing that is a general failing among them. Every Armenian, taken individually, is cautious, deliberate, unsure of himself, and has no will of his own. He waits for an example, for another to lead, and he will follow. Example, especially the example of successful work, has great influence over him. The Armenian always considers conditions. He does not care how those in foreign countries live. He does not adopt the example of foreigners, but waits for an Armenian like himself to show him the example. Therefore we will be the first to make an example of ourselves, and then I believe many will follow us. I know our people well. We have been tormented so terribly that we are ready to eat the flesh and drink the blood of the Turk and the Kurd. Our hearts are filled with bate, but our hatred is concealed."

Vartan and Tiutiukjian heard Hairabed's words with joy. Through him spoke the voice of the people.

"Happy is the people that knows how to hate." exclaimed Tiutiukjian with great animation. "He who does not know how to hate does not know how to love."

"My father says that the soil is not ready," said Hairabed. "He is really a wise man, and his head contains many good ideas, but because of his cautiousness his wise thoughts have become faults in him. He has deadened us with his counsel of patience and has kept us inert. In my way of thinking, boldness, self confidence, and almost foolish recklessness will accomplish more than the gentle and prudent reflections of the wise."

112

"Yes, while the prudent is considering, the fool crosses the river," put in Vartan with a laugh.

"That is quite right," observed Tiutiukjian. "The wisdom of the wise often deceives them, and of ten those who have been deceived by them understand that they have been fooled only when the kizir has finished with them. At one time our wise men in Constantinople considered it more profitable for Armenians to remain under the ignorant and disorderly rule of the Turks than under one which is enlightened and civilized. They thought that a civilized government would annihilate the Armenians by assimilating them; while on the contrary, prudent Armenians, profiting from the folly of the Turks, were able to compete with them in the struggle for existence, and to obtain the victory.

"This observation is quite in line with the theory. But the most correct philosophical theory sometimes proves wrong in the experience of life. History has its notable deviations. If a great civilized nation is able to absorb small nations, a great uncivilized nation may do the same with its small subject races. The difference lies only in the means used. One kills in a barbarous fashion, the other assimilates. I will speak more plainly. Until today none of us understood the secret policy of the Turks concerning the Armenians. I've repeat with childish short-sightedness: 'Our future is that of Turkey.' We looked at the disorder, corruption and barbarity practiced, but we did not see the hellish machinery hidden beneath all this. We saw oppression, murder, forcible change of religion, all the wickedness committed by neighboring tribes. We considered all that as temporary and accidental and did not know that these irregularities were secretly encouraged and fomented by men of high degree. We blamed the government, considering it simply weak and unable to control its lawless subjects. We did not know that government officials themselves excited these barbarians against the Armenians, in order to destroy the Christian element. Do you ask me why? Turkey understands very well that the existence of Christian subjects in her empire gives the Christian rulers a pretext to interfere in Turkish affairs every time, and to bring the Eastern question to the front anew. In order not to lose her territory, and to escape from the interference of the Christian rulers, the Turk is forced to annihilate the Christians. Because of the Christians she has lost many of her European states, and is about to lose the remainder. The only Asiatic country that she controls in its entirety is Asia Minor. Here the principal nationality that threatens the partition of that portion of the empire is the Armenian. Therefore, in order to stop the noise of the European Governments she must show them that no Armenians remain in Armenia.

"In that work of annihilation, the Turk has chosen those most fitted for the task, the Kurds and the Circassians. If we collect together the proofs of this during the past thirty five years, we shall be fully persuaded that this is true.

113

"We shall be persuaded that all the oppression, extortion, violence, persecution and rape committed against the Armenians; in a word, that all the barbarity has not been accidental. We are persuaded that under all this there lies concealed a premeditated, and definitely planned principle, and the intention to weaken, destroy and eventually annihilate the Armenian element. I mention only a few of the many proofs. In order to deprive the Armenians of any possibility of defending themselves, they snatched away their weapons from their hands. They tied and fettered their hands, while they gave weapons into the hands of the enemies of the Armenians. Then they saw that this was not sufficient to weaken the Armenians; they saw that this element, a thrifty and hard-working people was able to wrestle with its opponents, and to preserve its existence, through its wealth and material strength. Therefore it became necessary to impoverish it; to destroy it economically. They increased taxes, repudiated the paper currency in circulation, without notifying the people — in a word, they perpetrated various kinds of fraudulent financiering, in order that the money in the hands of the people lose its value, making them unable to pay their taxes, and in order that they might have a pretext to oblige them to pay in place of taxes, things essential to their subsistence — to deprive them of making implements. These means were still insufficient to accomplish the designs of Turkey. The people were long suffering. If they could not make a living in their native land, they would emigrate to foreign lands, earn money which they brought back and poured into the Treasury. So, what could they do? Turkey considered drying up the source of Armenian livelihood at one blow. Crafty land laws were devised, and the Armenians were deprived of the right to own real estate. The land owned by Armenians was given into the hands of Kurdish outlaw chieftains, Circassians, muftis, kadis and various "eshirat". These became the landlords, while the industrious Armenian became the slave or serf who tilled the soil. Numerous land disputes and law suits of the present-day, between Armenians and Mohammedans, have either received no attention from the Turkish Government, or if they have been tried, the decision has invariably been in favor of the Mohammedan. There are thousands of examples of this. An examination of any one of these decisions is sufficient to prove that the Government does not wish land to remain in the hands of the Armenians, but wishes them to be deprived of their inheritance from their fathers, in order, that more may emigrate to other lands, and by emptying Armenia of Armenians, fill their place with Kurds and Circassians.

"Now you see that there is a connecting thread in all these atrocities, a secret and hellish purpose. It is superfluous to speak of special instances, or to show that the local government officials have often tried to bring about famine by artificial means in the Armenian provinces in order to destroy by hunger those who have escaped the sword of the Kurds and Circassians. That is murder on a monstrous scale of which only the merciless Turk is capable.

114

"To exhaust them through poverty, to bankrupt them economically, to deprive them of all means of support, these are the chief weapons with which the Turk has tried to destroy the Armenian element. The Turk knows that it is difficult to destroy with other weapons a people whose strength lies in its industry. The Armenians of Zeitoon have no land on which to sow and reap. Their principal source of livelihood is from their iron mines, which they mine, and from which they make iron tools, or exchange the raw material for other articles needed by them, in the neighboring provinces. Several attempts were made by the Turks to snatch these mines from the people of Zeitoon, but the hardy mountaineers, by resisting fiercely, were able to save their principle source of wealth. The destruction of Van by fire may be considered an example of such machination. The Armenians of that city were well off. One night the Turks set fire to all the Armenian shops. Although the Armenians petitioned the government over and over, the local officials were unwilling to begin investigations as to the origin of the fire, and find the criminals, for the government itself was the criminal. We used to be astonished seeing how Turkey flattered the Kurdish and Circassian sheik who by reason of their irregularities cause the Government not a little trouble. Often they do not pay their taxes, and often they come down in hordes and raid certain provinces. Is it possible, we asked, that if the government wished to do so it could not control those robbers? Now we understand that Turkey needed such tools in her hands. Her intention is evident."

Tiutiukjian seemed to be pouring out all the bitterness of his soul this night. The suffering of a nation in agony, its unfortunate condition, and its dark future, which presented itself to him in somber colors — all this filled his soul with righteous indignation.

"Circumstances and the condition of life," he said, "force men to treat others as they have been treated, returning evil for evil. Man is the only creature which treats his kind more cruelly and unjustly than do the wild beasts. The wild beast kills his prey and puts an end to his suffering at once. But man tortures, oppresses, exhausts morally and mentally, sapping hit; victim's strength little by little, before he finally kills him. It is a frightful death. Only man is capable of murdering in this way. Such a death is dealt not simply to individuals, but to entire nations. Such a death threatens us. Is this not the purpose of the Turk, the Kurd and the Circassian regarding us? Is not this the reason that today Armenia is nearly bereft of Armenians?"

During Tiutiukjian's dissertation, Vartan listened sympathetically, and said finally, with an ironic smile: "The Armenians are a strange people. If one cannot say that it is impossible to destroy them, I can at least say that it is very difficult. This nation is like the many-headed mythological creature, the Hydra. When one head was cut off, another and a stronger one grew. During the course of ages, the Armenian has been so beaten, flattened and

115

hammered on the anvil of the universe, that he has acquired the hardness of iron. It is not easy to crush him; he is exceedingly resilient. The Armenians bore the barbarities of the greatest Mongol invasions compared with which those of the Mongol descendants in Turkey may be considered no worse than flies. Across the country of the Armenians passed the Mongol Khan, Tamarlane and Genghis Khan, and the bloody incursions of similar human monsters. They passed like floods and storms; they exterminated others, and were exterminated themselves, and finally they vanished, but the Armenians remained.

"The Mongol Turkey of today, by trying to kill the productive Armenian who fills the coffers of the Empire, in its ignorance, kills itself. Its present financial bankruptcy is the result of that attempt. Formerly, Turkey better appreciated the profitableness of the Armenian element for the establishment and prosperity of her Empire. Not only did she take especial care to ensure the comfort of the Armenian villages, but she entrusted the treasury department of the empire into the hands of Armenian financiers, and our bankers saved the empire on occasion, from serious critical disaster."

It was nearly morning, and our hotheaded thinkers were still talking. Then they began to talk of the necessary plans and preparations to be made. When the consultation ended, Tiutiukjian took from his pocket three calling cards and giving them to his friends, said, "I trust you implicitly. Now you may know who I am, and my true name." On the cards was printed the name, L. Salman. The father of Mr. Levon Salman, Toros Chelebi,* was an Armenian Catholic who became a Mohammedan. The reason for his changing his religion is a long story. We will say only this, that Toros was accused of having relations with a Turkish girl, and in order to escape death he was obliged to marry the beautiful Fatima. She died in childbirth and the infant, Levon, was left in his father's care. He was in great distress of mind at the thought of having his son trained and educated in a religion which had grown hateful to him. Salman pere, who had been given the name of Toros Chelebi, left his native city of Angora, and moved to Constantinople. Here no one knew him. He committed his son to a brotherhood of Freres, but he himself became an infidel. Little Levon grew up in a Catholic monastery, and when twelve years old was sent to Italy.

He received his elementary education from the clergy. He spent several years in the monastery of St. Lazare in Venice, and on leaving entered the Jesuit (Mekhitarist) monastery in Vienna. Finally love of a woman drew him out of that atmosphere and swept him into the chaos of Paris. Here, at first, his life was spent in idleness and pleasure-seeking. He joined various societies where there was much talk but little action. But when his

---

* Chelebi—a Turkish title given to Greek and Armenian merchants.

116

mistress's money was exhausted, poverty forced him to go to work. He wrote articles for the papers about the East, earning a meager income. But when the Eastern question rose to prominence once more, he deserted his mistress, left Paris, and went to Constantinople.

Chapter 22

A month previous to the arrival of Salman in the province of Pakrevant, a muleteer of Erzeroum called Hadji Misak, made up his caravan and set out for Erzeroum. He had obtained the title "Hadji" by reason of his having made two pilgrimages to Jerusalem, and, if God should spare him, he intended to do so once more, in order to reach the mystic number, three.

Hadji Misak was considered a good Christian; his zeal reached the point of superstition. He was acquainted with all the towns, villages and inns along the way. For more than twenty years this man had gone about in Armenia and Asia Minor carrying goods. He was a thick-set man of medium height, very quick in his movements. It is impossible to give an exact description of his features, for they were so concealed by his heavy beard that one could distinguish only his huge Armenian nose, and his sharp eyes, in whose depths there could be read great kindness of heart.

Wherever he went, the arrival of Hadji Misak's caravan occasioned general rejoicing. Was there any one who did not expect to receive something through him? The merchants expected goods; the wife, a letter from her absent husband. The officials, great and small, along the way expected this or that article or delicacy to eat, to drink or to wear. Often some wandering Armenian emigrant, near perishing by the wayside would be waiting for Hadji Misak's caravan to have compassion on him and help him on his way. Hadji Misak's prompt service and his willingness to help every man made him a general favorite.

He would be asked, "Hadji Misak, when you return, bring me a few pounds of cotton"; or, "Hadji Misak, my coffee is all gone. Bring me some more." "'Hadji Misak, see that this olive oil reaches my home." He would perform such services without a "para" of pay, even spending something for them from his own pocket. For these reasons, the authorities posted along his route were lenient with Hadji Misak. His caravan passed through the custom offices easily, and he was given no trouble.

A peddler or carrier, especially a well-known one, is trusted very greatly in the East. Bales of the most expensive goods are committed to him; Sacks of gold and silver without any papers or official documents, and he will deliver the consignment safely to the appointed parties.

Every town knew the time of the expected arrival of his caravan. So regular was his schedule that unless delayed by some unforeseen circumstances, his arrival would not vary an hour.

But this time Hadji Misak's caravan made slow progress. Although his bales appeared to be small, they were heavy. Most of the bales were oblong cases, bound with iron strips, and with PERSIA printed on them in English. The caravan had traveled principally by night. Hadji Misak said he didn't want his mules to suffer from the heat of the day.

In this caravan there was another person who gave his name as Melik-Mansoor. He was a merchant and claimed to be Persian-Armenian.

During the last twenty or thirty year,-, many changes had been introduced in Persia. and the adoption of European styles. A new business was thus inaugurated for Armenian traders that of purveying weapons. Melik-Mansoor was in this business, and the heavy cases on the backs of his mules were of this description. Little attention was given these articles in the custom-houses, as they were bonded through to Persia. Their route was by way of Trebizond, Erzeroum, Bayazid, through to Persia.

Melik-Mansoor was thirty six years old; he had a pleasant face; his cheerful disposition and his talkative tongue enlivened his conversations with Hadji Misak especially when he began on the interesting episodes which bad taken place in far distant lands. Such conversation enlivened the monotony of travel by caravan. The most interesting tale told by this Armenian "wandering Jew" was of how he lost three fingers in a fight with savages in India. Melik-Mansoor spoke many languages, both of the East and of the West, and in his constant dealings with men of every sort, he had learned all their tricks, and how to meet them. So, he was not what he appeared to be on the exterior. Hadji Misak treated him with marked respect, not only because he owed it to the owner of the loads he was carrying, but because he deserved it. The landlords of the caravansaries along the way always welcomed Melik Mansoor for he was generous and scattered gold right and left. Hadji Misak would expostulate, "You are throwing it away; another time we shall not be able to get as much as a cup of water from these robbers."

"No matter," he would reply with a laugh. "The glitter of gold will blind their eyes."

The caravan passed safely through Erzeroum, and a week later entered the province of Bayazid. Here Melik-Mansoor's loads began to be exchanged for others. The cases disappeared during the night, and in their place the animals were loaded with bales containing very different merchandise. These exchanges took place when the caravan remained at certain Armenian villages overnight.

Sometimes a stranger would appear and speak to Melik-Mansoor in some strange tongue, and then disappear.

At length the caravan approached the Persian frontier. It crossed the boundary and set foot on Persian territory. But by the time they reached here, not one of the cases marked PERSIA and TEHERAN remained on the backs of Hadji Misak's mules, and Melik-Mansoor, the counterfeit merchant, had also disappeared.

Chapter 23

The ordinary routine of life in the house of old Khacho had been greatly altered during the past few days. Salman, whom, the household still called Mr. Tiutiukjian, was not often at home. He and Vartan were away sometimes for days at a time. Hairabed and Abo appeared very much preoccupied and reserved. The brothers could not endure the two strangers whose behavior and "foolishness" displeased them. Old Khacho himself was busy with village affairs which daily grew heavier and caused him much anxiety. For this reason the landlord's oda seemed deserted and the nightly discussions there had largely ceased.

Only the life of the women of the family remained unchanged. That lonely separate portion of the Armenian family had no share in the talk, work and thoughts of the men. No idea outside of their housework and housekeeping occupied their minds. So they knew nothing of the consultation which took place in the oda. The landlord's oda, the village club, was not open to women. "It is necessary to draw on their strength which is confined within their four walls, then we shall surely succeed," Salman often said.

"It is early yet," replied Vartan, "they need preparation first. No reform in the life of a people is possible without the assistance of women. If our people have remained static the principal reason for it is because women have had no share in public affairs. The strength, the energizing force which has lain abortive within their four walls has yielded no results."

"In order to begin the work of educating our people we must certainly begin with the education of women. This time I have traveled all through Armenia and I have studied the Armenian woman with particular attention. The information I have gained has been very comforting. However much the men have grown deceitful and loose, and have lost their Armenian characteristics owing to the influence of the Turk, so much more has the woman remained pure, and has preserved her goodness and moral purity. There is no evil without some good. Women are shut within walls and although for centuries they suffered and degenerated, and were unable

121

to have a share in affairs, they still preserved the Armenian ethos. That is a great achievement.

"However much the man under the influence of Mohammedan elements has lost his moral superiority on the contrary the woman, far removed from that influence, has preserved the national ethos. In this way, unconsciously was preserved a permanent equilibrium. The women have supplied what the men have lost. This can be observed even in the commonest details. The abhorrence by women for Mohammedanism has become a veritable obsession with them. They consider everything defiled that has been touched by a Mohammedan; they will not eat the meat he has touched, the cheese he has pressed, the bread he has kneaded. But the men make no such distinctions. I have heard hundreds of stories of women and girls who have been seized by Mohammedans, who have finally made their escape, or, if not successful have committed suicide. But such examples in regard to men are very rare.

"There is another thing also which is most important. In many places, especially in cities, men use the Turkish language, but I never saw a woman who would speak Turkish or even know it. Woman has preserved the Armenian language in the home and taught it to the children. She imposes it even upon foreigners. All the Kurdish servants in the employ of Armenians speak Armenian. Woman has given us our language, our national ethos, and has preserved the moral foundation of the Armenian family. Now she is a pure, raw material in our hand, from which something wonderful may be made."

Such reflections and others of a similar nature were the subject of Salman's usual strain of talk during the last few days. But not knowing of his good opinion of Armenian women, the women of old Khacho's house did not take to him. We can understand how they were unable to recognize his inner moral and intellectual worth, but Salman had much on his outer shell which might attract the attention of a woman. But in the various stages of development and in different classes of people, women have different tastes in judging and liking the qualities of men. For this reason it is not strange that the young women of old Khacho's family accorded Vartan a higher rank than they did to Salman.

Once, in the quiet afternoon hour, the young women were sitting in the hall, each employed with her handiwork. One spun wool, another wound it, another was weaving a beautiful rug on a loom; another was sewing clothes for her children. They were all busy. The subject of their conversation was Salman.

"Sara," asked her sister-in-law, Parishan, "what is this man going to do in this village?"

"They say he wants to open a school," replied Sara.

"But he is not a choir-master," said Parishan, who thought that teachers are necessarily choir- masters.

"He is a choir-master."

"Then why doesn't he go to church and chant?"

Sara could think of no reply, and answered carelessly, "He is that sort of a choir-master too."

Abols wife the pretty Maro, spoke up. "People say that he is going to teach girls, too." Maro's speech caused a general laugh.

"What use is it for a girl to read? She won't become a priest or a bishop," answered Maro.

One of the young women turned toward little Nazlou saying, "Have you heard, Nazlou, that you are to go to school to learn Your a-b-c's?"

Nazlou was Hairabed's daughter, and she replied quite fearlessly, "What of it? I will learn, afterward I will go to church, put on a robe, and say the responses like the boys."

"There wasn't enough earth found to finish your head with when you were created," they said, in derision.

Parishan, who started this conversation, queried,

"Choir-master Simon has taught our boys. What do we want of another teacher? Hasn't he read as much as this man?"

"Certainly, he doesn't know very much," answered Sara. "Choir-master Simon has studied much, but he has one fault; he gets drunk and beats the children. Do you remember our neighbor Caspar's boy? He was beaten so badly that he had to be carried home, and the poor boy died after a couple of days."

"Whose fault was that? Without beating what will children learn?" replied another.

This conversation had some foundation in fact. Salman had been talking with the villagers those days, about opening two schools, one for boys and one for girls. He promised to get teachers, to have their children taught free, and even to furnish books and supplies without charge. But that which is free, is regarded with suspicion by the villager. For, that reason it was difficult to persuade the villagers, and they were especially angry about having a school for girls. The people being accustomed to getting their instruction from a priest, or a choir-master, considered it strange, unusual and even wicked (or wrong) to commit the instruction of their children to a man who did not go to church, nor sing chants, nor, as they had heard, keep the fasts.

Old Khacho, who opposed Salman in all his other views, agreed with him about the schools. Being the chief landlord of the village, he was able to win over the other villagers, and they gave Salman a piece of ground which he thought would be a suitable spot on which to build a school. The work was begun, the foundation was laid. Suddenly a tempest arose, and one morning they saw that the villagers had assembled by night and destroyed the foundations. That day, not one of the villagers came to work, even though Salman offered to increase their wages.

What happened?

As it appeared from the talk of the women, there was a chorister or choir-master named Simon in the village who taught school also, that is, during the winter he would gather the children in a stable and make them read psalms and lectionaries, but in the spring when the village work began, he dismissed his pupils who had no more schooling till late in the fall, and by that time they would forget all they had learned. This chorister was the son-in-law of the village priest Marook, and was always getting drunk, and was also a very quarrelsome man. He found the building of the new school injurious to his income, and worked upon his father-in-law to prohibit the enterprise.

One word was enough to excite the villagers and put a stop to the work. The priest informed the people, in a sermon, that Salman was a "Freemason" who did not worship the God of the Armenians and he would destroy the faith of the children. He added that it was a sin to teach girls to read; that Solomon the Wise, and John the Baptist had cursed woman, for a woman had John the Baptist beheaded. He also brought forward many proofs from the Bible saying that the death of the prophet Samson was caused by a woman. Eve deceived Adam and occasioned his expulsion from Paradise. Bringing forth many such proofs in his sermon, the father-confessor affirmed that it was dangerous to educate girls as they would learn too much and become devils.

Chorister Simon had a large following of women in the village. He had cast spells for them, he had foretold events, and so gained their confidence. The women stirred up their husbands still more to help keep the chorister so that he would not lose his income.

The priest and chorister Simon found a powerful ally in this disturbance, in the person of Thomas Effendi, who was violently opposed to all that is included under the name of school — schooling and education. Besides this, the chorister was his recorder who worked without pay. He wrote the tax accounts, and at harvest time accompanied the gendarmes from village to village, and collected the tithes.

All this caused much anxiety to kind-hearted old Khacho, but they were unable to shake Salman's determination. Returning home at evening, he said to Vartan, "I am going to treat those rascals the way the missionaries do. Whenever the missionary enters a community, his first opponents are the educated classes and the clergy. But at the same time his first followers are those persons who opposed him at first. The missionary entrusts various kinds of work to them, or rather no work at all, but simply pays them salaries. In this way the persecuting Sauls become the Pauls, of the new sect, and its most zealous advocates.

"That is true," replied Vartan. "What do you want to do?"

"We must be practical," replied Salman, with great self-confidence. "We must understand, what will attract a man. I would be much interested to know how much money that fool of a chorister received from his pupils. I will propose charging them double and giving him a position in my school, that is, a sinecure. I am sure that then he will come the following morning, with his spade and pick-ax, and will beg to labor with my workmen on the building."

"I think so, too," replied Vartan, "but you must butter the priest's mouth a little too."

"I'll do that, too."

In spite of t he unpleasantness that occurred that day, Salman was more cheerful than usual. The failures attending the beginning of the undertaking aroused his zeal, and bright hopes for the future filled his heart with boundless joy.

"Do you know, Vartan, what a great and prosperous future our school promises. This, only this, will cure our age-long wounds and will prepare the new generation for a vigorous, fresh life. The failure of our ancestors to train the young has left much work for us, it is true. They did not care for our present work at that time — but no matter. It is still possible to have hope that the future will belong to us. Only earnest and patient endeavor is necessary. I think that it is not sufficient to train the mind and ennoble the soul; it is necessary to train the body as well. You yourself have observed, Vartan, how slowly these children move, how lazy they are. It is necessary to strengthen their muscles and invigorate their nerves. With this aim in view, our school must give the necessary instruction. It must inculcate strength in the hearts of our youth and must invigorate their enfeebled spirits.

"I have something pleasant to tell you, Vartan. Today I talked with some Kurds. I spoke of their schools and the benefits of education. Great was my astonishment when they manifested all possible readiness, saying they would be pleased to entrust their children to the Armenians, since learning is such a fine thing. From their conversation it appeared that they do not wish to have their sons become robbers. And really, whose fault is it that their people have remained savages and have gained their livelihood by robbery and murder? We are to blame since until now, we have never tried to teach them. Our self-interest demands that of us. If we wish to be free from the attacks of wild beasts we must try to tame them and accustom them to a more peaceful and civilized life. Turkey has not tried to educate the Kurds, and that is easily explained, because the savagery of the Kurds has been very profitable to her. But we should try to educate them, for we are the ones who suffer. We will not meddle with religion, we will only teach them; after that 'water will find its level'."

126

Chapter 24

The signs of preparation for war, on the part of the Turkish Government, were quite evident; and this could be seen especially in the province of Pakrevant, which was not far from the Russian frontier. It had collected harshly from the villagers not only the taxes for the current year, but demanded back taxes also, and even for some years in advance. There was no limit to the complaints and cries of the people. Whoever was unable to pay in cash, was forced to sell his household goods and cattle, nor did they spare the oxen and buffaloes which were indispensable to the villager for his plowing, drawing his carts and moving his loads. This not being sufficient, the villager was obliged to prepare so many thousand "okes" of hardtack or they would take from him all the provisions from his home, such as barley, flour, cracked wheat, noodles, fat, cheese, rice, etc. The reply made to all the weeping and tears of the villagers was: "The Government has a war on."

These irregularities opened to Thomas Effendi a new and extensive sphere of activity. Being the imperial tax-collector, he undertook to collect the tribute and to find a portion of the provisions to be furnished for the army. Thomas Effendi had an extensive harvest-field opened to him, where he labored zealously with a sharp sickle. Now instead of two gendarmes he had received an official order to employ as many as necessary. All these outrages were inflicted on the Armenians alone, for the Mohammedans were working to take part in the war, and nothing more was demanded of them.

In addition, besides the plundering of the Armenian villages and having the accumulation of ten or twenty years snatched from them at one swoop besides their bitter poverty, they were smitten with terror, they were threatened with universal and frightful misfortune. The Mohammedan element exhibited a brutal ferocity toward the Christians, toward all the giaours. From the lips of each and all was heard the frightful word, "massacre"' The mollahs, muftihs, ghatis and the sheikhs had kindled the fanaticism of the turbulent hosts. They had excited them, preaching "a holy war." In Istanbul, the sacred banner would soon be unfurled and the "holy war" would be proclaimed, and all Islam must take up the sword against the Christians.

All this caused Salman great anxiety, for he understood perfectly the meaning of this frenzied tumult, and the fearful consequences to the Armenians of the region.

"The Bulgarian horrors will soon be repeated here," he said one morning to Vartan. "We must hasten to prepare the people for self-defense."

"And I can smell the stench of such barbarities," replied Vartan.

Talking together like this they came out of old Khacho's house, and turned their steps toward the house of the priest, Father Marook, with whom they intended to conclude the arrangements they had determined on a few days previously; that is, as Vartan said, they wished to butter the priest's mouth a little to keep him quiet, and to hire his son-in-law, Simon, the chorister, as overseer of the workmen, and to promise him a position later in the new school.

A sound reached their ears. A strange peddler was passing through the village, and calling out his wares one by one; he was inviting purchasers.

"Pretty girls, rosy brides, bring me your 'paras' and I will give you fine needles, colored thread, rings, etc."

The peddler was a huge fellow, dressed in rags from head to foot. The enormous pack of goods which he carried on his back in comparison with the size of his body, bore the same relation that a small sieve would on the back of a camel. The peddler's left leg was very lame, and when he swung toward the left, it looked as though that Goliath would fall to the ground, but the great staff giving him support helped him keep his balance.

When Salman beard his voice he seemed shaken as if by a shock. What tie was there between Salman and the wandering peddler? The peddler still continued to cry his wares and to walk slowly and unevenly through the village streets. Salman approached him and the eyes of the two strangers met. There was no conversation whatsoever between them, but they communicated much to each other. Vartan noticed nothing.

"He has found a fine time to sell his needles and thread. The poor villagers haven't a 'para' left, how can they buy anything?" said Vartan in disgust, as they moved away from the peddler.

"His pack, my friend, like the juggler's cases, have false bottoms," answered Salman. "In the lower one are found supplies which it is best to sell at the present time."

Vartan did not pay any special attention to that significant remark. His mind was occupied at that moment with a very different object. He was thinking about Lila. The sudden change of circumstance, the imminent disturbances made him very uneasy and he did not know how to manage Lila's case; where should he conceal her, what should he do with her, when he might be obliged today or tomorrow to begin a very different undertaking?

"Fine needles, colored thread, pretty beads," again they heard in the distance the lame peddler's raucous, long-drawn-out cry.

Just then Salman and Vartan met Thomas Effendi in the street. His beautiful horse stood near him as he prepared to mount. He was surrounded by a group of villagers, to whom he was giving orders and commands. Seeing Salman and Vartan, he left the group, and with his usual crafty smile turned toward the two young men and before reaching them said from a distance, "I have long wanted to see you, Mr. Tiutiukjian, Oh, how fortunate I consider myself, dear, compatriot, to have this opportunity of seeing you. Perhaps you don't know that I am from Constantinople also."

This flattery of the Effendi's seemed not only exceedingly strange but also very distasteful to Salman, whom he did not know in the least, and whom he now met for the first time. He made no reply. The Effendi, grasping his hand, said, "I hope you permit me to embrace you. I wish to assuage my longing for the land of my birth in meeting you."

Vartan stood apart, watching the comedy in silence. Salman did not know how to extricate himself from his embarrassment. The Effendi turned next to Vartan. Come here, my crazy friend, you know I have the heart of a child. I get angry one moment, I forget it the next. 'The Kurd doesn't call his "Koumiss" sour.' You are mine, whether good or bad, you are mine too. I have forgotten everything. Give me your hand."

Vartan found it hard to control his anger. But reflecting that the Effendi did not express this friendship without some special purpose, gave him his hand.

He turned again to Salman. "I am very angry at you Mr. Tiutiukjian," said he speaking in a more sprightly manner. "Have you heard the Turkish proverb, 'First see the landlord, then rob the village'? Thomas Effendi is an important man in this country. If you had consulted me in the beginning I

129

would have arranged all your affairs so that this unpleasantness would not have arisen. Oh, you young people, you young people, you have good hearts but you don't know how to go about your work. Am I not right?"

"I really don't understand what you are talking about," replied Salman.

The Effendi pretended that he did not hear Salman's remark and turning his head toward the group of villagers who were waiting for him, said, "Oh, donkeys, donkeys, when will you have any sense?"

Then turning to Salman again, he said, "Does a man put out the light of his eyes with his own hands? The villagers are like that. I beard of it today. I tell you, my hair stood on end. We have tried to have them start a school, be educated, have their eyes opened, 'not stay blind', learn to know the evil and the good, but they don't understand; with their own hands they have driven away the ass."

"We have tried," Salnian repeated in his mind. Who are the "we" which Effendi emphasized so significantly?

He continued, "I rejoiced with all my soul when I heard of your plans Mr. Tiutiukjian, and that is why I present myself to express my special gratitude. Our people are in darkness, we must bring them out into the light of the world. Only the school can save them. Don't let the disturbance which occurred a few days ago, discourage you. The beginning of every good work is filled with disappointments. You will find in me, your fellow citizen, sympathy and aid. Accept my small services. Today I have business in a village nearby. Tomorrow I will return, and I will go up myself and have the foundation of the school laid. There is no one here who will oppose Thomas Effendi."

"Thank you, Effendi," replied Salman. You are so busy that I did not wish to rob you of your valuable time."

"That is nothing," replied the tax-collector with great self-complacency. "I always have time for good deeds."

He shook hands with the two young men and took his leave.

"Insolent scoundrel," said Vartan after him.

"It is possible to gain something from such men," replied Salman.

"Do you believe what he says? Who knows what hellish purposes he has!"

The two young men had now reached Father Marook's house and knocked at the door.

"Lovely needles, threads of all colors, fine beads," they heard again the voice of the lame peddler passing through another street.

"Vartan, let us not go to see the priest today," said Salman to him.

"Why?" asked Vartan.

"I need to buy a few things from that peddler."

Vartan began to laugh at his companion's unusual eagerness.

"Come, there is something else," said Salman, in such a tone that Vartan could not surmise what his important business could be.

The two young men left the priest's door, crossed to the next street, and began to follow the peddler from afar. A group of village children were following him calling, "Give us mastic, give us mastic." He took out a piece of mastic and divided it among them.

"I saw that man a week ago, when I was coming from Van," said a villager to a neighbor standing near him.

"These peddlers wander everywhere," answered the neighbor, "but what a dreadful face he has. Look at him, Krikor, I shouldn't like to see him at night, I would think he was the devil."

The lame peddler went through all the streets. Occasionally he was called to enter some house and he would remain there for hours, but sometimes they had him open his case in the street and the village women gathering around him would bargain with him. So by night he was only just able to finish his trading and it was growing dark when he came out of the village. He left the main road which led to the neighboring village, and began to direct his steps towards a ditch which had been worn quite deep by the spring freshets, but which was dry. There was a change in his gait. He walked slowly, as before, for his load was quite heavy. But the man was not lame in the least, as he had seemed to be during the day. He began to descend into the ditch. Then he set down his pack, and laying two fingers of his left band upon his lips he gave a peculiar whistle. The other fingers of that hand were missing. A few minutes later Vartan and Salman appeared in the ditch. The latter embraced the peddler and clung to him long.

131

"Now let us be seated," replied the peddler in a happy tone. "I flooded Vasbooragan with my merchandise."

"Of course, without receiving pay."

"Without pay, I delivered my goods free."

Vartan listened in astonishment. He understood nothing.

"Now you understand," Salman said to him, "that my friend's pack like the juggler's has two bottoms."

"It would be interesting to know what was concealed in the principal portion of the pack," said Vartan.

"Weapons."

Now Vartan understood who and what manner of man the peddler was, for he had heard of him a few days before through Salman, and he also embraced him.

This man was Melik-Mansoor.

Chapter 25

Great men have great failings. Although Thomas Effendi did not belong in the class of great men, in the province of Alashgerd, he was considered a giant. Where no lions are found, even the fox is a large animal. This man also, however active and skillful he was, had his small failings. Passing the whole day in the pursuit of his business, he often passed the night without sleep in the enjoyment of his pleasures, and following the bad habits of Turkish officials, drank "raki", had boys and girls dance for him, and had a following of strolling musicians play for him.

Whenever he entered a village, the doors of every villager were opened to him. Who could refuse to admit that guest of high degree? On the contrary, the villager considered himself honored when Thomas Effendi stepped upon his door-sill. Although they gained nothing—for he ate and drank at their expense —it was enough that hereafter Thomas Effendi would look upon them with a "kind eye" as his hosts. One evening the "kizir" (tax-recorder) sent word to the house of a poor villager that the Effendi would be their guest. The owner of the house was the only carpenter in several villages. He made farming implements, he mended broken plows, yokes, carts, etc.. He was seldom at home, as he had to make the rounds of these villages afoot to find work. This evening also, he was not at home. The carpenter's wife answered the "kizir" that her husband was not at home and wondered how she could receive the Effendi?

"Your man isn't at home, but his house is," the "kizir" replied insolently.

Those men, called kizirs, are a trial to the dwellers in villages. They are the hounds of men holding government offices. They have keen scent, and are trained to know the best means by which to secure their prey.

The poor woman didn't know what to reply, and said nothing.

The kizir, considering his errand accomplished, turned away, saying, "The

Effendi will come when the lamps are lit."

The poor woman remained petrified at the door of her dwelling, and was at a loss to know what to do. Her husband was not at home; it was not proper for her to receive a stranger as guest. She went over to neighbor Oho's cottage and laid her case before him. "Brother Oho," she said, "the kizir has brought me word that the Effendi is coming to our house tonight. My man isn't at home. For the love of God, do come and manage the affair for me."

"What's that?" said Oho angrily. "Isn't there any other house in the village for him to visit?"

"I don't understand it," said the woman sorrowfully. "This is what the kizir ordered."

Neighbor Oho promised to receive the guest, and said he wouldn't leave the woman alone.

Thomas Effendi was so well-known in this province that be could be sure of being received in any place he considered suitable for his purpose. His taste in that regard was very discriminating. The main condition for insuring his enjoyment of the evening being, that the landlord be poor and somewhat foolish, and if not foolish, one who was fond of drink (two qualities which do not differ greatly), and the principal one was the face of a pretty woman be found in the house, which he could look at and enjoy.

But the lodging place he had selected for tonight did not comply perfectly with the Effendi's demands. The husband, Bedros, the carpenter, was an honest and industrious citizen who was neither foolish nor a drinker. Nevertheless the Effendi was not mistaken in his selection, for the husband was not at home. His wife was not bad looking, but his young sister was considered to be the prettiest girl in the village. The lamps were lit in the homes of the villagers. The carpenter's wife, Susan, had prepared the food at the fireplace. The carpenter's sister young Varvare, had fried a few chickens. Neighbor Oho had made various preparations, that nothing should be lacking, and everything in order to receive the honored guest. All was ready when the Effendi appeared preceded by the kizir. He had not brought the gendarmes with him this evening; he had sent them elsewhere to be guests.

Neighbor Oho received the Effendi with great respectfulness as he entered pompously and sat on the cushions prepared for him.

"Where is Master Bedros, I don't see him," asked the Effendi, looking about. "I wanted to see him. I have very important business with him."

Neighbor Oho replied that the carpenter had gone to a neighboring village to work.

"Alas, it's too bad that I can't see him. I had important business with him," the Effendi repeated, and he began to explain that in order to transport the supplies of the Imperial Army he needed many carts, and he wished to hire a carpenter to mend the carts whenever they broke down on the way, and there was no one more suitable for this than Master Bedros, and he wished to do him a "kindness" that he might make money at this job and have steady employment for several months.

Although the Effendi knew beforehand that the carpenter was not at home, and although he had no need whatever of a carpenter, for he used the villagers carts and oxen to transport the supplies without pay, without paying a "para", and if a wagon was broken, they, the owners, must repair it, the Effendi had a special purpose in saying what he did.

The poor carpenter's wife, Susan, hearing the Effendi's promise, rejoiced, and thought they might be able to gain much through this guest, although his having invited himself had been a trial and a very disagreeable task to her. It was necessary to please the simple woman's heart with some hope; that was important for the Effendi's purpose.

Only the Effendi was seated. Neighbor Oho was still standing up, waiting till he should receive permission to be seated. He was allowed that favor. The kizir remained standing and served as there was no servant or grown-up son. He had several attendants whom he had brought with him. The mistress of the house and the carpenter's sister did not appear. They remained apart, separated

from the place where the guest sat, by a low partition which did not reach to the ceiling, and answered as a screen.

But they were obliged to pay their respects to the honored guest. For this reason both Susan and Varvare came out of their hiding-place, and approached the Effendi, and crossing their arms, bowed silently to him from a distance. That was to show that he was welcome.

"Long life to you," said the Effendi, glancing at them sideways.

The face of the mistress of the house was covered with a veil, but the young girl's was open. They moved away and began to prepare the supper.

Profound silence reigned in the little hut. No one spoke. All waited for the Effendi to speak.

"What is your business at present," he asked Oho.

"I have no work, sir," replied Oho, scratching his neck. "God has punished me by sending several misfortunes in one year. My eldest son 'Evil One' carried off. My oxen have been destroyed. Now I can't use my plow, and so I'm out of work."

"Alas, very sad," said the Effendi sympathetically. "You are a good fellow, Oho, I know you. I won't let you stay out of work. I'll give you work. I need many men now."

Oho's joy was boundless. "Just give me work, sir, and you'll see how well Oho can serve you. 'The better the ass works the more barley he gets."

"Certainly, that's so."

The Effendi was one of those men who would puff up with such pride at times that he would swell up so that he couldn't enter the door of a house, but at others be would grow so small that be could almost crawl through the eye of a needle.

He must bribe neighbor Oho with some promise as he occupied the position of host tonight. And the simple-minded villager believed all he said, and expressed his deep gratitude saying, "God grant you long life, sir, God spare your hands to us forever."

It was supper time. Varvare appeared bringing the basin and pitcher, and gracefully set them before the Effendi, who began to wash his hands. Then she spread the table-cloth, set on the bread and the food. All they had prepared was set on the table at once, in their proper places. During all these preparations the innocent girl's shyness appeared mingled with timidity which were the ornaments of her secluded life, owing to her having known no strangers.

"My child," asked the Effendi of the young girl, "what is your name?"

She blushed, and looked from side to side for some one to make a reply for her. Neighbor Oho told him her name was Varvare.

"What a pretty name! Really it is a beautiful name," repeated the Effendi delightedly. "I have a sister who is called that also."

Now, something like a smile shone on Varvare's immobile countenance. She was glad that she had the name of such a great man's sister. In truth the Effendi had no sister whatever, but be wished to please Varvare too, by this means.

Only the Effendi and Oho sat at the table. The women of that region do not sit at the table with the men.

"The wheels of a dry mill don't turn," observed the Effendi. By this he intimated that he needed something to drink, and he ordered the kizir to go and bring some raki. Neighbor Oho begged pardon for not having provided any, but the mistress made signs that she would fetch some directly.

"No," said the Effendi, "it is my custom to furnish the wine and raki at every home where I am entertained."

This was true. In poor homes like this one he had the kizir go for the drinks, but he entered the charge on his expense accounts to be paid for by the village. And the beauty of that scheme was that by ordering drinks he could use as much as he pleased.

The kizir returned very soon bringing an immense jug of raki. "Now you may be seated and serve us the drink," said the Effendi.

The kizir sat at the lowest seat, setting the jug of raki near him. His was familiar with the Effendi's expression, "When I go to a house for 'keff' (to enjoy myself), "the first thing to do is to wet the house-owner's cotton," meaning his brain must be fuddled: he must get drunk.

Although the owner of the house was not present, neighbor Obo occupied his place. For this reason the kizir kept urging Oho to drink, offering him glass after glass.

Neighbor Oho was fond of drink, especially more so since his recent misfortunes, having lost his eldest son and, also, his oxen. So, in order to forget his grief, he bad become more addicted to drink. He accepted each glass and drained it to the last drop. The influence of the raki on the one hand, and the Effendi's promise to give him work, on the other, so warmed his blood, so rejoiced his heart that he forgot himself and began to sing a Turkish song.

"Nothing will spin with that (that's not enough)," said the Effendi, and he ordered the kizir to go and bring in the "chalghijis". The "chalghijis" were a local company of Armenian musicians who sang and played on various Asiatic instruments. They followed the Effendi everywhere, from village to village, for they knew that the Effendi did not pass a night without having his "keff", so they helped entertain him, and were paid by him. The musicians appeared shortly. They paid their respects to the company, and

137

seated themselves around the table. Now, the mistress of the house was obliged to bring on more food.

The Effendi condescended to inquire as to the "chalghijis" health.

"Thank you, we are all well," they replied.

After they had eaten and drunk, and were through, Varvare came out of her retreat again and removed the table. But the jug of raki was not removed. It had been refilled over and over all evening; glasses kept being passed around constantly. The musicians' heads grew heated.

"Now, let us begin," said the Effendi.

They took their instruments, and the little dwelling was enlivened with the discordant strains of Oriental music. The Effendi was enjoying his favorite pastime. In a few minutes the house and yard were surrounded by the wives and daughters of the neighbors, who began looking in through the door and the windows, attracted by the sound of the music. Nothing delights village women so much as music, which is a rare treat for them as usually it is only at a wedding or two during the winter that they had the good fortune to hear any.

Little by little the "mejliss" (gathering) grew more heated and more confused. General confusion was added to the drunkenness and music. As the proverb has it, "Even a dog could not know his master." Everyone had lost his head. Only the Effendi drank moderately and kept control of himself. During this interval the women and girls gathered outside grew bolder, and slowly drifted inside. They sat down near Susan and Varvare and listened to the music.

"Dance, dance," cried the Effendi, clapping his hands. "I want dancing."

Upon this, neighbor Oho who was hardly able to stand on his feet, rose, and seizing two small girls by the hands, dragged them fairly by force and stood them in their midst. The musicians struck up a local dance tune. The little girls were embarrassed, blushed a little and said, "We can't," but finally began to dance.

"Shapash, shapash[†] (dancing fee)," cried the musicians behaving more boldly.

[†] Shapash is a silver coin given the dancer by the guests which she must give to the musicians.

138

And the Effendi put a silver coin in the hand of each dancer and they gave them to the musicians. The dance, as usual, began with the smallest girls and was followed by the older ones. After the first two retired, they dropped their handkerchiefs on two other girls. This was a sign that they should succeed them. Thus the dancers constantly changed. The Effendi generously filled their fists with silver "shapashes" and the musicians played lively tunes.

The turn came to Varvare. The pretty girl excelled them all with her graceful dancing. Her every motion was graceful and of bewitching attractiveness.

"In our country," said the Effendi, "there is a custom among Armenians. When a girl finishes her dancing, she approaches the principal guest of the evening, 'kneels before him, places her bead on his knees and does not rise until she has received a fine gift." There is no such custom in Armenia, only among gypsies.

"That is a very fine custom," said the players, "that should be introduced here also."

"Varvare, you shall be the first example," said the Effendi, "come near, my child."

Varvare, abashed and confused, remained motionless. She wished the floor would fall and the earth swallow her rather than put her head on the lap of a stranger. But they urged her from all sides, and dragged her forward, saying, "Go, girl, don't be bashful. He will give you something." And finally, they forced her to kneel at his feet and place her pretty head on his knees. The Effendi stroked her lovely tresses and put two gold pieces in her hand.

While the Effendi was enjoying such "keff", one of his gendarmes came in and whispered to him. "We found the man you ordered us to seek."

"Keep him safe till morning when I will give you further orders," replied the Effendi in a low tone.

The gendarmes went away. Whom these orders concerned, no one knew.

The night was far spent. Little by little carpenter Bedros' cottage was deserted. The musicians took their leave. They carried the drunken, unconscious neighbor Oho to his house. The crowd dispersed.

In the carpenter's home only the honored guest and the kizir remained, and the latter had drunk so much that his only good eye could see no better than the one he had lost. Susan prepared a bed for the Effendi, the lights were extinguished and all went to rest.

What else happened that night? God only knows. But in the morning Varvare was very sad and for several days she did not cease weeping.

That same night, before dawn, another sad event took place. A young man was led in chains to a military governor who had recently come to this place for military preparations.

None of the villagers saw him, only Thomas Effendi gazed after him through the darkness and said to himself with devilish delight, "Go and blow your whistle all you please after this."

This youth was Tiutiukjian, alias Mr. Salman.

Chapter 26

At old Khacho's house no one knew what had happened to Salman, causing him to fail to return at night, and they felt very uneasy about him. Vartan, Hairabed and Abo were especially troubled, for they felt some evil had overtaken him. In the morning the three set out together in hopes that they might hear of him.

At noon, Thomas Effendi appeared at the house unexpectedly. His coming in this way, without a servant, without an officer, seemed very strange to the old man. Heretofore he had always come with his private attendants. He grasped the old man's hand, drew him aside, as if he had a secret to impart.

"Do you know," he said with feigned sympathy, "they have put that 'whistler' in irons, and taken him to 'Abraham's bosom?'"

The old man understood to whom he referred. He was horrified, and his limbs trembled so that be nearly fell to the floor.

"Hold yourself together - it is no time to tremble," continued the Effendi, "you have still more to hear." He told him that he had learned that last night Salman had gone to a village where a number of herdsmen gathered around him to whom he had talked of the "individual rights of man about the "work of cultivators"; talked against "tyranny"; had talked of bow men have secured for themselves "a freer and a more fortunate life"; and who knows what other crazy things he talked about? Suddenly, several officers entered and put him in irons. The government had long been seeking that "fool" for they had put some of his companions in irons in other places. Now this little mouse had also fallen into the trap.

Thomas Effendi told all this, but without revealing the fact that it was he who betrayed Salman.

He turned again toward the old man.

"Now we have a new problem," be said with a bitter smile, apparently trying to stab the wretched old man's heart still deeper.

"The gendarmes will soon come here to examine your house, and I came as a friend to warn you in time." He laid particular emphasis upon the word "friend". Upon hearing the words "gendarmes" and examine", the old man was terrified.

"There is still time to save yourself," the Effendi continued more coldly. "Just tell me this, has anything of his been left in your house?"

Terrible as was the news imparted to him, still the old man was a little relieved when he considered that such a "friend" as the Effendi had offered him a helping hand at such a dangerous moment.

"His saddle bags are here," be replied, fearfully looking around lest some one should bear him.

"Come now let me drag this donkey out of the mire," said the Effendi to himself, and then aloud, "Saddle bags! That is no small thing!"

He turned to the old man and fixed his wicked green eyes upon him. "Every moment is precious for us. Make haste, let us go hide those saddle bags before the gendarmes arrive!"

The old man, trusting the sincerity of the Effendi implicitly, took him to the oda and showed him the traveling "khoorjis" which Mr. Salman had left there.

"Lock the doors," commanded the Effendi, and opening the saddle bags himself, he began to examine their contents.

There were letters of introduction and various addresses. There were drafts on certain persons, by means of which Salman was able to obtain money when necessary. There were various instructions, documents, etc., also some leaflets which the young propagandist used to distribute to the villagers; in a word, there was nothing there but papers. The Effendi examined them with great care, and shook his head ominously.

"If they should fall into the hands of the Government," be said, "one of those papers would be enough to hang you and your sons, Landlord Khacho, and the Imperial treasury would swallow your property."

The old man stood petrified, and way, unable to reply. The last words had plunged him into a kind of a stupor.

"All this must be burned up," said the Effendi and be stuffed the papers back into the bag.

"I can't understand it at all; I haven't any wits left," replied the old man in a trembling voice, and his sunken eyes filled with tears.

Suddenly the Effendi changed his mind. "Why burn them," he reflected, "I must examine them well. I may need them. Why destroy them?"

He asked the old man, "Is there any secret place in this house, where this bag might be hidden temporarily?"

"There is." replied the old man.

There were several secret storerooms in his house, in which articles of value were hidden in time of danger. Because danger was never lacking in the land, several of them were full, and only one remained empty, which he could show the Effendi.

They took up the suspect "khoorjis" and went to a store-room in which were kept olives, oil, wine and similar store.-. The floor of the store-room was paved. The old man raised a couple of the paving stones underneath which a small iron door was concealed, placed horizontally over the entrance to a secret storeroom. The old man took a key from his pocket, put it in the lock, gave a certain number of turns and the iron door swung open. Now the mouth of an underground cavern was shown. They descended a narrow flight of steps.

It was impossible to see anything in the dark space within this cavern. The damp air was stifling. Leaving the "khoorjis" there they came out quickly. The old man locked the iron door once more, placed the stones in position and it would be difficult to suspect the existence of a subterranean store-room underneath them.

"Give me the key," said the Effendi. "I will keep it. There is no one you can trust more.

Without reflecting long, the old man gave him the key. Fear so overcame him that he was ready to accept every proposition made by the Effendi.

"I have much to say to you, Landlord Khacho, but the time is short, the examiner may appear very soon," he said hastily. "For the present I give you a few words of advice. No one is to know that I have seen you. All we have done must remain secret, even from your sons and all your family. When the examiners come, try as much as possible to 'appear undisturbed and honest. Let them search wherever they please, and walk all about. We have hidden the dangerous things so that the devil himself could not find it. Do not deny that Tiutiukjian has been in your house, only say that you do not know him and neither you nor your sons know why he is wandering around in this region."

With these instructions the Effendi came out of the store-room. "Now, show me another way for me to leave," he said looking about him. "I must try not to let them see me when I leave the house."

The old man conducted him to a gate in the rear by which the cattle went out and in.

"Now good-bye. I will return again after the examiners have finished their work. I will satisfy them by some means. Be easy."

The Effendi went away. On the way he said to himself, over and over, "Now your life is in my hands, landlord Khacho, and I'll do as I please."

It was an hour past noon. Vartan, Hairabed and Abo had not returned. The other sons were at work in the fields. The women were busy with their housework. preparing food to send to the workers in the fields. Villagers, for the most part, eat their noon meal away from home, and do not come home till supper time. No one knew what had happened.

Old Khacho was impatiently awaiting the examiners, as a prisoner awaits his death sentence; for he knew there was no escape, no chance of becoming free. He did not reveal the facts to the people of the house, not wishing to alarm them beforehand. Finally, a sergeant appeared with a number of gendarmes, guards and soldiers.

The rest of the family, having no information as to what had occurred, were not frightened by the coming of the soldiers. They were accustomed to receiving such guests often, and they sometimes came and remained for days, eating and drinking and then they departed. The lodging of Turkish soldiers in the house of Armenian villagers, especially in the landlord's oda, is a common occurrence.

"I am ordered to examine this house," said the sergeant addressing old Khacho.

"My house is before you, look where you please," answered the old man, trying to preserve some measure of tranquility.

144

The sergeant ordered the doors locked, stationed sentinels, and began to make his examination. He first entered the "oda", then the other rooms, looked in every corner, examined every article and found nothing suspicious. The women, seeing this, understood that something unusual had happened and began to weep and wail. The old man rebuked them, and they ceased and were quieted, thinking they had nothing to fear. After completing his search, the sergeant began to question him. "Did a man named Michael Tiutiukjian live here?"

"He spent only a few nights here," replied the old man.

"Were you previously acquainted with him?"

"It was the first time I had ever seen him."

"Then why did you admit him to your house?"

"I am the landlord of this town. You know the custom of this country. The landlord's house is a sort of a caravansary, a hotel, where many strangers find lodging. How can I know who comes and who goes?"

"Did he leave nothing here?"

"He left nothing."

"Did you not understand his purpose in touring this region?"

"He did not inform us. I know only that he was a teacher."

"Did you not know with whom he talked and with whom he consulted?"

"A teacher talks with everyone to secure pupils."

"Do you know, now, where he is?"

"I don't know."

"He is in irons!"

"All the better, if he is a bad man."

Just then someone knocked at the gate.

"No one may enter," commanded the sergeant.

145

The servant informed him that it was Thomas Effendi.

"He may enter."

The Effendi entered, and seeing the sergeant with his retinue, he pretended to be astonished, as though he knew nothing whatever of why they had entered the old man's house.

"Good may it be. What is the matter?" he asked solicitously.

The sergeant informed him of the nature of his errand. A hypocritical smile crossed the coarse face of the Effendi, and 'grasping the sergeant's hand, he said, "I pledge you my hand that nothing suspicious is to be found at Landlord Khacho's. You don't know what a fine man he is."

He led the sergeant to the oda but the gendarmes, guards and soldiers remained outside guarding the entrance to the house.

"Landlord," he said turning to the old man, "these men are hungry. Order someone to prepare some food. There must be plenty of arak you understand." He spoke the last word in Armenian. The landlord went out rejoicing. He thought he was out of danger.

But no, the danger was not past. The Turks would not let go of the old man's collar so easily. They would torment him; they would wear him out with months of imprisonment. Although no suspicious article was found in the old man's house for which they could blame him, and although there was no certain proof to consider him guilty, it was sufficient that old Khacho was an Armenian, and besides being an Armenian, he was rich. Such a fat prey is very attractive to the Turkish official.

Thomas Effendi had "cooked the broth" himself. It was he who had betrayed Salman to the newly arrived governor. It was he who suggested searching the old man's house, and for that reason it pleased him to rescue the poor old man from the net he himself had spread. But no - in order to accomplish his wicked designs, the Effendi tried to complicate the affair still more.

When the old man left the room to prepare the meal, the sergeant asked Thomas Effendi, "Effendi, what do you think? I think the man is innocent."

"You are aware, Bey," replied the crafty one, "that Thomas Effendi isn't a man who gives his judgment so easily. The affair is still in the dark. I was sure that some suspicious article was to be found in this house, or some preparations by means of which we could learn in how great a degree these

146

men are accomplices of the prisoner's plans, but I am surprised that no certain proof has yet appeared. I am most suspicious of two of the old man's sons and of a stranger guest of his."

"What stranger?" asked the sergeant.

"A young Russian who is an exceedingly dangerous character and a very bitter enemy of the Government. He wanders about in this region in the guise of a merchant, but he is really a Russian spy."

"It will be difficult to imprison him. if he is a Russian subject," replied the sergeant.

"In time of war, it is always permissible to imprison spies. You are aware that war is to be proclaimed shortly."

"I know that."

"I have already spoken with his Excellency, Pasha Effendi, the military commander; is it possible he has given you no instructions?"

"The Pasha Effendi only commanded me to put into execution all your plans."

"Very good," said the Effendi, with a pleased smile. "I will make the necessary plans. But there is one thing I will tell you later."

"I am very impatient to know," said the Turkish official, "I can't wait for 'later things'."

"Then I will whisper it to you."

The sergeant leaned toward the Effendi, although there was no one in the room but themselves to hear their conversation.

The Effendi said, "The old man is quite rich. You must milk him!"

Thomas Effendi, being familiar with the looseness of Turkish officials, knew well that the facts of a business (and all its details) do not interest these bribe-taking officials so much as the thought of what shape and course to give the business to be able to get more money out of the suspects. Thomas Effendi tried to gain something from the laxities of the Turks, and to give a turn to the machine he had invented to his advantage. For this reason he was very glad when he observed that the sergeant,

147

struck with his last words, asked, "Then, how do you wish to plan the affair ?"

"You have a good many men with you, sergeant. You will give orders to guard the old man and his two sons, one of whom is called Hairabed, and the other Abo. Besides this, you will order the imprisonment of the Russian spy who is called Vartan."

The sergeant made a note of the names, Abo, Hairabed and Vartan.

"The duty you performed today," continued the Effendi, "was simply examination, but the examination is not yet finished. Therefore, it is necessary for you to take the persons mentioned, under surveillance, until the examination which will be given in the presence of His Excellency, the Pasha Effendi."

"I understand."

"Still I must act as mediator, to pretend that I am the protector of the suspects, in order to ferret out their secrets. Do you understand?"

"I understand," repeated the sergeant.

Chapter 27

While Thomas Effendi and the sergeant were in the oda concocting their nefarious schemes, a very different conversation was taking place among the soldiers.

"Mahmood," asked one of the soldiers of one of his companions, "if we stay here tonight, which of these Armenian brides do you choose?"

"That plump, rosy little one is the one for me," replies Mahmood with gusto.

"But that lovely one with black eyes takes my fancy," said the first one with no less relish.

It appeared that when the soldiers entered the harem in their search, they had not paid so much, attention, to the articles they were supposed to discover, as to old Khacho's daughters-in-law.

The notice of some of them was attracted to the rich goods in the old man's house.

"My wife talks my head off," said an elderly guard, "she doesn't give me a day's peace, telling me constantly that I must get her a large brass kettle to heat milk in. I saw one here. It is just what she wants. When we leave, I shall certainly take it along with me."

A young soldier spoke up. "I saw a fine rug. It would be fine to lie on after a good full meal, smoking a 'narghileh' prepared by a pretty woman."

The old soldier who looked upon the spoil with an eye both to utility and to religion observed to the young soldier. "Such rugs are more suitable to use as 'sejjedehs' (prayer-rugs)."

A soldier full of envy and superstition said, "It is a strange thing, being a 'giaour' and having such lovely wives; to be a 'giaour' and have such a luxurious house. There isn't a piece of matting in my house for the children to sleep on at night. The 'giaour' ought to have this worn out girdle wound around his waist so that when he coughs it will be cut through in ten places."

The last remark is a Mohammedan proverb. In the east the thickness and handsomeness of a girdle is a token of wealth and honor. The Armenian, being a 'giaour' according to the Mohammedan, should be so poor that he should have such a worn and ragged girdle, that it would fall to pieces when he coughs.

Likewise, the Armenian has no right to have pretty wives, since he is a 'giaour' because whatever is good or pretty should belong to the Mohammedans.

Some of the soldiers had entered the old man's beautiful garden, and like a bear or a hog in a vegetable garden, they had trampled and destroyed the beautiful flowers which had been so carefully cared for by the "brides" (daughters-in-law) of the landlord. They had seized the branches of the trees, and broken them off trying to reach the fruit. They had eaten the ripe fruit and dropped the unripe ones into the dust and trodden on them. Old Khacho saw this from a distance and it grieved him very much. He loved his trees as he did his sons. He shook his wise head as the old Persian proverb came into his mind, "When the captain takes an apple from a vineyard without pay, his soldiers root up the whole vineyard." The Turk is capable of such barbarity. He has no pity on living plants, has no pity on living men. The Turk eats the fruit of the tree and destroys the tree. The Turk takes a man's earnings from him, and kills the man. As the Turks have ruthlessly consumed the forests of their country, they have similarly annihilated the foreign races of the Empire.

The old man saw the same barbarity in his house, but he kept his peace. He entered the kitchen where the women were preparing the meal. Poor man, he was already imprisoned in his own house and in his prison he showed his keepers the sacred duty of hospitality.

"What are these men? What do they seek, and why have they turned our house topsy-turvy?" asked Sara, tearfully.

"God knows," replied the old man sadly, and commanded them to serve the meal soon.

The women were in a terrible fright. They had withdrawn into the house to escape the stares of the soldiers. They knew something strange must have

150

happened, for the Turks to behave impudently in their house. They had seen many such guests before now, but the honor of the house had always been respected.

Hairabed and Abo, who had gone in the morning with Vartan to hunt for Salman, had not returned yet. The other sons of the old man, hearing in the field of the irregularities of the Turks, hastened home. They were very angry, not at the Turks, but at their innocent father.

Slaves always attack the weakest. They considered the barbarities of tyrants natural, but they blame slaves like themselves for "angering the master". For this reason there was no limit to the insults and reproaches which they heaped upon their father. They blamed their father for allowing such dangerous men as Vartan and Salman to be in his house, and they were ready to go and tell the sergeant all they knew thinking this would lighten their offense.

"You have demolished your house with your own hands," said his sons.

"Let it be demolished," said the father with anguish, "when such unworthy sons as you live in it. You are worthy of curses and annihilation since your feelings of self-respect, honor and freedom are dead. The men against whom you are angry, they are my true sons and I don't care very much if for their sake I lose all that I have."

The last words of the old man were spoken concerning Salman and Vartan. The sons were still more incensed. The prudent father, fearing that they might commit some folly, or let fall some careless word from their lips, quieted them saying they had no occasion to fear, that it is always possible to stop the mouths of Turkish officials with a few pieces of gold, and he added that Thomas Effendi had promised to use all his efforts to prevent any harm from coming to them. The sons were somewhat relieved. It always exercises a great influence upon such persons to use the names of great personages. Thomas Effendi had promised, therefore he would be able to perform anything.

Just then Thomas Effendi appeared at the door of the oda and he called from a distance, "Landlord Khacho, be quick, you must feed these gluttons."

"It is ready, Effendi," replied the old man, "they will serve it immediately."

The old man's sons began to prepare a separate table in the oda, and another under the shade of the trees outside for the soldiers. The latter were becoming more and more unbearable. On such occasions, in the house of an Armenian, the Turkish soldier becomes exceedingly exacting.

151

His taste is critical, his appetite is keen, and he demands such food and drink whose names alone he knows, but which he has never once seen. The landlord's reply, "we have none," is received with curses. Although such behavior did not occur on this occasion, still the old man's sons were tormented trying to pacify the demands of their shameless guests.

The sergeant and Thomas Effendi ate together in the oda. The old landlord did not wish to sit with them but remained standing like a servant, wishing in this way to show special respect to his guests. The old man's sons served at the soldiers' table. For the present, the wine and the abundant stores of the landlord's kitchen kept them occupied. Taking advantage of that circumstance, the old man approached Sara and said to her privately, "My child, take these keys and hide all the things that are of value. You know already where to hide them."

"I know," replied the poor woman, and her eyes filled with tears. That precaution was a sign that a great danger threatened them.

"Listen, and be brave. Hold your heart firm," continued the old man. "Our house has often passed through such trials. With God's help, it will all pass. We must only be patient. After biding the goods, send the young women with their children to their father's homes, while you must take Lila with you to our townsman Zako's house and remain there till we see how this trial ends."

Some of the old man's daughters-in-law were from the village of O..., but others from near-by villages. For this reason it would not be difficult for them to seek protection temporarily in the homes of their parents. Only Sara had come from a distant place. Her parents were in Bayazid. For this reason the old man proposed townsman Zako's house for her; a neighbor in whom he had great confidence.

"There is another thing; listen Sara," he continued. "Hairabed, Abo and Vartan went this morning to hunt for Mr. Tiutiukjian. It appears that they don't know what has happened to us and when they return they also will fall into danger. Send a man quickly to find them and tell them to hide somewhere and wait for my instructions."

The last words pierced the poor woman's heart still more deeply. Then her dear husband was threatened with danger, also, she reflected. What fault had he, what had he done? But Sara was so wise, there were few of her husband's undertakings of which she was ignorant, from which she feared some disastrous result.

"Whom shall I send?" asked the woman sorrowfully, and her anxious eyes again filled with tears.

Sara's question was not uncalled for. In time of danger, when brother denies brother, and even treats him as an enemy, on whom could she rely? Sara had heard with her own ears, a short time ago how angrily Hairabed's brothers had spoken of him, and how much they were stirred up against him.

The old man understood the reason of Sara's anxiety, and sadly answered her.

"I know that no one of us will go. I know that in time of danger all forsake one another. But Vartan's two servants Sako and Gegho are in the house. They are brave and faithful. Make haste and quickly explain the business to them, then they will go and find Hairabed, Abo and Vartan, and tell them all that is needed. It will suffice if they say that Mr. Tiutiukjian is imprisoned, and our house is being searched', and they will understand the rest."

Having finished giving his orders the old man came out of the harem, confident that prudent Sara would perform all according to his desires.

In the court-yard, the old man observed that the government representatives of law and order, the soldiers, having enjoyed the abundant viands of the villager's table, drinking his wine and whiskey, now presented a scene of disorder - a very Babel of riot. He closed his eyes and passed on. He did not wish to see their unrestrained lewdness, and he was unable to punish them.

At this time the conversation in the oda was not a little interesting. The sergeant drank much and ate much. The conversation on official affairs with the Effendi became more and more personal.

"How many wives have you?" asked the sergeant.

A rare smile crossed the Effendi's ugly face as he replied, "They asked the ass how many wives he had and he showed the whole herd."

When the Effendi began to illustrate his meaning with anecdotes of donkeys, that was a sign that he was enjoying the happiest moment of his existence.

"But I think Christians are forbidden to have more than one wife," observed the sergeant.

"And so are Mohammedans forbidden to drink wine and raki, but you have drunk more than I," replied the Effendi, pleased with his fitting reply.

153

At this moment old Khacho entered, bringing in his hands two boxes of "rahatlokoums" and Smyrna figs which he placed on the table saying, "After dinner it is good to sweeten the mouth with something." He hastened out of the room once more.

"The old man appears like quite a good fellow," said the sergeant after he had gone. "I am astonished that he has allowed such men in his house as the Russian spy and the revolutionist from Istanbul."

"The donkey's ears are long, but his wits are short," replied the Effendi in his usual style.

"If there are fools in the world, there are those who are called 'good'. The old man is of that sort."

The Turkish sergeant was a man of nobler feelings than the Armenian Effendi. He said complacently, "I think our new military governor will milk him well."

"No doubt. I would call a man a fool who did not try to gain something from such a fine cow."

"You know him. What sort of a man is he? I have seen him only once."

"I know him very well," replied the Effendi, with the manner of a man of affairs. "I have known him ever since he was a Kaimakam in the province of Dikranagerd. For more than ten years he robbed, and pillaged, then he went to Constantinople and returned there as a Pasha."

"What sort of a man is he?"

"He tears a dead ass to pieces, to pull off its shoes."

While the Effendi and the sergeant were engaged in conversation; while the soldiers were singing, pushing each other around and dancing in drunken abandon, the women of the house, taking their infants in their arms, fled by the back gate toward their fathers' houses. Tears streamed from the eyes of the poor wretches to whom it seemed as though they were being taken into captivity, and that they should never again see that home where they had been so fortunate, so loved.

At that time, Gegho and Sako, both armed, went out by the same gate, and mounting their horses, departed.

Thomas Effendi, with all his cunning, had not thought to imprison these

154

two thieves, who were Vartan's hands and feet, who might ruin his evil plans.

Chapter 28

Thomas Effendi considered that he had only half attained his purpose. His principal object still remained unaccomplished. He had known before that Stephanie was a girl. Father Marook, the priest who baptized her had informed him one day when he had been invited to dine with the Effendi, and becoming dulled by drink, revealed the secret which he had sworn never to reveal.

From that day, Thomas Effendi had loved Lila. But what was love in this morally dissolute man? Was it a natural desire? He ate, drank and was satisfied, and behold his need passed. He was content when his passions are satisfied. Love was only animal lust in him. Passing his life with Turks, he had acquired all their characteristics. A pretty girl, a lovely woman is enticing objects to the Mohammedan, as playthings are for children. The child is attracted and pleased with his toy as long as he is not wearied of it: when he grows weary, he breaks the one in his hands and wants another. Woman was an article for the Effendi; an object which he appropriated only for his temporary enjoyment and for his temporary satisfaction when he saw a prettier one, he was already to leave the first and try to obtain possession of the second. His last choice had fallen upon Lila. But why did he attempt to reach his purpose by such dishonorable and wicked ways?

Could he not propose to her father, directly, for her hand ?

Thomas Effendi had acted according to his nature. In all the needs and duties of his life, he had his peculiar way of attaining his ends. Thomas Effendi was an oppressor. The oppressor does not attain his ends by direct means. The oppressor is that kind of a hunter who spreads snares, places nets, sets traps, to catch his prey. He had tried to trap an innocent girl's love by wicked cunning. He had tried to put Lila's father into such an inextricable predicament, that he would be forced to give his daughter to the Effendi in spite of himself, contrary to his wishes.

Thomas Effendi had looked upon Lila as one of her father's possessions: as one of the fruits of his cultivation. As a tax-collector, he knew what means must be employed to wrest the fruits of his labor from the villager. He knew that until you torment and abuse a villager and wrest from him all his power of resistance, he is not willing to let out of his hands the fruits of his labor, or his property. With this idea, Thomas Effendi tied and bound old Khacho with such complicated knots, that only he could loosen them.

Betraying him and his sons as civil offenders, as accomplices of disturbers of the peace, as men who entertained spies in time of war, Thomas Effendi also had a secondary purpose. To show by this means his faithfulness and his great services to the Turkish government. On the other hand, to say to old Khacho, "See, if you don't give me Lila, you and your sons will be hanged. Your house will be burned and your riches confiscated. Only I am able to save you and my reward must be beautiful Lila."

The scoundrel could do all that. He had evidence in his hands, which was very clear proof of their treason. This was the traveling bag hidden in a store-room in old Khacho's house in which were concealed Salman's papers.

The key to the iron door was in the Effendi's pocket, but he did not wish to have his wickedness reach its extreme limit. Yet he was confident that it would be easy to obtain Lila's father's consent. But he saw a more powerful adversary before him. Vartan.

Commencing from that day when Vartan snatched from Stephanie's hand the pipe she offered the Effendi and angrily threw it out of the window, commencing from that day when Vartan had attacked the Effendi so fiercely on Stephanie's account, the Effendi believed that there was a secret understanding between Vartan and Stephanie, and that the two loved one another. Besides this, he knew that Vartan received much sympathy in the old man's family, and that they would be very glad to give their daughter to him for wife. But even if they should not consent, it was enough that he loved the girl; and Vartan being a contrabandist, would do with her as he did with illicit goods, that is, he would run away with her some night.

And Vartan had the courage and boldness to do so. The Effendi had considered all this. Therefore, what must be done to frustrate the young man's intentions? He must remove him in some way from this country, and send him away under the surveillance of Government soldiers that he might not be able to take Lila with him. This was the reason why Thomas Effendi betrayed Vartan as a Russian spy.

But why did he order only two of Khacho's sons imprisoned — Hairabed and Abo? Was he aware that they sympathized with Salman? He could not have had a suspicion that an Armenian villager was capable of thinking of obtaining his freedom. He knew only this that the old man's other sons were "as meek asses" but if any of them would dare to oppose his desire to marry Lila, they would be these two, Hairabed and Abo, for the Effendi had long observed the fierce opposition of these two brothers to him. For that reason he ordered them imprisoned, to stop their noise.

So Lila's fate was in this uncertain condition. Each of the three was planning to obtain her by his own peculiar wiles. Fattah Bey, the Kurd, being a bold and fearless robber, intended to snatch up his prey in a high-handed fashion just as a bold eagle darts down from the clouds and seizes the fawn grazing among the rocks. While Thomas Effendi the Armenian tax-collector and extortioner, meditated, twisting his folds around his prey, like the boa constrictor, and squeezing and strangling it, in order to be able to swallow it. But Vartan, that self-confident and bold contrabandist, as we said before, thought of running away with her if they should not be willing to give her to him. But which did Lila love? We know that.

But the Kurdish Bey was occupied with his military preparations and did not think often of Lila. Vartan was occupied with Salman. Only Thomas Effendi had so managed his affairs that he promised himself success.

After dining, the sergeant had drunk so much that he went to sleep immediately. His soldiers still stood on guard. The old man's sons, Hairabed and Abo, had not yet returned home. Thomas Effendi considered this a very suitable time to talk about Lila with her father. He left the sleeping sergeant in the oda and went out. "I have begun. I must finish," he reflected. "Sitting on a donkey is a shame, but falling from one is a double shame."

He found the old man sad and weary, sitting alone in the garden against a wall warming his chilly limbs in the afternoon sun. The soldiers had jostled him insolently, insulted him and made obscene jests. They had seized the skirts of the Kurdish servants who tried to pass them and obliged them to talk and jest with them. They had beaten the servants to make them obey their orders. The old patriarch had seen this indecent behavior in the house where the sanctity of the family had always been maintained, where even the impudent glances of a strange young man would not pass unpunished. But now he saw a gang of scoundrels before his eyes, who gave orders as if in their own house. "What condition is this?" reflected the old man. "Why do we live? Why does the earth not open and swallow us? Why do the heavens not fail and bury us? What life is this, to see dishonor before one's eyes and to remain silent? For whom has God prepared the fires of Hell? For whom are the lightnings of the Heaven? Why do they not punish the scoundrels?"

Thus he groaned and raised his tearful eyes toward heaven. But no reply was heard from heaven. He saw some of the soldiers bring various articles out of the house. But Sara, after seeing the other young women off, still remained in the house, and was trying to snatch the great copper kettle away from the hands of a soldier. But he struck the poor woman on the breast with his fist and the woman fell to the ground. "My household furniture is divided before my eyes, without asking the will of the owner. And why, in what am I to blame? Because I have received a guest into my house who preaches that the labor of the villagers, the belongings of the peasant should be protected. They punish me because I gave shelter to a man who talked against violence, merciless oppression and brutal cruelty. Who preached to us that we must try to manage our own affairs; and try to shake off the yoke of the foreigner.

"What introduced this thought among us, if not violence? If they had left us in peace, if they had not insulted our families, if they had not wrested from us our earnings, if they had treated us as men, and not abused us as beasts, then we would have been content. 'The father of the love of freedom is oppression,' the young man said, 'and its mother is injustice.' Now I understand the meaning of these words. The tyrant prepares enemies for himself. If the Turk did not treat us like this, we would love him, even though he is not of our flesh and blood."

Thus the old man meditated, and his heart was overwhelmed, like a storm-tossed sea. But what could the helpless lion do against so many wolves? He realized the desperateness of his condition and had no courage to make plans or seek means of escape. He repeated the well-known proverb, "One hand alone can't clap." "If all the villagers thought thus, then we would have some chance."

Thomas Effendi found the old man in this turmoil of soul, and called to him from a distance, "The affair has gone badly, very badly, Landlord Khacho. The ass is too deep in the mire to be pulled out."

The old man did not bear his remarks, but seeing him, rose to his feet.

"Be seated," said the Effendi, placing his hands on his shoulder in a friendly fashion. They sat near ach other on a piece of carpeting which served as a cushion.

"When are these men going to leave," asked the old man, pointing to the soldiers, who had not yet ceased from their unseemly behavior.

"They took the fool to a wedding, 'this is better than our house, he said.' Where should they go, and why should they go? Is food or drink lacking?" said the Effendi laughing insolently.

159

This raillery wounded the old man's already sorely wounded heart. The Effendi observing this, turned the conversation.

"Don't worry, Landlord Khacho, as long as the Effendi lives he will not let a hair of your head fall."

"Why won't it fall?" asked the old man somewhat angrily. "Don't you see them destroying my house, before my eyes? They are dividing my furniture before my eyes, and I have no right to prevent it." Again he pointed to the soldiers.

"That is their custom. When the butcher enters the slaughter-house the dog snatches up a bone.' You know very well yourself, landlord Khacho, that when the Turk enters the house of the Armenian, he does not draw back his hand empty. But the thing isn't theirs. Thank the Lord that it is only your goods, not your lives which suffer."

The old man shuddered. He had grown so sensitive that every word affected him greatly. "What is there, what?" he exclaimed, quite out of patience. "If there is anything else, tell me. Why do you torment me? If I must die, let me die quickly."

"I will tell you, I will tell all, Landlord Khacho; be patient," replied the Effendi, easier now, and speaking with more animation, he explained his meaning with a fresh proverb from his store of such tales, saying, "The ass would not kick against the goad unless he wished to have his leg pricked." From this he drew the conclusion that Armenians should not oppose the Turks, and especially not in time of war. And citing the burning of Van as an example, he began to prove that it is great folly to disobey the Turks. He explained why the Turks of Van had burned several thousand Armenian shops and plundered them of their goods. "Because," he said, "the Armenians there were spying for the Russians. After all," he added, "in this war, the Armenian need not expect gain from the Russians." And again returning to the subject of faithfulness he said the Turks are not as bad as we think; the fate of the Armenian is linked with that of the Turk, and for this reason every plan of revolt must be considered "folly". And for this reason the Effendi considered Salman's behavior "craziness", and he would not be at all sorry to see him severely punished. He was only sorry that on his account some other men would be exposed to danger of punishment also.

"What men?" interrupted the old man, turning pale.

"You and your two sons, Hairabed and Abo, and your other guest, Vartan," replied the Effendi.

The shock was severe enough to paralyze the old man, but a life full of trials, continual danger and suffering had so pierced and wounded his heart that he was able to endure the Effendi's frightening words and, preserving his composure, he asked, "What faults have we?"

"Bless you. You ask such simple questions that even a child would not ask them. Do you think you don't know yourself what faults you have?" replied the Effendi, with bitter insolence. "What fault is it of a well man if he is treated as a sick person, only because he has come from a community smitten with plague or cholera and wishes to go to some other community to escape the sickness. But he is seized on the frontier, forced into a hole and given so much smoke and fumes that he dies."

"Then it is necessary to thrust us into a hole, is it?" asked the old man, his wrinkled face working frightfully with anger.

"Yes," replied the Effendi, coldly. But he had come to make a proposal for Lila, to request her hand and declare his love. Why did he forget that, and why did he torment the pitiable father in this way? As we said previously, Thomas Effendi wag trying to place the old landlord in such an inextricable position, and bring him to such a pass that he would be obliged to consider that their salvation depended upon the Effendi, and Lila must be sacrificed to attain that salvation. For the Effendi knew that the old man would not readily consent to give him his daughter for 'wife, especially after those words which he had heard from Vartan, that the Effendi had left wives in various places and he had been unable to deny the truth.

But the Effendi, observing that he bad passed the limit by discouraging the old man to this degree, began to comfort him, saying, "They will keep you in prison for a few days it is true, but that is only because of regulations. Thomas Effendi has planned the affair so that no harm will come to you."

The old man made no reply. He saw a great difference between the Effendi's talk of the morning and that of the present. A dark suspicion entered his heart.

Chapter 29

After Vartan, Hairabed and Abo left home in the morning, they bad no information whatever of what had happened there in their absence. They did not know of Thomas Effendi's wicked plans, nor of the search by the commissars, nor of the lawless behavior of the soldiers.

They passed through several villages where Salman had been. They had inquired everywhere about him, and finally they entered the village and found the house where he had spent the previous night. The landlord appeared to be a good man. He said that be did not know what became of the poor youth, only that he had sat and talked about all sorts of things with the village good-for-nothings till midnight. When the young people went he was left alone. They gave him food and a bed, and he slept in the oda. In the early morning the young man was missing. He did not know where he had gone. Vartan and his companions entered the room where the young man had spent the night. There they found a scrap of paper on the floor, on which had been penciled hastily only a line, "I have been taken to prison," and the initials, L. S.

Vartan read it, and giving the paper to Hairabed said, "I expected that."

The three stood petrified. This event made a frightful impression upon them. They immediately pictured themselves two great losses - one, that a young man full of good desires bad become a victim of his inexperience, and the other that his imprisonment might bring to light and destroy that agreement which they had pledged themselves to labor for in spite of sacrifice.

The landlord gazed in astonishment upon these three men, wondering why that scrap of paper caused them such sadness. They said nothing and went away.

It was now evening. The herds and flocks, lowing and bleating, had turned homeward, raising a thick cloud of dust. The joyous villagers also, laughing and making jests with one another, were returning home from their pastoral labors. None of them was interested in the fact, nor gave any thought to the two evil deeds which had been committed in the village. The night before a young man was imprisoned and a maiden was dishonored, both by the band of the same man; one who bore an Armenian name, and who enjoyed the respect of the Armenian people.

"The villager," said Vartan, to his companions, "is a grown-up child. When a child falls and bumps his head against the wall, he cries as long as he feels the pain; when the pain ceases he forgets all about it, and as if nothing had happened, begins to laugh and play once more. It is difficult to deal with such large children," he continued. "They have received the same blows for centuries. They have bumped against the same wall, fallen in the same muddy spot, but they feel nothing; they forget tomorrow what occurred today. They go to work again, happy and careless, never thinking for whom they are working or what they have to cause them joy.

"Thomas Effendi," he continued, "knows these people very well when he calls them 'asses' and those who are thinking about them 'fools'. Go, tell that villager that that young man who so wisely discoursed to you concerning the individual rights of man, and of what labor is, and how it may be safe-guarded, tell him that young man has been imprisoned and possibly he will soon be hanged, and you will hear from all the same remark — 'he was crazy'.

"But I think this," said Vartan, resuming, "I am sure that Thomas Effendi has had a finger in the betrayal of Mr. Salman."

"I think so, too," replied Hairabed.

"We must prove it," said Vartan.

It was nearly dark. The old men and women were enjoying the cool of the evening outside their houses. Vartan and his companions made haste to depart from that village.

"Fine needles, colored thread, pretty beads, came to their ears the voice of the lame peddler.

He was coming along the other side of the street, swaying and limping, as Vartan had seen him a few days before, and with his enormous pack slung on his back, and holding a thick stick in his band, like the club of Hercules.

Seeing Vartan and his companions, he said, "Fine gentlemen, buy something. It is evening and I will sell them cheap."

163

"What have you?" asked Vartan, approaching him

"I have everything," replied the peddler, setting down his pack.

Vartan, as though examining the goods, surreptitiously slipped the scrap of paper Salman had written on and left at the villager's house, into the peddler's hands. The peddler gave it a glance and replied almost immediately, "Yes, I know it."

"What can be done?"

"We will meet and talk it over."

"Where?"

"Go away. I will find you."

The conversation attracted no attention. Hairabed and Abo who stood there, heard nothing.

The peddler saddled his pack again and turned toward the house of a villager, saying to himself, "I have sold enough today, now I must rest."

Vartan and his companions continued their journey. The lights were burning in the village homes (or cottages).

They passed the door of carpenter Bedros. Neighbor Oho was standing there. When an Armenian villager sees some one passing his door at evening, whether he be a stranger or friend, it is the custom to invite him in, saying, "Be my guest". They heard that invitation from many villagers and passed on saying, "Thank you". But they stopped before Master Bedros' hut, not because neighbor Oho invited them to be guests, but because they heard a strange sound from the carpenter's house, as though some one was calling for help. They entered immediately. The sound came from the stable which was quite dark. Abo hastily seized a light which was burning in the hut, and the three entered the stable.

This was the picture that appeared before their eyes. A young girl had slipped the end of a noose around her neck and hung from the ceiling of the barn. A woman held her feet and raised her up so that the noose would not strangle her.

"Let go, let go," the girl repeated faintly.

"Varvare," cried the woman sadly.

They quickly cut the rope and took down the half-strangled girl from the gallows she had herself prepared. If they had been a moment later, all would have been over for the woman's strength was nearly spent.

They brought Varvare to the cottage, in their arms. She was unconscious. They placed her in the bed they had prepared for her. Spasms crossed her livid countenance, and from her set lips came the words, "Let go".

The poor woman went to the girl, and embraced her saying, "Varvare, dear, why did you try to kill yourself? What sin had you committed? Let God Punish the scoundrel."

Vartan and his companions understood that a mystery was concealed by the behavior of the young girl. But it was difficult to solve it, for Susan told them nothing, and there was no one in the house save themselves and two small children.

Hairabed was acquainted with the man of the house, Susan's husband. Master Bedros had often come to old Khacho's house, and repaired his farming implements. But Hairabed saw his wife for the first time. And even if he had seen her often, and had been acquainted with her, still a village woman would not speak freely to a stranger. She only blessed and thanked them for helping her and begged them to send for her husband.

"Where is he?" asked Vartan.

"In that near-by village," replied the woman. "He has gone to work there."

They agreed to go and find some one to send after Master Bedros. Just then Varvare opened her eyes and asked for water.

Susan gave her water, of which she drank much. The girl's livid face was waxen now and her eyes were blood-shot. She put her head on the pillow again, and drew the coverlet over her face. Her low groans could be heard from beneath the coverlet. Sad and heartbreaking though the sound was, Vartan and his companions rejoiced for they thought they saved the girl's life.

Outside, they found a boy to whom they gave a few copper coins to go and call Master Bedros. Neighbor Oho was still standing at his door. He again invited Vartan and his companions to be his guests, saying, "Bless you gentlemen. Where are you going this dark night? Oh, if you only knew what 'keff' we had last night," he added, "we will do something tonight, also."

165

"What 'keff'?" asked Vartan.

Neighbor Oho began to narrate with great enthusiasm how Thomas Effendi had been guest at Master Bedros' house, and he was also called there. "Chalghijis' had played, girls had danced; they had eaten and drunk much and had a fine time, and he finished his story with these words, "God is my witness; this Thomas Effendi is a very fine man; he had so much raki brought, one could swim in it."

"And he got you all drunk, didn't he?" asked Vartan.

"Bless you, who wouldn't be drunk after drinking so much," answered Oho with a laugh. "The 'keff' is in getting drunk."

"Was the master at home?"

"I occupied the place of master of the house."

'But after you got drunk, the Effendi occupied your place didn't he?"

"I couldn't say. They brought me home on their backs."

Leaving Oho they went on their way. On the way Vartan said to Hairabed, "Now I understand why that poor girl tried to hang herself."

"And I understand now who must have betrayed Salman," said Hairabed. "There is no doubt," said Vartan, "that Thomas Effendi betrayed him. He is such a crafty man that it is impossible that he did not suspect Salman's intentions, and betray him with the notion of serving the Turkish Government. Having been in this village himself that night, it is very easy to understand that he must have ordered his arrest. If we have learned to know the Effendi's character, these are truths that there is no reason to doubt."

Silence reigned among the three companions. They bad been walking quite slowly. Each was engrossed with his own thoughts, and by what means the life of the young man could be saved.

"All you have said is right," said Hairabed, interrupting the silence. "Now what must be done?"

"I am quite well acquainted with the loose ways of Turkish officials, how careless they are, how inexact, how negligent in the performance of their duties," replied Vartan, "and for this reason, I think it will be easy for me to rescue Salman. I have two servants, whose bravery you admit. Our horses

166

are ready: this very night we will mount and go where they have taken him; we shall be able to find him, and if we find no other possible means of rescuing him, we will use force. I have long known what cowards Turkish officers are."

"We also are ready to go with you," replied Hairabed and Abo. "We will not let you go alone."

"Your going with me will not only be superfluous, but dangerous," replied Vartan. And remembering the words of the peddler, be thought they should wait for him a while, and said to his companions, "Let us sit here. We are walking so fast it is hard to talk or think."

He did not seem weary; sorrow and sadness seemed to have bent him with their weight. And a tempest seemed to rage in his heart which was increasing in fury. They left the highway and withdrew to one side where they sat in a leafy shelter near a melon patch.

None of the peasants bad remained to guard the melon-patch for the fruit was not ripe yet, and there was no fear of robbers. A peasant's leafy booth is a good retreat for the weary traveler. There he finds shelter from the beat of the day, and from the rainstorms which often occur in this region. The night was quite clear, although there was no moon. The lights of the village of o... could be seen in the distance and occasionally the low warning bark of dogs was heard. Vartan continued the interrupted conversation. He repeated that every means must be used to free Salman from his imprisonment which would certainly end in his death. But he considered it dangerous to have Hairabed and Abo share in this undertaking, principally because such an undertaking must either succeed or fail. In either case Hairabed and Abo would not escape the revenge of the Turks. For this business, he said, might end with fighting and bloodshed, and possibly murder, and if Hairabed and Abo shared it they being natives would not escape punishment, and besides themselves, their relatives and all of old Khacho's family would be punished. But there was no such fear for Vartan, himself. Being the subject of another government, and a stranger, he might accomplish his purpose and then leave and depart from this country and no one could find him, especially in this disturbed time of war.

Listening to the long explanations from Vartan, who was a man experienced in many bold enterprises, Hairabed and Abo replied, "We will disguise ourselves and no one will be able to recognize us."

"It is all the same, whatever you do. It will be found out. Men like Thomas Effendi are not lacking here, who will betray you. The Armenians here, if they can gain the favor of the Turks by any means, will not spare anyone even though they injure their fellow-countrymen thereby. The Armenian is his own enemy." He spoke these last words with deep feeling. The events of this day and the sad impression they had left had been a great strain on his nerves. On one side, the imprisonment of his esteemed young friend, on the other the indifferent hard-heartedness of the people; on one hand, the affair of poor Varvare, on the other, the wickedness of Thomas Effendi filled his heart with indignation although he had not yet learned of the false accusations that detestable man had made against the family of old Khacho, that same day.

In this distress and turmoil, he had almost forgotten Lila that lovely being, who held the first place in his heart. Suddenly, he fancied he saw her sadly entreating him, saying, "Where have you gone? Why have you left me? Have you gone to rescue your beloved friend? I am also your beloved - you promised to take me away from this country - this place is bad I am afraid of the Kurds."

In Vartan's heart a fierce battle of feelings arose. Two beings stood before him. One, the girl he loved; the other, his beloved companion. Both needed his help; the lives of both were in danger.

Vartan had no clear knowledge of the misfortune which threatened Lila from the Kurdish Bey. But he knew what snares Thomas Effendi had spread to trap her. He knew that to reach his evil purposes he was not accustomed to regard the means.

There was silence for a time. A similar reflection occupied Hairabed at the same time. He knew of the love of Lila and Vartan. He intended his sister for that young man. Now Vartan was going to rescue his friend. He would either be killed himself or would save him from the hands of the Turks. In either event he would lose Lila. Perhaps before his return, the Kurdish Bey would have carried Lila away. It seemed that Vartan did not know that and could not know it, for they had not yet informed him of the Kurdish Bey's intention. Why not tell all to Vartan? But how should he begin? Vartan had not informed anyone in old Khacho's family that he loved Lila and wished to marry her. Only Sara knew that secret, and she only by accident. The sudden succession of events one after the other had given Vartan no time to open his heart. Now a new and dangerous undertaking separated him from Lila. Now Hairabed's hopes that Vartan would save his sister were annihilated, the hope that he would take her to a far country, where the Kurdish tyrant's hand could not reach her.

On the other hand, the loss of Salman did not torment Hairabed any less. He loved that devoted youth. He sympathized with him more than Vartan. Now to leave him in the hands of the Turks to wear his life away in a dungeon or to be tortured and killed, that, also, would be cruel. And this cruelty seemed more severe and bitter to Hairabed principally for this reason, that he would furnish Vartan a reason for holding back from the undertaking, that he would weaken his resolve to rescue Salman, if he revealed to him the fate which awaited his sister from the Bey.

The complex and confusing turn which affairs had taken had plunged both Hairabed and Vartan into disturbed meditation. Both Lila and the imprisoned youth demanded speedy assistance. But which should they attempt first? This question gave them difficulty.

But what was Abo, the courageous son of this peasant family, thinking about? In fact, he was not thinking at all. He was one of those men who go in whatever direction they are led, so long as it is not toward evil toward which they are disinclined. Abo was a good tool to employ in saving things from a conflagration. His actions depended upon the skill of his master.

Vartan's confession simplified the matter a little. Vartan without concealing a single point revealed to the two brothers his love for Lila. He told them that he had promised to run away with Lila, and she had expressed her willingness. He said that he felt obliged to put into execution such a strange procedure, only because he had no hope that Lila's father would consent to give Lila to him for a wife: for he had observed and was persuaded that old Khacho had set his mind upon Thomas Effendi and intended to have him for a son-in-law.

"It is superfluous to speak of that man," he continued, "for you both know what he is, and you have learned more about him today. To give a daughter to Thomas Effendi is the same as delivering her to a wolf or dog. But one thing torments me," he continued, "I must go after Salman as I informed you. I cannot give up that undertaking. Love for such a companion and friend has placed a heavy obligation upon me. Besides this, I hold myself partly to blame for his having fallen into this difficulty. I encouraged and abetted him. I rekindled the flame which burned in his heart. By this means I hastened his fall, therefore it is necessary for me to rescue him."

"On the other hand," he continued, "there is a great obstacle before me. I don't know what I ought to do; can I leave Lila? Perhaps today or tomorrow Thomas Effendi will so manage the affair that Lila will become the wife of that monster. What will become of poor Lila?"

Hairabed replied that Lila told Sara everything, and his wife had related it to him, and he had long known of their having come to an understanding. And he and possibly all his brothers would be glad if Vartan would make haste to escape with Lila with all speed. "Not because of the Effendi," he added "but there is another and more imperative reason which calls for Lila's being taken out of our country quickly."

"What other reason is there?" asked Vartan, and his eyes blazed with anger.

Hairabed related in detail the intentions of the Kurdish Bey; he told of his wife Koorsit's opposition to her husband's will; told by what means Koorsit had made known the Bey's intention, and her advice to remove Lila from this country; in a word, Hairabed told him all that had happened in connection with Lila up to this day which Vartan had not learned before.

Vartan heard Hairabed's story with great indignation and his words pierced his heart like poisoned arrows.

"And you knew all that and kept it from me?" be said deeply agitated. "And you were waiting for the Kurd to come and snatch your sister from her father's house in broad daylight, and you were going to listen with your eyes open to how he had dishonored you!"

Now Vartan understood the meaning of Lila's sad and despairing words, which he had not been able to explain till today; be understood why Lila, in the dead of night when he first met her in her father's garden, when the hours spent together should have been sweetened with kisses, when they should have talked of love and boundless happiness, instead she had shed tears from her beautiful eyes, and in mortal terror bad said these words, "I won't go near the grave. I am afraid of graves, I am afraid of Kurds. Save me and take me to some other country." So she knew what a sad fate awaited her and with deep sympathy had related the story of her friend, Narkiss, how she had been carried off by the Kurds, and how unfortunate and sad she was now.

There are moments under the heaviest blows of misery, danger and a bitter sorrow, when a man grows bolder, obtains a more enduring and undismayed heart and is more resolute. He begins after that to despise the blows of misfortune when they attain a certain degree, when he has nothing worse to fear.

Vartan was now in this condition. He did not any longer combat with ideas, feelings and the turmoil of spiritual and mental torture. - Now he was at rest. Everything was decided all at once for him. Now he knew what he ought to do. The love of his friend overcame the love of woman. By losing his friend, the idea would perish, the idea of freedom for the oppressed and wretched villagers, in which was included not only Lila's safety and honor, but that of many thousands of women. Why care only for Lila? Why desert the general good to follow the good of one particular individual, he thought.

"After all," said Vartan, "I must repeat what I said a few moments ago. I

170

must go after Salman, and I must try by every means in my power to save his life. But certainly, I must not leave Lila uncared for. We must make plans for her. This is my plan, listen."

"No plan is necessary," they heard a voice say as the gigantic form of the lame peddler appeared from behind the booth.

Vartan rejoiced to see him; but it produced a very unpleasant impression upon Hairabed and Abo that this wandering fellow should have overheard their secret conversation. They knew nothing about that strange man yet. But when they saw that Vartan shook hands with him with great friendliness and seated himself close beside him, then the two brothers felt relieved, especially when Vartan said to them, "Do not fear, he is one of us."

But Melik-Mansoor was not the ragged, wandering peddler, clad in rags, whom they had seen a few hours earlier. Vartan himself was hardly able to recognize him in his present transformation. He wore the "Laz" national costume and was completely armed.

"I am not able to remain with you long," he said hurriedly. "You are aware that Mr. Salman has fallen into the net and he must be extracted."

"We were just speaking of that," said Vartan.

"You may rest assured about him. He will be set free today or tomorrow," he said rising. "You must continue our general business. Good night for the present."

"Do you go alone?"

"No. My companions wait for me there."

He pointed toward the mountain where in the darkness, they could dimly distinguish a group of horsemen.

"Who are they?" asked Vartan.

"A few mountaineers. Au revoir."

Vartan wished to ask a few more questions, but he had gone. Hairabed and Abo were astonished. They did not know who or what that disguised man was. Vartan imparted to them such information as he had heard about him. The two brothers were now convinced that that skillful man would be able to rescue Salman.

171

They rose and proceeded toward home. But Sako and Gegho, Vartan's two attendants who had been sent by old Khacho's advice to warn Vartan and his sons not to return home, these faithful followers, although they had searched for them all day, had been unable to find them to let them know what awaited them at old Khacho's house.

"Gegho," said his companion Sako to him, "it is a bad affair. We must try not to be captured so that if anything happens to our master, we may be able to go to his aid."

"I think so too," said Gegho.

The two fellows decided to watch over Vartan from afar and keep away form the old man's house.

Chapter 30

The night was nearly over when Vartan, Hairabed and Abo returned home. They did not yet know what had happened in their absence. Entirely unsuspecting, they entered, and immediately the door was clapped shut behind them. Two soldiers stood there on guard. The sergeant and his unruly men were in the oda. Several gendarmes wandered about in the courtyard sniffing about like hunting dogs, looking for something. The sons' wives had been taken to their parents' or neighbors' houses. On such occasions when a family comes under suspicion and is placed under military surveillance, the women are sent away from the house.

Seeing all this, still Vartan and his companions did not comprehend what this motley crowd could signify. For the quartering of a group of soldiers in the landlord's oda, as well as in any Armenian peasant's house, was a common thing in this country. And whenever a villager received guests of this kind, he was obliged to send his wife and daughter and his sons' wives to spend the night at a neighbor's to save them from the lust of his guests, if the guest was kind enough to allow it instead of pointing his sword at his host's neck and compelling him to keep his wife at home to entertain him and wait upon him.

One of Hairabed's brothers, meeting him, said angrily, "Do you see what a trick that Salman has played on us? Now answer! From the first day I would have seized that whelp by the scuff of his neck and pitched him out of the house, but you wickedly opposed me and would not let me. Now, come, answer!"

Hairabed said not a word. He understood that his brother's curses concerned Salman. He understood the sad occurrences.

"Boy, we have fallen into the snare too," said Vartan to him bitterly. "Only this was lacking."

173

Immediately several gendarmes approached and seized them and led them to the captain in the oda. Thomas Effendi was not there. After making his arrangements he had left and had settled himself in the house of the village priest, as his guest. There was no one in the oda save the sergeant and old Khacho; only a few soldiers were standing at the door. Vartan entered and took a seat beside the landlord, not waiting for the sergeant's permission. Hairabed and Abo remained standing.

Vartan's behavior seemed rude to the sergeant, and he asked him insultingly. "Where are you from, you Armenian?"

He spoke the word "Armenian" as a slur.

"From Russia," replied Vartan controlling his agitation.

"What business brought you here?"

"I trade in this region."

"Have you a passport?"

"I had, but it is lost."

"That is easy to prove. You have only to tell which custom house you passed on the frontier, and your name will be recorded there."

"I am a contrabandist. Men engaged in this profession do not go near the custom houses. I will say this also, that I never had a passport originally."

"That might be excusable if you were simply a contrabandist, but you are charged with another crime."

"What is it?"

"You are a spy."

"That is true. It seems Thomas Effendi has informed you. He is really a very truthful man," said Vartan sarcastically.

"It is true all the same, whoever informed me," replied the sergeant, preserving the dignity of an official personage. "We do not allow suspicious persons in our country, especially in war time. They will keep you here tonight, and in the morning you will be taken to the military commander. He will determine your case."

"Then what is the need of all this cross-questioning when my fate is to be decided by the military commander? You are able to imprison me and nothing more. But it is your custom. The lowest soldier here, even, when he is sent after a criminal performs all that the highest court should do."

Although the sergeant was offended, he made no reply.

He called four gendarmes and ordered them to take Vartan and guard him. He made no resistance but allowed them to handcuff him.

After they had taken Vartan, the sergeant turned to Hairabed and Abo. "It is not necessary to ask them anything," he stated. "Their crime is apparent. Go and guard them well."

Old Khacho was in a state of stupor. Half asleep and half awake, he seemed to see all this in a dream.

Why had the Effendi deceived him? Was all this mere form, as the Effendi had persuaded him to believe ?

They took Vartan, Hairabed and Abo and locked them in a building which served as a granary. The walls and floor were of stone, solidly joined together to prevent mice from entering and destroying the wheat. The windows were narrow and barred with a grating of iron to prevent the birds from entering. This building was very suitable to be used as a prison. An oil lamp was burning in one corner, and shed its light in the dusky arches of the granary.

Hairabed and Abo were silent. Deep dejection together with great terror was pictured on their countenances. They were familiar with the cruelty of Turkish officials who, making a pretext of an insignificant fault, and often inventing the charges themselves, and slandering the just, were always ready to fleece and destroy the innocent, especially if they were Armenians and somewhat well off. But now they had enough proof to consider them guilty. But how bad they learned this? Who could have betrayed them? They had no clear ideas as to that.

Vartan seemed to feel at his ease. His quiet resembled the quiet of a storm-tossed sea, after a tempest.

"I will explain all this to you by a parable," said he to his fellow-prisoners. "The trees of the forest carried word to their king that a tool had appeared which destroyed them mercilessly. 'What is the tool called?' asked the king. 'It's head is of iron, but it's handle of wood,' replied the trees. 'That is a very dangerous tool,' replied the king, 'since the handle is of us.'

175

"The handle is of us," repeated Vartan emphasizing the first word. "Our oppressor, our robber, our tormenter, our enslaver, our destroyer and the demolisher of our house, the tool with a handle of ourselves, of Armenians.

"The Thomas Effendis, beginning with the village tax-collector, up to the great lords of the Sublime Porte, are such handles in the lands of our enemies. These evil and dangerous handles have never been lacking in Armenian history. When you see the fatherland and the people betrayed into the hand of a foreigner, there you will find the finger of an Armenian. When you see the Armenian king betrayed and sent into exile, and the gates of the capital opened before the enemy, there you will find the finger of an Armenian. When you see the soil of the fatherland stained with the blood of the Armenian, his dwellings destroyed by fire and his children taken captive, there you will find the finger of the Armenian. When you see religious, political and holy church conspiracies, there you will find the finger of an Armenian. In a word, all wretchedness and persecution and every kind of brutality and barbarity which we have suffered from our enemies, the hatchet of an Armenian man has always had a share.

"The Armenian himself undermines the foundation of his national institutions and with his own hands he destroys his consecrated establishments. Why do we blame the foreigners?"

Hairabed and Abo heard Vartan's words with sad hearts. The latter asked, "Therefore all our hopes are ruined. Our building, still in its initial stages, incompleted, is ruined."

"I seem to have foreseen that it would end this way, and it was folly to expect any other termination," replied Vartan. "Salman himself was also in doubt and scarcely believed in the work he had begun. I remember his discouraged words, word for word. When that enthusiastic young man once said to me, 'When the idea of stirring up a people is not only a visionary phantom of a few individuals, and has not yet become general, has not yet been spread abroad among a portion of the populace at least, it is possible to annihilate it all with one blow — when the leaders are destroyed. But the populace is another thing. It is impossible to destroy the mind which dwells in the populace.'

"'We' he said, 'will now perform only the work of the sower, but not of the reaper. We shall leave the harvest to the future descendants.' And that is the reason why in the last days he attempted to establish more permanent, more suitable institutions, such as schools. Salman's activity had no revolutionary purpose. He had no revolutionary spirit, but later it took the form of preparation for the future. Once he turned to me with a peculiarly happy smile, such as I had never seen before on his stern face. 'Vartan,' he said, 'we who are undertaking the work of educating a people, are still ignorant ourselves. We still have much to learn from the people themselves. The people are great teachers. There is boundless philosophy in a single proverb of theirs. Listen,' he said, 'how the people express the condition of their relationship with the Turks. "Be friends with the dog but don't drop your stick".' And truly, the principal requisite of how to behave with Mohammedans is summarized in that proverb. They gnaw and bite, and in order not to be wounded by their teeth, one must always keep his stick in readiness. And that is the reason why Salman tried to arm the people, and place them in a position to defend themselves."

Hairabed and Abo listened with deep interest. They seemed to have forgotten their individual grief and the sad fate which awaited them in the morning. And now they were thinking of the general suffering. They had often heard such ideas expressed by Salman, but they had not clearly comprehended them until now.

The prison seemed to have aroused Vartan's eloquence. He talked without ceasing. He had entered prisons and had been released many times in his life, but the prison had always left a gloomy impression upon him. But now he felt a sort of satisfaction. He was like a condemned prisoner on the point of being put to death and looked with deep contempt upon an unjust world and derided the folly of men, saying to himself: "Behold all your power, what can you do more than this? You kill my body, but you cannot kill the ideas I have disseminated."

"Be friends with the dog, but hold on to your stick," continued Vartan. "From this condition of vital affairs are born monsters — monsters like me. It seems, my friends, that you do not know me as I really am. But because, perhaps, this will be the last night when I shall be able to talk with you, listen. I am one of those men who very early learned to return evil for evil. My hands have often been stained with blood, but never with innocent blood. I was once a monk, but I only learned so much from the Old Testament, 'an eye for eye'. When I read that Moses, the prophet of Jehovah, destroyed whole tribes in order to purify the Promised Land, and caused the children of Israel to dwell there in their stead, I reasoned that the same ought to be done to the Turkish, Kurdish and Cherkez tribes who tyrannize over us Armenians in our remaining inheritance.

"This is the same natural law which Salman explained using plants as an example. One kind of plant chokes and destroys another kind and occupies its place. If we do not wish to be annihilated in the struggle for existence, we must have strength and ability for resistance, and that characteristic is called self-preservation. Salman's principal aim was, to develop that quality in the people. I early acquired that characteristic. Perhaps the moralist calls me immoral, criminal, a brute; perhaps the priest considers me a sinner, but no matter. I must act as life demands. But when men

177

cease to be evil, when peace and Christian brotherhood reign upon earth, I am ready to be the best of men."

They talked on for a long time, until the oil in the lamp was exhausted. The flame flickered a few moments, smoked and became extinguished. The prison was enveloped in darkness.

Chapter 31

The same night that Vartan, Hairabed and Abo were philosophizing in the prison, and meditating on the unfortunate conditions of their unfortunate fatherland, Thomas Effendi was at the house of Marook, the village priest, and after dining, chatted and jested merrily with the priest.

He was the same priest who had caused Salman so much trouble, but now, hearing of his fall, grieved, not because a prominent laborer would vanish from the defenses, but because the loss of any Armenian was a sorrow to him. The father-confessor was not a bad man and if he had been opposed and had desired to ruin Salman's work, it was because he considered it harmful. He was a common villager in his youth. He had learned to read and write, more or less, at St. John's Monastery. He did not succeed in making a living in the village. He grew poorer and went to seek his fortune abroad. He met with no success abroad either. At one time he was a coffee-maker in the city of Van. His affairs went badly. Without having earned a para he returned to his native place.

Finding no other means of making a living here, he became a priest.

That evening, the village school-master, the famous chorister Simon, who was the priest's son-in-law, was also invited to the priest's house. This man had a high opinion of his learning (the villager also had the same) and he was prouder still of the fact that he was the priest's son-in-law.

The subject of conversation was the events which had transpired that day at old Khacho's house, which had terrified the villagers greatly and had disquieted the priest still more.

"The ass is convicted, the horse eats, Father Superior," said the Effendi continuing the interrupted conversation. "This is the universal order of the world and as it always will be. What God has planned, man cannot change. God has created one master, the other slave. One judges, the other eats.

The Armenian has learned to work. The Kurd and the Turk have learned to eat. If there were no one to eat, the laborer could not live. The Turks keep us with their sword. We must keep them by our labor. God has given the Turk a sword, but the Armenian a spade. The one cannot take the place of the other."

"That is true," replied the priest crossing himself. "Our Lord Jesus Christ also said thus in the Holy Gospel, that not a leaf falls from the tree without God's will. Without His will, not a hair falls from man's head. All is in His hands."

"That's so, it is true," affirmed Simon, also crossing himself.

They next began to talk about the more severe oppression of the villagers owing to the war. The priest regarding the robbery entirely from the standpoint of his personal gains, complained, saying that the Government taxes had been so much increased that the produce of the villagers was entirely exhausted, and if anything was left, the Kurds would carry it off. For this reason, he was paid very badly, for he often performed baptisms, weddings and funerals without receiving a para. The villagers promise to pay later; but they will either be unable to, or they will deceive him. For this reason the priest has many credits now in the village, and he is determined not to christen, marry or bury hereafter unless he receives his fees in advance, for he also is a man and must live.

"Father confessor," replied the Effendi, speaking in a business-like manner, "you do not know the villager as well as I do. God has given the villager a soul, but he can't take it away, but when the angel of death stands at his head with drawn sword, then he gives up his soul. We cannot follow that example. Unless the villager sees that 'blessed stick' he will not pay. Prepare the list of your dues, hand it to me and I will give it to one of my soldiers. He will collect them. I will not allow you to lose a single para."

"Blessings upon you, God grant you long life," replied the priest. "The account is in readiness."

"Read it. Let me see how much it is."

The priest drew from his bosom a sheet of paper, soiled and yellow with age and nearly worn out. This was his account-book. On the four pages were written in large characters, forming crooked lines, the father confessor's dues. He held the paper near his eyes, and tried to read it, but could not. He gave the sheet to the teacher, saying, "Take it, Chorister Simon. Read it. My eyes do not see well."

Chorister Simon took the account, coughed a few times and began to read

180

it in a rhetorical voice as though he were reading a will. "I christened Muggo's daughter. 5 piastres due. I married Khubo's son. 10 piastres due. I received 80 bales of hay, value 3 piastres. Paul's wife was sick. I went to her home, read three healing chapters, 3 piastres due. Sako's son fetched the cross out of the water. Parso gave 80 piastres that he might fetch it. I did a favor to Sako and made it 20. Money due me 20 piastres. He said I will give you grain at harvest. I went and demanded it. He didn't give it. The kizir is witness."

And thus, one after another, was the lengthy story. It was not an account, but the man's church business dealings during past years and although depicted in a jumbled fashion, still it was proof of how a village priest is occupied.

"It is a legal account," said the Effendi, interrupting, unable to listen patiently until the chorister should bring his "reading" to a close. "Entrust me with that paper, Father-confessor, and I will have it all collected. The villagers of N.... delayed in presenting their 'fruits' to the monastery. They did not give them on time. The bishop wrote to me and I had them all collected in one day. Then I obtained a paper of blessing from the monastery."

This way of collecting his dues seemed so natural to the priest that he not only agreed to the Effendi's proposition, but he bestowed blessings upon his precious life, and expressed his gratitude repeatedly.

But why did the Effendi undertake to perform this service? He was one of those men who do no kindness to anyone without a purpose, without some personal gain. Now what prompted him to be so kind, and even promise not to take his tithes from these sums, which was customary when any sum was paid by order of a government official?

"May the blessings of Father Abraham descend upon you, and may you increase," said the priest, hearing the Effendi's last promise.

Chorister Simon had a similar list of dues in his bosom. He too had money owing him from his pupils, and he meditated presenting the account to the Effendi. But the priest whispered to him, "Let him collect mine, afterwards yours."

The family of Der Marook was very small. His only son had died, leaving his widow with two small children. The daughter-in-law had not re-married, but remained in the priest's house and cared for the little orphans. The father-confessor had been deprived long since of his wife and led a strictly celibate life.

That evening, the bride (daughter-in-law) after giving her guests their dinner, was occupied with her child who was very sick. Seated near his bed, the pitiable woman looked sadly at the sick child, rubbed his hot palms, and listened to his heavy breathing. In this child she seemed to see again the young man whom she had loved, and in this child the unfortunate mother found comfort after her husband's death. She hardly heard, and paid no attention to the conversation in the house but was absorbed in pity and love and saw nothing but her sick child.

But the priest, rejoicing over the Effendi's promises, wished to have a more perfect time rejoicing, and ordered his daughter-in-law to fill the bottle of raki which was empty.

Although supper was over, the custom of the place demanded that when a special honor was to be given to a priest, the drinking should continue.

The bride was in such distress that the priest repeated his command twice before she was able to understand what he wanted. She found some raki and filled the bottle. There was always a supply of this at the priest's house. But how should she prepare the "maza" — there were no sweets in the house. It would be a disgrace to let it be known. Everything necessary for a guest must always be found in an Armenian home. She thought she would borrow some of a neighbor.

It was very dark outside, and rain fell in torrents. The poor woman went out into the court, crossed the muddy yard, and mounted the terrace to climb over into the neighbor's yard. She heard the neighbor's gate being pounded furiously, and threats were being poured against them by some Turks outside with commands to open. But from within they swore that the ones they sought were not there. But whom did they seek? What Turks were these who sought to enter an Armenian house at this unseasonable hour?

Zoulo, this was the name of the priest's daughter-in-law, hearing the commotion in the street was in great fear, and she could neither go to the neighbor's nor return home from fright, but remained dazed and motionless on the flat roof. At that moment she heard a barely audible whisper. The speakers seemed to her to be climbing the neighbor's stairs and did not know which way to run.

"Carefully, Stephanie."

"Where shall I go, Sara?"

Zoulo recognized them. Her fright was over. Her heart was filled with courage when she saw these poor creatures were in need of help. She had heard of the sad events which had taken place at old Khacho's that day. She knew that the women of the family were hiding in various houses in the village that night. But now they were seeking them, and why? Zoulo understood why.

Therefore the Turks knocking at the neighbor's gate were none other than some of the soldiers who had imprisoned old Khacho's sons.

Sara and Stephanie now reached the priest's property, and like deer chased by the hunter, surrounded on all sides, they did not know in which direction to turn. The rain poured down on them. The doors of the villagers were closed and they were asleep. It was past midnight.

Just then lightning flashed and it's momentary flash was followed by a fearful clap of thunder. The lightning enabled them to distinguish Zoulo standing on the terrace. Stephanie seeing her indistinctly, thought that one of the Turks had climbed there. She fainted from fright and fell upon Sara's breast. Zoulo came near. "It is I. Do not fear," she said.

"Ah, Zoulo. Is it you?" said Sara trembling. "For the love of God give us a place. They will catch us, they will carry us off."

Zoulo was at her wits' end. Where could she take them? Where could she hide them? These were suspicious guests for them; the priest would object to receiving refugees like these. Nevertheless Zoulo thought she ought to help the wretched creatures. She knew the dishonor which would be theirs if they fell into the hands of the Turks. On the other hand, a heavy responsibility threatened her if she should furnish a hiding place to these criminals whose only crime was that they were women. Zoulo knew all that, but sympathy outweighed the feeling of fear and uncertainty and the imminent danger gave birth to an inspiration for saving them.

"Come," she said, taking Stephanie's hand, and with Sara helping her, they both raised the poor girl who was still unconscious.

They began to descend from the flat roof. Just then a terrible commotion was heard which was drowned immediately by the voice of the storm. It was the sound made by the Turks bursting open the door of the neighbor's gate. A hay-loft was next door to the priest's house. A small door from his yard opened into it. Zoulo led the fugitives there. Sara and Stephanie hid themselves in the hay.

"I will come again, soon," said Zoulo, and locking the door of the hay-loft, she went away.

On account of the noise of the rain, neither the priest nor his guest heard what was happening outside; while Zoulo on her return informed them of nothing. She only went up to the priest and whispered to him that all were asleep at the neighbor's and she had not been able to borrow anything with which to make "maza".

"I'll find something," said the priest, and rising went to the cupboard and began to rummage among the things there.

The Effendi, taking advantage of the priest's absence, turned toward Zoulo and said, "You are 'maza' yourself. What do we want of other 'maza'?"

Chorister Simon had drunk so much that he did not bear, but Zoulo, wounded by the Effendi's remark, replied, "Insolent!"

The Armenian woman endures every trouble and opens not her mouth under provocation, but when her honor is assailed then she loses her patience. Zoulo much disturbed, went and sat beside her sick child, who had awakened from his sleep. The child was comfortable, and seeing his mother near him, said, "Mother whip Toros, he has taken my knuckle bones." Toros was the sick child's elder brother; probably the boy dreamed that his brother had taken them. His mother quieted him, saying, "See, Light of my eyes, Toros has given them back. Here they are. The mother drew the playthings from under the child's pillow and put them in his hands. The child began to play with them with his feeble hands. The mother looked on and rejoiced. She forgot the Effendi's insult, she forgot everything, because now her child seemed better.

But a new unpleasantness arose to disturb the mind of the poor woman. After hunting a long time in the cupboard the priest did not find the thing he had hidden, and he asked Zoulo what had become of a piece of sugar he had hidden there which was gone. The daughter-in-law replied that she had taken it and had made a sherbet for the sick child a few days before, as he had a high fever and needed a cooling drink.

"He might have drunk it unsweetened — he might have taken it bitter," cried he angrily. "Didn't you know the sugar was for guests? Now what shall we do?"

Zoulo made no reply, but tears began to fall from her sorrowful eyes. The priest, Der Marook, was not really a bad man, he was even good. But goodness in ignorant men often is unintentionally changed to evil. Besides this his office had made him more or less severe. Priests, physicians and executioners who deal frequently with the dying are not very much concerned over life and death. For this reason, the sickness of his grandson did not concern the priest so much as his desire to show hospitality and to gratify a man like the Effendi especially as he had promised to have all the father-confessor's dues collected.

"Mama, why do you cry?" asked the sick child looking at her with sympathy. "Don't cry, I'm well now."

The mother forgot all her sorrow and wiped the tears from her eyes. Nothing is so comforting as the loving words of a dear child and its innocent prattle. Now Zoulo began to think about Sara and Stephanie, and wondered what they were doing; whether the Turks would enter suddenly and search and find them. But the unwanted guests still continued their drinking. She was waiting for them to finish and go to sleep so that she might be able to go to Sara and Stephanie.

But she must at least learn how the affair at the neighbor's house had ended. Zoulo was unable to control her impatience longer for that thought disturbed her greatly. Making some excuse, she rose and entered a small room which they called the "secret chamber" which served as a store-room. A narrow slit had been opened from this room directly into the neighbor's house. Openings like this were found in nearly all the village houses and in time of danger served as a secret channel of communication. If anything happened in a neighbor's house, they would call through the opening, and the next neighbor would hear. Between houses of intimate friends these openings were so large that small articles could be passed back and forth. Often they passed a lighted candle through the aperture, when the neighbor had no matches,

Zoulo stood before the opening and could look into the house and hear the following words, "We will kill you if you don't show us; where are they? They told us they were over here. You have hidden them! Be quick, or we will take your women." These threats were made by the Turks.

Neighbor Zako had fallen at their feet, and begged and cried, saying, "God and heaven and earth be my witness that they are not here; don't kill me. Behold my house is before you. Take whatever you please."

This was a repetition of what took place in Sodom when the evil men of the place came to Lot and demanded that he give up his guests to them. The kindhearted patriarch had begged them not to molest his guests and promised to give up his daughters instead. But the God of Israel was hard-hearted and sought revenge, and punished human wickedness by burning the dissolute city with fire and brimstone. And the God of Armenia saw wickedness worse than in Sodom, and left the sinner unpunished.

Zoulo trembled with dread as she looked and listened. She heard a commotion and saw neighbor Zako totter and fall to the ground. They extinguished the light. Zoulo could see nothing more, but only heard confused cries, "Oh, alas, let go — don't kill me, I am dying! Where are you taking me?" These were the cries of neighbor Zako's wife and daughters.

"Be still, you wretch," was the reply to these cries.

Chapter 32

Returning to her place, Zoulo found the guests in the same condition. They were still drinking. The priest was chanting while chorister Simon followed him, and the Effendi hummed an accompaniment. They were enjoying themselves. What matter what happened at the neighbor's house! Zoulo thought of informing them — perhaps they would assist them — and going up to the priest she whispered what she had seen in Zako's house. But she did not tell that she had hidden Sara and Stephanie in their house. An inexplicable instinct sealed Zoulo's lips on that subject.

According to the custom of Armenian women, she did not speak to the guests but whispered to the priest briefly what had happened, and the others heard nothing. But seeing the startled face of the priest, and the uneasiness which the woman's conversation occasioned him, the guests asked to know what had happened.

"Beasts, beasts," cried the priest, raising his bands toward heaven, "May the curses of the twelve apostles and the three hundred and sixty six patriarchs be upon you — cursed roots of evil!"

"What has happened?" repeated the Effendi.

The priest related what Zoulo had told him, and begged the Effendi to help the poor wretches.

There are men who in time of danger, misfortune and trouble, which overtake others, instead of thinking of means of deliverance, instead of quickly reaching out a helping hand, begin to examine the reasons for the misfortune and consider their conscience eased when they find someone was to blame. Of necessity, this judgment is meted according to the understanding of each man. The Effendi not only did not consider the occurrence unjust and immoral, but justified it with his belief that they deserved punishment. With this idea in mind, he inquired, "Tell me

187

Father-confessor, would an innocent man do what landlord Khacho did in keeping such suspicious men in his house who were turning the heads of the villagers, preaching all kinds of foolishness?"

"It is folly, it is great folly," replied the priest, "but how are the poor villagers to blame? Because of a few crazy fellows must the Turks throw them all into the fire? Our neighbor Zako is much to be pitied; he is so timid that he is afraid of his own shadow. Why do they afflict him? Why do they tyrannize over his family? What cruelty they practice!"

"The green wood is burned together with the dry — that is the order of the world, Father-confessor. Who distinguishes the wet from the dry?" replied the Effendi, astonished himself at his wise remarks. "When God sends chastisement to punish men, the innocent child goes to the grave with the old sinner. The evil and the good are mingled together. The vengeance of governments is the same, when it is necessary to punish a community. Harm comes to the villagers, I told you, Father-confessor, to all the villagers,"

The priest found no reply to make. The proofs brought forward by the Effendi were very cogent. In time of cholera and plague when men are punished for their sins, is there any distinction made between the just and the unjust? The dry and the wet are burned together. The priest thought of all this. He even forgot neighbor Zako, and the last words of the Effendi brought something to his mind which lay close to his heart. He said, "If the houses of all the villagers are plundered as they have robbed old Khacho today, I shall surely lose my dues."

"Be easy about that, Father-confessor," replied the Effendi. "I'll have it all collected soon. But tell me this, Father, isn't Khacho to blame himself for this punishment?"

The attention of the villagers had been centered upon the events in Khacho's house that day, but nevertheless, they all blamed him. "What business has a weapon in the hands of an Armenian?" they had said. "If you give a child fire he will burn his fingers." The opinion of the priest did not differ much from this. 'He replied to the Effendi's query, "I know one thing, my son. When the Jews came with sword and spear to seize our Lord Jesus Christ, the apostle Peter drew his sword, smote the servant of the high priest and cut off his ear. Then our Lord Jesus Christ spoke to Peter saying, Put up thy sword, for he who lives by the sword shall perish by the sword.' We should not forget this counsel if we do not wish to sin against the Christian faith."

"Honor to you, Father-confessor, you have comprehended well," said the Effendi, "but did you read those pamphlets?"

"I read them. One got into the hands of the chorister Simon. He brought it to me and we read it. But we made nothing out of it. I said — blessed men! You have written — write something understandable that will profit soul and body. That man may read and repent of his sins. What is the use of such crooked and twisted things as these? Chorister Simon, didn't I say so? You read them too."

"I did not approve," replied the teacher, having a chance to show his learning. "It was all evil. If they had written the lives of the fathers, the people would read and be profited. But I am glad that Vartan was punished, he is a very proud fellow. Once he stepped into my school, and said, 'What business have you to be teaching — you harm the children, go tend donkeys.' Was that a proper thing to say, as though he had read more than I?"

"The donkey's kick hurts more than the horse's," said the Effendi. "This Vartan has wounded me often, also."

Thus the priest, the chorister teacher and the government official each expressed his opinion about sad events and not one of them paid any attention to what was being done in neighbor Zako's house. Not one of them lamented over the condition of landlord Khacho's family tonight. That man to whose benevolence so many of the villagers were indebted now had become the object of their anger, because of his behavior, which according to their opinion, was reprehensible. Everyone was in the grip of terror and expected a tragic and terrible fate. Only Thomas Effendi, the author of all these villainies, was happy, and with especial fiendish pleasure felt great satisfaction in his heart because the seed he had sowed promised to yield the fruit he longed for.

"I repeat," he replied with the manner of a man of affairs, "that the villagers are harmed seriously. Times are bad, preparations for war are going on everywhere. In such disturbed times such appearances are punished by the Government."

Hearing the word "war", the priest was terrified, not because war threatened the villagers with trouble and misery but because he thought of his dues once more.

"If it begins," he said, "the villagers will have to pay so much taxes that it will be difficult to collect my fees."

"Rest easy, Father-confessor," replied the Effendi, "I will not allow your dues to remain till the war begins."

Then chorister Simon drew near the priest's ear and reminded him again

189

of the dues from his pupils and again received reply to be patient. One talks of the part where the pain lies. The question which interested the priest and the chorister was the collection of their fees.

"Although the ass is good-for-nothing, its hair ‡ cleans clothing," said the Effendi. "You must know that proverb, father. The villager is like this. Although he is clothed in rags and walks barefoot, the clothes worn by the rich is bought with the price of his sweat. Although he goes hungry and often can't find a bite of bread, he decks out the tables of the rich with all sorts of luxuries. But you Father, do not seem to know how to gain profit from the villagers. If you did you would not have so many dues and you wouldn't have given us whiskey without 'maza'."

The last remark touched the priest and he replied bitterly, "What can I do, Effendi? The hands of the priest are tied. They haven't given us a stick as they have you, with which to beat the villagers. Our weapon is very weak. What can I do? To tell the truth my heart is filled with rage sometimes and I lose my patience, and begin to curse them. But the villagers have become so unbelieving, that they are not afraid of my curses even. What other weapon have we? But they are not to blame, either. What have the Kurds left them that we should be able to demand anything of them. Cursed be those Kurds. If it were not for them I should not have many fees due to me. Now that war is to begin the Kurds will be fiercer and bolder than ever."

"The ass is still an ass, but the mule is worse," replied the Effendi in his usual style. "The Kurds are as bad as mules for they are illegitimate."

The night was nearly over. Zoulo, sitting apart near her sick child, listened in displeasure to the conversation of the guests, which was very tiresome for her. She waited patiently for them to finish, to cease drinking wine, in order that she might be able to go to Sara and Stephanie to see what condition they were in.

But the Effendi did not intend to sleep yet. He had much more to say to the priest and only the presence of Chorister Simon hindered him. For this reason he remarked that he would like to go to sleep for he was obliged to rise early in the morning on account of important business. The chorister, bidding him goodnight, left. After he had gone the priest said, "He knows more than seven bishops, the poor fellow, but alas, he likes to drink too well. Did you see how well he read off the account of my dues?"

"Are you speaking of Chorister Simon?" asked the Effendi. "Yes, he read well."

---

‡ Because Mohammedans consider swine unclean, they use clothes brushes made of donkeys' hair instead of pigs bristles.

190

But the Effendi was not interested either in Chorister Simon or his extensive learning. He was seeking a pretext to speak of a subject for which he had expressly come to the priest's house so eagerly this evening.

Just then the priest took off his half-worn cloak as he had become quite heated both from the wine and from the heat of the room. The sleeve of the cloak was torn accidentally. The Effendi said to him, "Your cloak is much worn, Father, why don't you have a new one made?"

"Bless you, how can I have one made? You know how my fees remain unpaid. And this cloak belonged to the departed Garabed Effendi. He died and they gave me this from the clothes he left. I have been wearing it ever since for seven years. Because of my sins none of the rich has died, so that I might get new clothing."

"I'll have a fine one made for you; you are a good priest," said the Effendi, "wear it and give me your blessing!"

"May the blessing of the three hundred and sixty six patriarchs be upon you, my son," said the priest, beginning to intone a prayer. "But I have another request, Effendi," he added. "You are our crown and glory. We rejoice and praise God every day that he has given us Armenians such magistrates as you; one who has access to mayors, judges, governors and pashas, and can speak freely to them. For the love of our nation and for the love of our holy faith, I beg you not to leave landlord Khacho and his family in the hands of these miscreants. If you are willing you can save them. They are poor and wretched. They are Armenian Christians. Help them. Whatever their crime may be, we ought to conceal it, because they belong to us and are of our blood. I don't approve of what they have done either, but 'who of you have not sinned'?"

Although the priest's words made no great impression upon the Effendi, still they gave him an excuse to impart to him what he bad long sought to say to the priest.

The Effendi replied that he was ready and willing to rescue the landlord's family from their difficulties and he would not allow a hair of his head to fall if the landlord would on his part grant the Effendi's request. And, reminding the priest of the secret imparted to him a year ago about Lila, the Effendi said that he had loved this girl since then and desired to make her his wife. If the landlord would grant this desire of his, he was ready to help him. But, if he refused, he would be obliged to let justice have its lawful course, which would certainly result in the landlord's whole family being destroyed and his property confiscated by the Government. And, thinking that the priest occupied the place of a father in the community, the Effendi begged the priest to undertake to interview old Khacho and

191

speak with him about it, before it was too late, while there was still time to direct the course of affairs and prevent the evils which threatened them.

"May my order be my witness," said the priest with hearty pleasure. "I will go to him tomorrow morning early and arrange everything as you wish. Khacho ought to thank the Lord and offer several lambs in sacrifice to the saints that such a man as you desires to become his son-in-law."

A crafty smile appeared on the face of the Effendi, and he replied as if in jest, "When you do all this, then your old cloak will be made new."

"But my fees?"

"Don't worry about those."

Chapter 33

The sad and terrible night was over. In the morning, old Khacho's house resembled such houses of mourning from which several persons are carried to the grave at once. First they brought out Vartan. He was tranquil. His countenance did not betray so much as a hint of agitation. Nothing seemed to have happened to him. Only his lips wore a sarcastic expression, as though he were saying, "What do these fools want to do?" When they seated him upon a horse and wished to fetter his feet and tie them together under the horse's belly, he made no resistance, although it is agony to be obliged to remain motionless in that position.

"That is unnecessary," he remarked, "If I wished to escape, your chains would not prevent me."

The soldiers paid no attention, but fettered him. Not content with this, they tied his arms together, behind his back, and with two soldiers holding the ends of the ropes, they prepared to set out.

Besides these two soldiers, three gendarmes accompanied him. Although the vulgar crowd is interested in such scenes, none of the villagers appeared to see how they were deporting the man who had labored and worked so hard for them. They all avoided the old man's house as though it were a dwelling afflicted with the plague.

None of the women had remained in the house. All were hidden in various places. Hairabed and Abo were in confinement, their turn would come next. Khacho's other sons who were free did not show themselves. Only the father came out to see Vartan off. After the last misfortunes, the old man was as one dead. The bitter persecution, the tyrannical injustice and brutal cruelty had quite worn him out. He approached and embraced Vartan, but his heart was too full for utterance. A few tears said much more than his tongue.

"Keep a stout heart, old Father," replied Vartan with an even voice. "He who has fallen into the water is not afraid of getting wet. Good-bye."

The soldiers did not understand what was said, and driving Vartan's horse before them, began to move along. The old man watched them for a long time, till they were out of sight.

Plunged in sad reflections, he returned to the house. Why did they take Vartan only? Why did they leave Hairabed and Abo? Why didn't they imprison him, instead of leaving him free, although under surveillance? The old man did not yet know the details of Thomas Effendi's program. He had arranged the affair so that if the old man did not accept his proposition about Lila, then he would pour out the full measure of his vengeance upon the poor man's family. He had caused Vartan to be exiled and had betrayed Salman because he considered them dangerous to the Turkish Government he served. But be had no such suspicion about old Khacho and his sons: he only included them in the charge because by putting them in an exceedingly difficult position, he would have a pretext to play the role of protector and deliverer, and thus make them indebted to him, so that afterwards he might request the hand of Lila, as the reward of his services.

These were the bargaining schemes which moved the Effendi to cause this great injury whose disastrous results he was not able to foresee for all his craftiness. But Thomas Effendi did not appear that morning. The old man wished to see him, wished to hear a final word as to how all this was to end. He still believed the Effendi's promises. He still clung to the statement, "Landlord Khacho, I will not allow a hair of your head to fall."

Instead of the Effendi, Der Marook appeared as his ambassador, for he had promised to go to the landlord in the morning and speak about Lila. In moments of misfortune, although the presence of a priest brings comfort, it made an unpleasant impression upon the old man. He had a peculiar superstition in regard to priests, and he always considered that the sight of their faces presaged disaster. The priest drew him gently aside, telling him he had an important matter to speak about, and that relieved the old man a little. The two sat down together in a remote part of the garden in the shade of the trees.

The introduction to the priest's embassy consisted of a string of comforting phrases, in the form of a sermon, with proofs drawn from the Scriptures. He spoke of the trials of Job and said that God often allows his servants to fall into various kinds of troubles in order to strengthen their faith; it is necessary to have patience, and not to become discouraged, for He will deliver believers from the hands of the ungodly at last, and cause them to inherit everlasting glory, and so on.

Bringing his lecture to an end, the father-confessor approached the real object of his visit, and in the usual manner of intermediaries in negotiations of marriage, he began his propositions with a parable. He said, "Once a prince went out to hunt, and being overtaken by darkness, he was unable to return and remained in the forest in the hut of a shepherd. He was pleased with the shepherd's hospitality, but especially taken with the shepherd's beautiful daughter. The next day the prince returned to his palace and told his father that he wished to marry the shepherd's daughter. The father thought his son was crazy, and was very angry with him. But after holding out against him for a long time, when he saw that it was impossible to persuade his son, he sent one of his chamberlains to negotiate with the shepherd. The chamberlain returned saying that the shepherd was not willing to give his daughter to the prince. The king was astonished and sent another chamberlain of higher rank than the first. He also brought the same reply. The king next sent his prime minister's vizir and he also received a refusal. At last, the king, at the end of his resources, went himself, and returned unsuccessful like the others. The shepherd rejected him also. The king was astonished. He called together his lords and counselors and consulted them. One of them who was a man of experience and very wise, advised the king to send a shepherd like himself to the shepherd, saying that a shepherd understands the language of a shepherd and he can persuade him. They selected one of the king's shepherds who without fine clothes or preparations Of any kind, took his shepherd's crook and bent his steps towards the shepherd's hut. The father received him kindly; they ate and drank and had a pleasant time together. Finally, the shepherd made known the king's request saying, "Why didn't you want to give your daughter to the king's son?" The father replied, "Blessed one, I am a man myself and have my preferences. When did the king send me a proper man like yourself to ask me to give my daughter to his son?"

Bringing the parable to an end, the priest added, "I also am a shepherd, and you are a shepherd, landlord Khacho, for we both manage people instead of sheep. I am the village priest, and you are the village landlord, and I have come to you with a proposition, as from shepherd to shepherd."

"What proposition," asked the old man, displeased, offended by the inappropriate words of the priest at this hour of grief and anxiety.

The father-confessor, replied that God had been pleased to comfort the old man in his present trouble and to open a door of deliverance before him. Thomas Effendi begged for Lila's hand, and promised to deliver the old man from the troubles which had overtaken his family. He should praise the Lord that a man like the Effendi had reached out a helping hand to him.

Skillfully as the priest had conducted his argument, still he did not meet with the success he expected. Perhaps at another time and under other conditions his words would have met with acceptance, for the old man had himself long ago thought of giving his daughter to the Effendi. But now circumstances wore a different aspect. Now when his two sons were in prison, when he was guarded by soldiers, when the women of his family were unprotected and hidden in the houses of strangers, when his two friends, Vartan and Salman had been delivered into the hands of the Government, when his household possessions had been plundered before his eyes, at such a time they brought him the proposition of a scoundrel, who had himself prepared these misfortunes.

All at once, the eyes of the old man, which had been bound until that moment, were opened. He saw the pit which the wily Effendi had dug with his own hands. He recollected Vartan's words telling that the Effendi had married wives in various places, and had deserted them. Wouldn't he try the same trick on Lila? He had some secret motive, which presented a succession of crafty performances, which were all bent toward the purpose of finding some means of entrapping Lila.

The Effendi was the first to tell him of Salman's imprisonment. Whence did he learn it? When it had occurred secretly in the darkness of night and not one of the villagers in the whole province knew it. The Effendi was the first one to tell him it would be necessary to have his house searched and by feigning to be his friend and boon companion, was able to deceive the old man, was able to obtain possession of Salman's papers, and locking them up in a secret chamber in the old man's house had kept the key himself. With what intention? Couldn't he have taken the papers himself and destroyed them? But he left them in the old man's house in order to open the secret closet, if necessary, and delivering the papers to the officers, say — "Behold the proof of these men's conspiracy!"

The entire past unrolled itself like a panorama before the eyes of the old man, and he was horrified to realize that he had been tricked. Therefore he replied bitterly to the priest, "Father-confessor, your fable was not very appropriate for the intervention you attempted, but even if Thomas Effendi were really a king, still I would not give my daughter to such a scoundrel. Come what may, I consider it better that my house be ruined and my whole family destroyed, than to obtain freedom at the hands of that scoundrel, who brought all this upon me. I understand now, I understand it all. He tricked me but he can deceive me no longer after this."

The anger and the dark sayings of the landlord seemed incomprehensible to the priest, for he had no knowledge of the facts of the case. And the landlord did not deem it necessary to give him a lengthy explanation especially when he considered that he was Stephanie's godfather and that

196

no other outsider knew that she was a girl; therefore who could have told the Effendi that she was a girl but the priest himself?

He departed from the old man's house quite displeased saying to himself, "God first takes away a man's wits, then his wealth."

The Effendi was waiting impatiently at the priest's house. When the priest returned, he inquired immediately, "What news do you bring?"

"I don't know what to say," replied the priest, abashed. "The man is demented."

"Did he refuse?"

"Yes."

"I expected that." The heavens seemed to fall upon the head of the Effendi and crush him under their stupendous weight. 'His eyes grew dim, he trembled and fell to the ground. He remained there stunned, for a long time. Occasionally he raised his hand to his forehead, beat his head and tore his hair, saying, "Now what shall I do, what shall I do?"

There is nothing in all the world which so humbles a man as love. The most frightful human monsters who have caused the earth to tremble, who have stained the earth with blood, who have kept nations in fear and dread, have been humbled, have bowed their knees before some beloved woman. Only then have they been men and have exhibited all the weaknesses of man.

Thomas Effendi loved Lila now. He loved her with a true and passionate love. All his savage, brutal cruelty melted, and vanished before this love. When the devil loves, he becomes an angel. The Effendi, being in love, began to repent.

He had never loved before in all his life, and now we can explain the dark side of his character where there was nothing sacred for him in life. Learned as he was in worldly affairs, good accountant that he was, and fiendishly cunning in attaining his ends, so harsh and unmerciful in business dealings, now love for Lila inflamed his heart, and dropped there that fierce spark which caused light to shine in a darkened soul. He looked upon his deeds and was horrified. "What have I done?" he muttered, and tore out his hair again.

Until that moment he had not appreciated the enormity of his crimes; until that moment he had considered it legitimate to use every means to attain his purpose. At first he had thought to play a little trick on the old man, and like a child, took a bit of fire in his hand wishing to frighten him with it, to make him do what he demanded. Suddenly a fearful conflagration came from that spark and he was unable to extinguish it.

"Ah, what have I done?" he cried again.

The priest regarded the Effendi's agony with dread and thought he was in his death-throes. And indeed, he did grow weaker, fell in feverish convulsions, and his lips trembled dreadfully. He remained in torment like this for a long time, until finally opening his eyes and turning to the priest, he said, "Whatever old Khacho said is true, Father-confessor. I am unworthy of his daughter. What bond can there be between a criminal like me and an innocent angel. Curse me, father, I am deserving only of curses."

He fell into a stupor once more. The priest thought he had died.

"Oh my fees," he cried, "I have lost my fees!"

Chapter 34

Let us return to the beginning of our story. Now, I think the reader knows who that young man was who at the time of the siege of the fortress of Bayazid took the letter from the commander Ishdogvitch and, pretending to be crazy, went among the besieging Kurds and passed through the camp of the enemy safely and a few days later delivered the letter to General Lord Lucasoff.

The reader also recollects that the young man, declining the General's offer to keep him and give him the office of bodyguard, left the Russian camp and hastened to save the life of someone. The young man was Vartan. Let us see where he went. Mounting his horse which he bad taken from a Kurd he had killed in a valley, Vartan began to travel toward the province of Alashgerd.

There were the persons dearest to his heart. There was the family of old Khacho, with whom he had passed so many happy hours. There was beautiful Lila to whom he had given his whole heart. There were his beloved companions with whom he had sworn to devote himself in a sacred cause - all were there who were sacred to Vartan, who were devoted to him. But in what condition did Vartan leave all these when he was taken away in chains by the Turkish soldiers to the commanding officer?

Old Khacho and his sons were imprisoned, his family was scattered and each hidden in a different place. Lila's fate depended on her two pursuers, on Thomas Effendi's and the Kurdish Bey's brute-like conflict. Salman was imprisoned. Melik-Mansoor went with his companions to rescue him. Did he succeed or not? Vartan knew nothing about these things.

A month and a half had passed since then and he had no word concerning them. What changes there had been in that month and a half, what events had taken place! The Russians had proclaimed war against the Turks, General Lord Lucasoff's victorious soldiers had conquered Bayazid and the whole province of Alashgerd and approached Erzeroum. The oppressed

199

downtrodden Armenian people, passing under Russian control began to draw breath more freely. Suddenly the fortunes of war changed. General Lord Lucasoff was obliged to leave the places he had taken and return to the Russian frontier. And Bayazid which he had taken April 18th, went back to the Turks June 27th.

Vartan had no information concerning the later events. He did not know what had happened during the time of General Lord Lucasoff's soldiers' occupation. He was ignorant of the wretched migration of the people of Alashgerd, and the sad reason for it.

In that short time great changes had taken place. Two and a half months, ago, Vartan, surrounded by Turkish soldiers, had been taken in chains to the governor. Before they reached there, Vartan's two attendants, Sako and Gegho, overtook them and making a bold attack succeeded in rescuing their master. Vartan was wounded in the fight and was carried across into Russian territory almost in the arms of his attendants to a village in the province of Sourmali. He had only just recovered when he entered the Armenian militia as a volunteer. His two servants, Sako and Gegho, entered the same service. They were both killed in the siege of Bayazid. But we know by what means Vartan left the fortress.

Now sad and lonely, he entered that valley where the village of o.... is situated. What a view that valley had presented a few weeks before! How fresh and beautiful were the fields, the valleys and the green hills! The entire extent of the valley was covered with fields of ripe grain, which tossed and waved like a sea of gold. On the slopes of the hills, scattered about like ants, grazed the herds of cattle. One heard the sweet and tender melody of the careless shepherd's pipes. Lavish nature and man had hand in hand produced the miracle of earth. But now, everything was changed. Now the entire valley had become a desolate wilderness. A conflagration had burned and devoured all the fields of grain, covering the whole surface of the plain with black ashes. Who had perpetrated this wickedness? Who had annihilated the productivity brought about by the farmer who had expended so much sweat and labor upon it? Vartan was puzzled. He turned his eyes upon the once beautiful and populous villages. They also were each a heap of ashes; here also the fire and conflagration had left their traces of destruction. Life had ceased everywhere. The joyous song of the laborers was no longer heard from the fields. No cattle grazed in the meadows; all was still. Everything was in a state of silent death. It seemed as though the destroying angel had passed over this wretched country annihilating everything which had been created by man's industry. What had happened?

The July sun was scorching hot. It was late in the afternoon when Vartan entered the village of O.... It resembled one of those legendary spots which, being cursed by some witch, has suddenly turned to ruins. The houses in which life once pulsed and where people had lived, had now become their tombs. Everything was buried under mournful, unsightly heaps.

Vartan passed through the familiar streets like one out of his senses. Here and there he saw portions of corpses. Surely a terrible catastrophe had occurred here, a frightful tragedy. He passed by the church. There was nothing to distinguish the house of God from the ruins around it.

He approached old Khacho's fortress. Only the outer walls remained and these were broken down here and there. 'He entered. A sad scene presented itself. The garden was bare of trees, bare of leafy trees under whose shade he had passed such happy hours with lovely Lila. Where was she now? Vartan had come for her. He sought her in these mournful ruins. Did the Kurdish Bey snatch her away, or did she fall into the hands of Turkish officials. Vartan was overcome with horror.

Suddenly a frightful object appeared. The man of iron seemed to crumble beneath a crushing blow. The blood rushed to his head and everything turned black. He saw no more. He felt no more. He mechanically seated himself upon a mound and holding his head in his two hands, remained long in deep confusion of mind. Suddenly a fair vision appeared to him, sad, hopeless and tearful, as he had seen her that last night in the silent garden when with her arms clasped around her lover's neck in entreaty, she cried, "Take me away! Remove me from this land. I am afraid of the Kurds."

Why didn't Vartan take her? Why did Vartan leave her? Vartan was not able to think more. He was bound, held in a state of stupor, his mind ceased to f unction.

What bitter memories these mournful ruins awoke in him? Not long ago, a splendid family lived a peaceful life there. What had occurred? Where was that family? He looked toward the living-room of which only the charred and blackened walls remained. The ceiling had fallen. Here all day long, the old man's numerous daughters-in-law, daughter, and grandchildren chattered, wove, and worked in lively fashion, and were always happy, having no anxiety about a livelihood. Now neither the noise of children, nor the careful mothers' gentle voices were heard.

He turned his glance upon old Khacho's oda which was entirely demolished. He remembered those noisy nights when together with Salman, the landlord and his sons had disputed in warm debate in that room. They had thought and prepared a hundred plans to rescue the wretched people from their present misery and to create for them a more fortunate life. But now he saw that everything was lost; both plans and planners had vanished.

Suddenly some men appeared. Until this moment Vartan had not seen a human creature in the whole region. Men appeared among the ruins. This heartened Vartan. He approached them. A few wretched Kurds, with pickaxes in their hands were digging in the mounds of the ruins. Vartan recognized them. They were old Khacho's shepherds and their families. The men dug while the women hunted for objects. Many things still remained un-burnt under the ruins of the house destroyed by fire.

"God give you strength," said Vartan greeting them as laborers are used to being greeted.

"Welcome," they replied.

"What do you seek?"

"You behold it with your good eyes," replied the Kurds, continuing their work.

Vartan, turning to one of the Kurds, asked, "Do you remember me, Khulo?"

"Why shouldn't I recognize you, sir? You were the friend of our landlord Khacho; you often brought goods to sell to this house, and you never failed to give something to your servant Khulo's children. See, this is something you gave her" and he pointed to the red calico dress worn by his wife.

Vartan began to inquire what had happened to their family, why the village had become a ruin and what had become of its inhabitants.

The shepherd dropped his pickaxes wiped the sweat from his forehead and sat down. He seemed to want to take a rest and tell the story.

"May it not happen to our enemies even, what happened to this house," he said with compassion. Really, we don't know it all. We were not here. We had taken the sheep to the mountains to pasture. When night came we drove the flock to the village. My wife had a bad dream that night and I was expecting some evil to happen. Before we reached the village, suddenly a troop of Kurds attacked us and began to seize the flocks. I ran with my companions to the village for help. We saw it was full of Kurds. We hastened toward this house. We saw that it was on fire likewise and it was impossible to enter from any side."

"What became of the people of the house?"

"May it come upon the heads of our children, if anything bad happened to them. Landlord Khacho, Hairabed and Abo were not at home. They had been taken to the judge many days before. They say they are in prison. None of the women were at home either. Only the other sons remained, and what became of them, we do not know. We came and found the house on fire."

"Our master, old Khacho, was a good man," continued the shepherd. "He feared God so much he would not tread even on an ant. They were all good in this house. They didn't even disturb the flies. They cared for us as for their sons. Cursed be those 'erishats' (the wild Kurdish tribes who are as cruel to their own race as to others). They overturned everything. They destroyed everything."

"What became of the villagers?"

"They massacred part of the villagers, some they took slaves. But many fled and escaped."

A drowning man is glad to clutch at a straw. Sad and terrible as was the shepherd's story, still it gave Vartan a ray of hope. They were not all lost, he thought. Vartan understood that old Khacho and his two sons, Hairabed and Abo must have been imprisoned; they may have escaped the barbarity of the Kurds, if they had not been murdered there. He knew that when the examiners took the old man's house under surveillance he sent away all the women from the house who were certainly hidden at their friend's and relatives' houses; and they must certainly have taken Lila with them, and so she would have escaped the disastrous misfortunes which overwhelmed the house. But what might their fate be if the same disaster happened in those houses where they had taken refuge?

There was one comforting point in the shepherd's words. "They massacred some of the villagers, some they took slaves, but many fled and escaped," he said. Perhaps Khacho's family was among those who escaped, thought Vartan. Perhaps Lila was among them. But where did they go? Whither had they escaped? This question tormented Vartan. The shepherds were unable to give a clear explanation.

These events had taken place at night and so suddenly that everything was shrouded in darkness. But Vartan had noticed on his way that in the entire province of Alashgerd no Armenians remained. It was impossible that all had been massacred or taken captive, therefore a general migration must have taken place.

In which direction? Toward what country?

Chapter 35

Leaving the ruins of old Khacho's house, Vartan didn't know where to go. The information he had received from the shepherds was so indefinite that it was difficult for him to take a decisive step.

It was now evening. The sun sank in the western sky. Vartan saw everywhere the same sad spectacle, ruins, desolate villages, fields lying uncultivated and nothing more.

"Is there not a single Armenian left in all this province?" he asked himself.

Suddenly a human form appeared in the empty expanse. It climbed slowly with uneven steps up the steep mountain side, sometimes stopping, sometimes gazing about him, and sometimes clinging to the rocks to keep from rolling down. Thus he reached the summit of the cliff he sought, which overhung an abyss. The last rays of the setting sun outlined his small body, which stood motionless, like a statue, looking from the summit of the crag down upon the extensive valley, in which within the last few days so much crime had been committed, so much devastation dealt. A long time he gazed and seemed to decide to do something which was exceedingly difficult for him.

Vartan's curiosity was aroused by this sight which presaged a strange sequel. He drew rein and watched from afar. Vartan saw the figure standing on the summit of the crag make despairing gestures, gaze again on the ruins of the extensive valley, then covering his eyes with his hands, throw himself down from the top of the crag into the abyss which yawned below. The small figure rolled over and over like a ball, striking the rocks again and again as it rolled downward.

Vartan urged his horse forward and in a few moments reached the foot of the mountain to give assistance. The body still rolled downward, but did not reach the bottom of the abyss. The brambles growing from the clefts of the rocks, caught him. Vartan was glad. He hoped to be able to save the life of the would be suicide. He looked up, saw that the body had rested some fifty feet above, held fast by the briars. How should he bring it down? This was now the object of his concern.

He dismounted from his horse, and began to examine the surface of the cliff which rose like a fortress wall, seeking for a path by which he might ascend to the bushes. There was no way to make the ascent. The body remained there motionless, giving no sign of life. What could have driven that wretched creature to attempt suicide? Vartan's sad surroundings had taken such a hold upon his feelings that he imagined he read a secret in every trivial object.

He realized that it would be impossible to save the wretched creature without endangering his own life, but he might not be dead; it might still be possible to help him. The feeling of sympathy caused him to forget himself, and he attempted a dangerous undertaking. He saw that by grasping the clumps of bushes or the stones jutting out from the cliff it might be possible to climb up, if they were firm enough to support the weight of his body. Vartan was as supple as a snake and nimble as a cat. He seized the nearest stone which he had selected and began to claw his way up. He had climbed only a few yards above the ground when suddenly the stone he hung from crumbled to bits and he rolled backwards. "It is not feasible from here," he thought, and paid no attention to his hands which had been scratched on the sharp stones and were bleeding.

Vartan's nature was such that difficulties fired his ambition the more, his pride was involved and he was determined to succeed. He must make haste. The sun was setting. Soon it would grow dark and prevent his success. He had an idea. He took the long rope which was tied to his horse's saddle. It was one of his weapons to whose end he had tied a ball of lead. He threw the ball up, and the end of the rope was twisted firmly around the branch of a tree not far from the spot where the man had fallen. Grasping the other end of the rope, he began to ascend as quickly as a spider, and in a few moments reached the spot where the body lay.

He raised the body, and how great was his astonishment when he discovered that the body was that of Thomas Effendi. For a moment passionate feelings of anger, disgust, hatred and revenge arose successively, out of his heart. He was ready to cast that odious creature into the abyss below that his remaining bones might be shattered, and that he might become the food of beasts, reptiles and birds of prey.

But was it possible to treat so cruelly an inanimate body? That was foreign to Vartan's nature. He carefully lowered the body with his rope and descended after it.

Vartan's first care was to discover whether he was dead or alive. He had several broken bones, his, head and face had struck upon the rocks, and were scratched and bleeding; he still breathed, but he lay there inert. This miscreant who had caused Vartan so much sorrow, who had been the cause of the ruin of thousands of homes, and the desolation of an entire province, stirred Vartan's pity in his present condition.

Perhaps, if the Effendi had fallen into his hands under different circumstances, Vartan would have killed him, but now he had before him a battered body which aroused his pity, and demanded his aid. Vartan had had much experience with the wounded, and had often been wounded himself, so he always carried with him the necessary dressings. His first care was to bind up the wounds on the Effendi's head and face, and stop the loss of blood.

Night had overtaken him. The heavens were overcast, and wind, lightning and thunder presaged an approaching storm. Vartan wished to find some shelter. He raised the body, tied it onto the horse, but he did not know which way to turn. Not an Armenian remained in the nearby villages. He recollected that there should be Kurdish villages not far from that place. He directed his steps towards one of them, leading his horse by the bridle.

Now the young man began to comprehend that this man had attempted suicide in order to flee from the pangs of conscience. He had repented of having been the cause of so much grief, bloodshed and ruin.

Vartan's memory had not played him false. He perceived a glimmer of light through the darkness. There must be a village there, but it was still quite distant. Now the rain increased in violence. He took off his cloak and carefully covered the body of the Effendi with it. It was late when he reached the village. The houses, as they usually are in Kurdish villages, were huts dug out of the hillside. Vartan approached the nearest hut and pushed open the door. Behold a fortunate people who have no fear of robbers and sleep without locking their doors, he thought.

No light appeared in the hut. The people of the hut were asleep. Vartan began to knock. In a few moments a woman's voice was heard from within.

"Who are you?"

"The guest of God."

The word guest was sufficient to admit them. The woman immediately lighted a lamp and admitted them. She had undressed and gone to sleep for her only clothing was a red shirt which reached only to her knees. The woman helped Vartan and together they carried the Effendi and laid him upon the divan.

"Is he sick?"

"No, he is wounded."

The young woman immediately brought a case in which there were various dressings and a few surgical instruments neatly arranged.

"I am the doctor in our house," she said opening the case. "When my husband is wounded in a fight, I cure him. Formerly, my mother-in-law was the doctor, now, she is old. I learned from her."

Although Vartan had great confidence in the Kurd's surgical skill, he thanked her, saying that he had a little knowledge in that line himself, and had already cared for the wounded man as much as was necessary.

Although this reply offended the young woman a little, as she wished to show her skill, still she did not interfere when she saw that the patient's wounds were bandaged.

"Now I must care for your horse, the poor thing was left outside."

"Do not take the trouble," said the young man. "Only show me where to tie him."

The young woman took the light and conducted the guest to a place in the courtyard. Vartan looked around and saw that the yard was surrounded only by a low fence.

"Is there no danger here?" he asked.

"What fear?" replied the woman with a laugh. "The thief does not steal from a thief."

"Blessed are ye," said Vartan to himself. He looked all about and saw that there was no one in the hut but the young woman and some children who were asleep on the floor. But their footsteps awoke the old mother-in-law who had been out of sight. She raised her head, sat up in her bed, asking, "Saro, is it you? Have you come, my son?"

"It is not Saro," replied the young woman approaching her. "It is a guest."

The old woman on hearing that it was not her son, laid her head on the pillow again, and went to sleep.

"Her eyes do not distinguish anything. She thought that her son, my husband, had returned." "Where is your husband," asked Vartan with interest.

"Near Bayazid. He has gone to fight. There's not a man to be found in our village; they are all there. It is only two days since I returned from there. I went to bring plunder."

"Did you bring much?"

"Not a small amount. We must be content with what God gives, be it much or be it little."

"Free daughter, free people," thought Vartan. "How simple your life. Are you to blame that they have taught you to regard booty as honest gain? If you had been brought up in other conditions, with your gifts you would have been one of the wonders of womankind." Vartan now turned toward the wounded Effendi and felt of his body. He was warm. His breathing was more regular, and he occasionally emitted muffled groans. The Kurdish woman began to beg to look at the patient. Vartan allowed her. He knew that surgery was well known among the Kurds, to whom wounds and blood were common affairs, and their cure is one of the vital necessities for them.

"There is no danger," said the Kurdish woman, finishing her examination. "The wounds are insignificant, but he has some broken bones. It seems that the patient must have fallen from somewhere." Vartan made no reply.

"Now I ought to prepare you something to eat."

The young man only just now realized that he was hungry, for he had not eaten all day. But there are moments, when although a man feels hungry, he has no appetite to eat. He was in this condition. Grief and sorrow had fed him.

"No preparation is necessary," he replied. "Only give me a piece of bread and cheese."

Vartan's modest request wounded the hospitable feelings of the Kurdish woman who wished to prepare a hot meal for him.

"Don't spare us," she said smiling. "We are not as poor as formerly."

"Yes, Bayazid enriched you."

"Besides Bayazid, we had a fine harvest here. Last year sickness destroyed all our cattle, and we were left without a crust of bread, but God has made it up to us this year. All the Armenians of this region emigrated and left most of their riches to the Kurds."

"Where did they go?"

"I don't know, but they went in such haste and their migration was so sudden that they did not have time to take everything with them. They tried to escape quickly lest the Turks massacre them."

"Did they escape?"

"Many who remained were massacred."

The terrible facts were being made clear to Vartan, little by little. There had certainly taken place a general migration of the Armenians from this region; but in which direction, and why? The Kurdish woman was unable to give him any definite explanation. Vartan fell into deep meditation. He quite forgot his hunger, and did not even watch the pretty Kurdish woman who had lighted a fire in the "ojak" and began to prepare some eggs for him.

Some other time, in a happier frame of mind, no young man would be able to look unmoved upon the pretty woman's trim figure, beautiful even in a simple shirt. Having risen from her bed, she did not even wear a veil, and only her heavy brown hair bound about her forehead like a wreath. Such a head with such luxuriant hair! Such a face with such bright eyes belonged only to a mountain sprite who sees her beauty mirrored in the clear streams.

Chapter 36

The night was half gone. The lamp still burned in the Kurd's small hut. The simple patriarchal family slept. All within the same four walls. On one side the old mother-in-law snored; next to her the children, who tossed uneasily and talked constantly in their sleep. Next to them lay the mother. This free and simple mountain girl thought it quite natural to go to bed in sight of a strange guest. Because of the warmth of the hut, she had thrown off the quilt and her beautiful bosom was half-exposed, over which her heavy tresses fell like a veil. Her sleep was quiet, like the sleep of an innocent lamb.

"Now I understand why the first human pair lived quite naked," thought Vartan. "They began to cover themselves when they felt what sin is. This people do not yet know what sin is, and for this reason, the idea which in the language of the world is called shame is unknown to them. Behold a beautiful race in its primitive simplicity. It is possible to make something wonderful of them. The wild plant grafted upon a more cultivated plant yields remarkable fruit. What would result if this vigorous strain were to be mingled with the Armenian race?"

All were sleeping. Only Vartan was awake. He sat thus for a long time, and sad disconnected thoughts arose in his mind. Sometimes, in his heated fancy, he seemed to be seeing the emigration of the people of Alashgerd. A transplanted tree does not often take root in another spot, and grow as it should, but withers away. This people were withering away owing to its many migrations during the centuries. It had not settled permanently as yet. Behold still another migration! That is according to Nature. A tree which has not taken deep root in Mother Earth, is not able to withstand the tempest. When fierce winds blow, it is torn out by its roots, cast into the abyss, and destroyed.

Sometimes, in his fancy, he beheld the animated countenance of Salman. He seemed to hear the young man's eloquent discourses. He was talking unceasingly, in a sweet, reasonable way. Although the ideas he expressed were immature, they gushed from a warm heart, filled with earnest faith.

Sometimes Vartan's mind pictured in fancy Melik-Mansoor, that powerful adventurer, who was always eager to plunge into every stormy dangerous disturbance that presented itself to him.

Sometimes he thought of old Khacho, that virtuous patriarch, who had so much love and pity for all who were committed to his care; who was always denying himself of rest and comfort, in order to wipe away the tears from the eyes of some unfortunate person.

Sometimes he thought of the old man's sons some of whom, under the heavy burdens they bore laid upon them by circumstances, had lost all expectation, or hope of individual freedom, or of better conditions, while others made a protest against the prevailing irregularities, injustice and oppression. His mind was agitated and, wandering about, laden with all these thoughts and passing through immeasurable darkness, at last paused at one point, from which it did not deviate. That point was Lila.

Now the Effendi occupied his attention. His breathing had grown steadily heavier, his hands moved constantly and from his compressed lips, indistinct words and deep groans were heard. He was delirious. Vartan could hear him but could not understand anything. He appeared to be tormented as by spiritual conflict. That continued for a few moments then he began to grow easier little by little. At that point he raised his head, sat up in his bed, opened his eyes and looking wildly about, laid his head down once more and closed his eyes.

"Oh, if there were only an Armenian here," Vartan heard him cry.

"There is," replied Vartan coming near.

"Give me your hand."

Vartan drew back in revulsion.

"Now where am I? Who brought me here? Why did they bring me out of Hell so soon? It was good there, very good. In waves of f ire, in a fiery ocean, I floated. The thousand-headed vipers choked and throttled me in their embrace. I see them now, alas. Behold, they writhe in the burning flames there. They heap themselves upon one another. How sweet it is for a criminal to be tormented in the claws of such monsters! To be torn, but to be unable to protect himself and to know himself deserving of still more horrible torments."

He opened his dim eyes once more, gazed at Vartan, but did not recognize him, and turning to him continued, "To me was assigned, my friend, the most horrible part of Hell, and I am proud of it. I was unable to attain a high position on this earth, but there I succeeded. No one was able to dispute my right. I saw Vasag, Metiroozhan, Vcsd Sarkis, Cain and other criminals like them — they envied my glory. Oh, what great satisfaction there is in floating in waves of fire, to feel their frightful heat: to burn, to roast, and never be consumed to ashes. It is fine, that it is endless. Everything is good in eternity.

It was not difficult for Vartan to understand of what these imaginary phantoms were the expressions. But in these words he observed the confession of a repentant heart. For this reason he forgot all his hatred towards this wretched man, and taking his hand he said, "Restrain yourself, Effendi. You will soon be well. Your wounds are not so dangerous."

"I hear a familiar voice."

"The voice of Vartan."

He shuddered and pushing away Vartan's hand, he said, "Take your hand away from me. I may pollute it. Go away from me. I may poison you. Vartan, I know you. You are good, but at the same time you have a hardened heart. Exercise all your cruelty and kill me this moment. You will have rendered me a great kindness. Leave my carcass in the fields of Alashgerd, which I myself turned into a desert. Let the wild beasts tear it to bits. Oh, be so kind as to throw my carcass into a ditch and cover it with earth. I will find a way from there to the abyss, to the place of everlasting and unquenchable fire and torment. But no, no, I am not worthy of the soil of Armenia. My odious carcass would pollute its purity."

"Compose yourself," repeated Vartan. "You will not die. I will use every effort to keep you alive."

"I thought it would be easy for me to die and close my eyes forever in order not to see the evil I have done. But no, the vengeance of Heaven is more powerful than worthless man. It has left me that I might longer see these lands of which I have become the first destroyer; that I might longer see the huts of the wretched villagers, which I emptied of inhabitants, to see and to be tormented with the bitter sting of conscience; that is a fearful torment. I became the tool of the destruction of the entire province, but I was unable to kill myself." He uttered the final words with deep and melancholy bitterness which revealed his spiritual suffering, showing how weary he was of life, and how he longed for the oblivion of the grave.

Just then the hostess awoke.

"Your patient appears delirious," she said. "Don't you want something?"

"Nothing is needed. He is feverish. It may pass soon."

The Kurdish woman approached the patient, and looking at him attentively, asked, "I think I know this man. Isn't he Thomas Effendi?"

"It is he."

"Poor man! A few days ago I saw him, barefoot, bareheaded and ragged, wandering about near us. When anyone went near him, he screamed, cried aloud and fled. They said he was crazy."

Vartan then for the first time recollected that he had seen the Effendi in just the condition the Kurdish woman described when he first saw him. He showed all the signs of lunacy even then, before he had thrown himself down from the top of the crag. But why bad he become insane? In a character as demoralized as the Effendi's were mental torments able to cause that degree of suffering?

"They say that the Effendi loved a girl and in the emigration of the people of Alashgerd, the girl was lost. They said that unknown persons had stolen the girl."

"What men? What girl?" exclaimed Vartan deeply agitated, and a frightful look appeared on his face.

"I don't know. That is what they said"

Vartan's question was superfluous. It was forced by his curiosity which he could not restrain, which happens to hopeless men. Vartan knew who was the object of the Effendi's raving. Now he had lost her. Now they had stolen her. With this the remaining sparks of hope in Vartan's breast were extinguished, leaving in his stricken heart only the ashes of sad memories.

The night had passed imperceptibly. Day was breaking. The joyous song of birds was heard from outside. The stormy, rainy night was succeeded by a roseate summer morn.

Suddenly a girl ran in joyously through the door of the hut. It seemed that she had come far, for she was wet from head to foot, and the edges of her long skirt were bedraggled with mire.

213

"Chavo," exclaimed the woman of the house, embracing her.

"Sister," cried the girl, presenting her rosy cheeks to her lips.

Vartan seemed to forget his sorrow for a moment and began to watch the two sisters embrace one another. The newcomer was a tall girl, slender and quite good looking. She had also her sister's bright black eyes, which were now made more bright and sparkling with happiness. Both her face and her name seemed familiar to Vartan, but where and when had he seen her? It was difficult for him to recall her.

"Do you know what has happened?" asked the pretty girl. "After this Chavo is going to stay with you. She will stay with you a long time. The mistress has set Chavo free."

Glad as she was to hear that her sister Chavo would remain with her for a long time, she was puzzled when she heard that her mistress had dismissed her. Why had she dismissed her when formerly she had spared Chavo with great difficulty whenever she begged to visit her sister.

"What has occurred?"

"Don't be frightened, nothing bad has happened." And Chavo began to relate that her mistress had dismissed her only temporarily, to dwell with her sister, until she should send for her again. The mistress had given Chavo money, clothing and many fine gifts and Chavo had brought them all with her.

"See, I will show them all to you," she said.

She began to open the bundle she had brought with her to show the gifts she had received. But the older sister, not content with the explanation Chavo had given, asked, "What has happened? Why did she dismiss you?"

"Chavo will tell you afterwards. It is a long story. As long as the story of Leyly and Majnoon." Then she said she was very tired. She had traveled all night. The cursed rain had given her much trouble, and now she was very hungry and tired. She begged her sister to give her a little milk to drink. Her sister hastened to take the milk pail and ran to the corral to milk the cow and bring her sister fresh milk.

Only at this moment did Chavo observe that there were guests in the house, and her eyes met Vartan's interested gaze.

"Charming Chavo, you are Koorsit's handmaid, are you not?"

214

"That is correct."

"The wife of Fattah Bey."

"Exactly."

Vartan now found the end of the tangled thread, and asked, "Has the Bey a second wife — an Armenian girl ?"

"He would have had one if Chavo had not stolen her away."

"The Armenian girl?"

"The Armenian girl, Lila, Stephanie; she had two names."

Vartan's heart began to beat with joy. Where did Chavo take the stolen girl? Chavo took her to her mistress and her mistress sent her secretly to the Russian boundary. Vartan's countenance brightened with inexpressible joy, and forgetting himself, he embraced Chavo not knowing how else to express his boundless gratitude.

"Kiss Chavo. Chavo saved her."

"Chavo is my sister," said Vartan and he gave her another brotherly kiss. The elder sister entered, bringing the foaming milk-pail. Chavo took it from her band, and drank half of it without stopping. The warm milk satisfied her hunger and thirst.

"Now tell me," said the older sister to her.

Chavo began to tell in her own peculiar manner how her mistress' husband, Fattah Bey, had long loved the Armenian girl who was the daughter of landlord Khacho of O.... .The mistress did not wish the Armenian girl to become the wife of the Bey, for she was beautiful and might possibly rule over his heart. Incited by jealousy and envy, the mistress had tried in every way to prevent that marriage, but the Bey had violently opposed her, and when the Bey returned from the fighting at Bayazid, he had made ready to go and bring the Armenian girl. Then the mistress sent Chavo with two of her trusty servants beforehand to the village of O.... to go and take Lila out of the country before the Bey could reach there.

Chavo found Lila in the house of the priest of that village in hiding with her brother's wife, Sara. Sara knew already of the intention of the Bey and when Chavo told her Koorsit's plan, she agreed to it gladly, to take Lila and escape from the village that night with the servants sent for her. They conducted Lila to the Russian boundary and the Bey was left "cursing and raging". His wife began to laugh at him in secret, and to rejoice at having snatched the beautiful Lila away from him. The servants returned after a few days and reported that they had taken the girl in safety. But Chavo's mistress told her to go and stay with her sister temporarily till the Bey's anger should cool.

Chavo's story so much interested her sister, and more especially Vartan, that not one of them noticed that the sick man was equally interested in it. When Chavo concluded, they heard him say, "Now I can die in peace. Lila is saved."

Vartan went to him and held his trembling head, which after a shudder, dropped to the pillow.

"The starving ass smelt barley, but before he reached it, he breathed his last," — these were the Effendi's last words. The Kurdish woman and her sister also drew near.

"He has died," said Vartan.

"Poor creature," the sisters exclaimed.

Chapter 37

The July sun was burning hot. The whole expanse of the heavens seemed filled with fiery needles, which were scattered in all directions like sparks and scorched everything. The heat was intense. The birds, weary and faint, hid among the thickest of the trees on which not a leaf stirred in the dead stillness of the air. Only flies, insects, and tiny microscopic gnats entered the fortress shamelessly, and millions of groups buzzed and hissed. They entered men's mouths, noses and ears, when they breathed or stung exposed parts of men's bodies worse than did the fiery beams of the sun. A strange scene was presented to old Vagharshabad then. In whatever direction one looked, an immense multitude was gathered together, women, girls, old and young, all half-naked, all poor. They were spread out there. The streets were full of beggars outside and inside the wall of the monastery of Echmiadzin, under the shade of the trees around Lake Nerses as far as the monastery of Kayaneh to the end of the forest kept by the same Catholicos. Wherever there was a patch of shade, sufficient to protect one from the burning rays of the sun, everywhere one could see the same pitiable, wretched groups. These were the emigrants from Alashgerd.

Three thousand families, leaving their native land, their homes, lands, all their possessions had tried to escape from the sword and fire of the Turks and had found an asylum here. There was not a house in Vagharshabad where ten to twenty families of these wretched people were not piled one on top of the other. The stables, hay-lofts and court-yards were full of them. It was not sufficient to feed this immense multitude, but it was necessary to cure them as well. Leaving the highlands of Alashgerd, this unfortunate people had descended into Ararat in the frightful heat of July and had succumbed to all kinds of illnesses.

It was midday, that hour when in summer the peasant ceases from his work in the field, when the plowman and the oxen stop in some shady spot to rest. The more fortunate creatures, after an abundant meal, have retired to their cool rooms. At that hour of the day, among the great number of Alashgerd poor people who begged from door to door, one claims our

217

special attention. This is a young girl not more than sixteen years old. Her face was thin and drawn, and having lost her natural color, she had become a jaundice-like yellow, and she looked like a faded rose, near its sad dissolution. In her black eyes, deep melancholy was depicted. Her pale lips showed that she had not entirely recovered from illness. This mournful face, which must once have been of wonderful beauty, even in its present state was attractive.

The demon of misfortune seemed to have played a mischievous trick upon this delicate creature and concealing her in tattered rags, had tried to caricature and obscure her beauty and grace. But with this it had made her more interesting and attractive. The worn and tattered clothing barely draped her half naked body. She seemed to have received each separate garment from a different person, for they differed from each other in style and color. Besides this, some portions were too large and some too scant, one shorter than usual, another too long.

She went with slow tottering steps down one of the village streets. Her bare feet were burned by the earth, heated so by the rays of the sun that it was like red-hot irons. She had with her two little children who clung to her hands like two cherubs. She walked far, her head bent, silent, without a word she stood at the doors of houses and without venturing to enter she waited for hours until some of the people of the house should notice her and give her a piece of bread. It would seem as though her proud lips had not yet learned to beg for, charity. She appeared to have been born and bred in more fortunate circumstances, but now by reason of sad conditions, she had fallen into a different state.

Misery, humiliation, loss of former comforts, all filled her heart with indescribable bitterness which wore upon her body and marred her face more than the disease which had already begun to destroy her body.

She passed from door to door, but no one paid her any attention. At last overcoming her bashfulness, she stepped over the sill of a house and meeting the mistress, she said timidly, "A bit of bread."

There was in her tone notes which expressed the sorrow of her heart. The mistress replied, "Curse you! which one of you can we give to?"

The girl looked about her, and saw, it is true, there were many like herself. She was ready to depart instantly but she delayed. She did not think about herself, although she was hungry; but she thought of the two little children, who had eaten nothing and she thought about their sick mother who lay in her bed, half famished.

She wiped the tears from her eyes and tried to repeat her entreaty. Just then a little house-dog leapt out from the door and attacked the poor girl's skirts with his sharp teeth. She ran out in terror, leaving a portion of her clothing in the dog's jaws. The two little ones lifted up their voices wailing; they were nearly heart-broken.

Tying up the loose ends of her clothing, she now turned toward the monastery. The two little ones forgot their tears and fright in their joy over a piece of watermelon rind they found lying in the road. One of them ran and picked it up, and wiping off the dust and dirt on his skirts, began to gnaw on it. The other child tried to snatch it from him saying, "Give me some, I am hungry too." A battle waged between the two. The young girl pacified them by dividing the rind equally between them.

Just then a young man was passing hastily by them. Seeing the girl with the two children, he recognized them and said, "You are not entirely well yet. I told you not to go out; you have walked out again."

The girl was embarrassed and did not know what to reply. It was true, she was not well. She was so weak, she was hardly able to stand on her feet. The young man looked at the children who were still munching on the watermelon rind. He snatched the rind from them and tossed it away and said, "How can you eat that?"

The children were less bashful than the girl and with the tears running down their faces, they replied, "We are hungry."

"Don't they feed you at the monastery?" the young man inquired of the girl.

Instead of replying to the question, looking downward with her beautiful eyes, she said with difficulty, "If it is possible, could you provide some other place for us so that we might leave the monastery?"

"It seems that the good-for-nothing bishop doesn't take good care of you."

The girl made no reply, and continued to look downward as she did not wish to turn her revealing gaze toward the inquisitive young man, taking care lest he should read from her face what she was obliged to hide in her heart.

"I understand," replied the young man greatly disturbed. "Now go. It is not wise to walk around in this steamy heat; you are ill. You may grow worse I will come to you in an hour and I will arrange everything so that you shall receive good care. How is your brother's wife?"

"She is still the same. She was more restless last night," replied the girl

219

mournfully. And now raising her bashful eyes to the young man, she asked, "You will not leave us at the Vank, will you, sir?"

"Very well. I will find some other place for you," said the young man, as he hastened away saying to himself, "Poor creature, how soon you have tired of your Vank."

The Young man was a physician, the son of a wealthy landowner of Vagharshabad. He had completed his course of studies in the University of St. Petersburg and like a knight who has just entered the order, he had set out to seek adventure and to show his heroism in his profession. The emigrants from Alashgerd with their multitude of sick, opened before him a wide field of activity. The fresh, unwearied zeal of the young man full of good purposes found great satisfaction in the labor of helping those miserable creatures. In him was united skill as a physician, with kindness. He not only visited them without pay, and distributed medicine free to the sick, but he also looked after their lodging places and their food. This was the reason why the young girl appealed to him so earnestly begging him to provide some other place for them.

After the physician left them, the girl continued toward the Vank. Swaying, tottering, she was barely able to drag her feet along. She stopped a few times, and sat down in a few places to rest. They called to her, from cafes and bars opposite the Vank, promising to give her money. "Those men are worse than Kurds," she said to herself, and rising to her feet, continued her journey.

She went on into the garden, passed near the principal entrance of the Vank, circled the western side of the wall, and came out by the gate which leads to the lake and the forest. She entered Ghazarabad by this gate. That portion of the Vank, on feast days, served as a guest-hotel for the numerous pilgrims, but now it was filled with the sick from Alashgerd. She entered one of the cells in the lower story. In that damp cellar, deprived of air and light, on the red brick floor, lay a woman. She had no bed, nor bedstead. She had a bag of straw under her and a piece of sacking over her.

The two children ran to embrace their sick mother and began to kiss her emaciated hands. But she did not reply to her children's caresses for she was asleep or rather in a stupor. The young girl motioned the two children not to disturb their sick mother, but to go and play outside. They went obediently, and sitting near the door of the cell, began to build houses for themselves of dirt, pebbles and sticks and amused themselves.

But the girl herself lay down on the bare floor and propping her head on her arms in place of a pillow, turned her tearful eyes toward the sick woman and gazed at her. She was so weary and weak, and in such anguish

220

of spirit, that she longed to sleep a little and rest a little, but unwillingly her tears choked her and she was unable to close her sorrowful eyes.

She longed to close her eyes forever and not see the light of the world, which had become darkness for her. What misfortunes had she not borne, what sufferings had she not endured! She had lost father, brothers, relatives, and a comfortable home, all that was valued by her, all that was dear to her. While now, in a strange land, alone, unprotected, left to the will of destiny she wandered from door to door. Her only support and her only protector, on whom she placed her hope, was now sick and might die today or tomorrow. What would her condition be after that? Who would care for the unfortunate children of the unfortunate mother? If only she were well, if only she were able to work, then she would do everything. She would care for the orphans. But she had no strength, she was weak and ill also, and daily was growing more worn and emaciated and she awaited her longed for final moment, which delayed its coming.

The wretched girl was struggling with these sorrowful thoughts and her hot tears rolled down her pale cheeks when a cry was raised outside and a harsh voice disturbed her still more.

The two little children had made little houses near the door of the cell and were amusing themselves. Just then a thick-set monk with black robe, black cowl and black face — there was nothing white about him, seeing the two little ones roared fiercely, "Begone, brats. Why are you spoiling the floor?"

The children were slow to move, and the monk rushing upon them was on the point of trampling them under his feet if they had not hastened into the cell screaming. The screams of her children brought the unconscious mother to herself. She embraced them both and began to quiet them without knowing the reason of their tears. Just then the troubled face of the monk appeared at the door of the cell.

"Begone this moment from here," he shouted angrily. "How many days is it since I have told you to find a place for yourselves and to get away from here, and you still stay?"

To whom did he speak these words? The sick mother heard nothing. She held her children in her embrace, whom she seemed to see for the first time. For two days she had been in a state of stupor. Now the voices of her darling children had aroused her. To whom did the monk speak?

No one in the cell was able to hear or understand his words. The young girl was terrified by his voice and fainted. While the little children huddled, in fright, in their mother's arms, trembling. Another voice interrupted the monk's anger.

"What thunder-bolts are these, Holy Father?"

"Welcome, Mr. Doctor, how are you? Are you well?" How are you feeling?" asked the monk smiling, and putting on an ingratiating smirk.

"Never mind how I am feeling just now," said the head-physician, looking the monk straight in the eye. "Tell me this, what grievance have you, Holy Father? Why were you so angry at these poor creatures?"

"May you be my witness, there are no grievances here. I only said they should find a place for themselves and leave here. You know that it has been agreed not to keep emigrants more than two days at the Vank. New emigrants arrive every day. The first must go to give room to the second."

"Where shall they go? You can see that they are dying."

"What can I do? These are my orders."

The holy father was the supervisor of the Vank, a loud-mouthed monk, with whom every man liked to jest, especially the head doctor who took special delight in ridiculing the clergy.

"You don't deceive me with these words," he said. "Speak out, Holy Father. What has given you a pain? Is it the light in the girl's eyes?"

"Oh, let me alone blessed one. What things you talk!"

"Begone, begone," said the chief physician and entered the cell. The visit of the physician was especially comforting to the wretched family when after giving the necessary medicines and instructions, he told them that he had arranged to have them removed speedily to a priest's dwelling where they could find every convenience, both as to lodging and food.

"But quickly, if possible, very quickly," begged the sick woman with a grateful voice.

"Rest easy, in a few moments they will take you there," replied the physician and went out to see the other patients in the Vank.

"Lila, do you see, my child," said the sick woman to the young girl who sobbed with her hands over her eyes. "In the bitterest moments of misfortune, still God does not forget the needy, and He sends His angels to

222

comfort them. Do not weep, my child. The dark and stormy night is followed by a glorious morn. A day will come when you will find joy once more."

"After all this, dear Sara," replied Lila with bitter tears, "after all this, only death remains for me."

Two men entered the door of the cell. The conversation between Sara and Lila was interrupted. The newcomers were the physician's servants who had brought bread and food. Besides this, they had brought a bundle of women's clothing for Lila and Sara, and children's clothing for the two little ones. Sara and Lila did not touch the food, they had no appetite, but the two little ones pounced upon it and began to eat greedily. The servants waited outside till the meal was over.

Lila dressed herself and changed Sara's rags and the two half-naked children were clothed. Then the transformed family emerged from the polluted atmosphere of the Vank and turned their footsteps towards the dwelling prepared for them by the head physician.

Chapter 38

"The Illuminator's wind" arose and the fierce heat of midday gave place to the cool of evening. This kindly wind was the life-giving spirit not only of Vagharshabad, but also of the whole province of Ararat, which blew towards evening every day during the summer. And it is not unbelievable — this popular tradition — that our father, the Illuminator, appointed it to keep his people from sickness.

The monks of the Vank, after their comfortable noon naps, came out of their cells and enjoyed themselves strolling two by two around Lake Nerses, in beautiful walks which were shaded by the thick branches of the trees. One noticed immediately that the fathers taking their ease did not form groups, but walked in pairs, or entirely alone. They resembled those creatures who keep themselves aloof from social life, only because they are afraid to go near each other. Suspicion and disagreement separated them, and this was called brotherly union!

The lake was situated near an artificial mound which had been built of hewn stones. From its foot to the Vank extended an old cemetery. New graves had been dug in some places, and in others the bodies thrown into a ditch and covered with earth. They used spades and pick axes. The priest, reading the service, or reading nothing, ran from grave to grave and had at last found rest in the grave. They were lance. No friends to weep, no relatives to mourn and conduct the spirit of the departed to the realm of the dead. One would think they were rejoiced that wretched men were released from the troubles of life and had at last found rest in the grave. They were burying the emigrants from Alashgerd.

"How many have died?" asked one monk to another walking beside him.

"It is all the same for them," replied the other indifferently. "There they would be killed by the Kurds and the Turks. Here they can die themselves. But we have strayed from the question," said he, taking up their interrupted conversation. "I repeat, that it is not necessary to believe him,

224

not in the least. He has approached us and has posed as an intimate friend, he has shown sympathy and has a thousand and one tricks, but that's all hypocrisy. He tries in this way to discover our secrets and make them known in certain quarters. He is a spy, simply a spy, and that is the reason why he is so well received 'in the upper Jerusalem'. It is very probable, as he hopes, that he will soon be made a bishop, and the head of a rich diocese."

"All you say is correct, but he will not secure the last two honors.' The Fourth' is very generous with promises but exceedingly niggardly in performance. He intends only to give that fool's head the reins, temporarily, as long as he is needed; afterward, they will cut off his tail and turn him loose, and give his office to a more suitable person. See, they are bringing in two more bodies to bury."

"Let alone your dead as you love God."

"But he isn't one of those foxes who is easily deceived."

"The crafty fox falls into the trap with both feet."

"Be careful. Let them pass."

On the opposite side of the terrace appeared two other monks who approaching the first, likewise discontinued their conversation. They were both members of the Synod. When they had moved some distance away, they continued their conversation once more.

"We must appoint the auction now. It is the best time."

"Why?"

"Because we know who those are who have taken possession of those lands belonging to the church through taxes. Messrs. N., M., and K. who have always been the tax collectors of those lands, now have gone into private business, one in Alexandrapol, another to Iktir and the third, the devil knows where, perhaps to his own place. In their absence we can profit. If we set the auction for now, it is very simple. The tax will remain charged to Mr. Satarlian, who will take it in his own name, necessarily, but we will be his secret partners."

"But as far as I know, Mr. Satarlian has not sufficient ready money to be able to show the correct amount."

"I know that, but that will not upset the transaction. We will give the

225

pledge and he will present it as his."

"Have you any ready money?"

"I have interest-bearing notes."

"It is all the same. Therefore, we will raise the question of the auction at the next meeting. But I am afraid that 'the superiors' will interfere."

"They are not able. Have they not done the same thing themselves that we are thinking of doing? If the 'little devil' puts in his finger, I will speak a word in his ear, and he will shut up."

Thus some in the brotherhood were talking about intrigues they practiced, others talked of their secret speculations, but none gave a thought to what was occurring around them. None thought about the people of Alashgerd, who having lost their homes, left friendless and uncared for, were dying off like flies. No one was interested in the question as to what had been the reason for the emigration of these poor creatures, or what their fate would be in a foreign land.

Several monks, seated together, according to their daily custom, were drinking tea as they sat on fine Persian rugs. The young novices a little distance from them were gambling together and laughing and jesting as they made elaborate preparations for tea. There was cream, butter, white bread, rum and everything else.

The cool of the evening and the pure air of the forest whetted the appetites of the holy fathers. They drank, they ate, they made merry without reflecting that under the trees of the same forest, by the damp riverside, hundreds of hungry families were huddled.

"This is fine rum. What a rich aroma it has. Where did you get it, Holy Father?" asked one of the monks tasting the cup of tea mixed with rum, with great enjoyment.

"Where did I get it?" repeated the holy father from whose cell had been brought the fragrant drink. "Don't you know that my cell is one of those shrines where gifts come on their own feet?" (There is a legend that wild beasts come voluntarily to the door of half ruined shrines in desert places, and the shepherds catch them and offer them as sacrifices.)

"I understand. It is fine to have such powers of attraction."

The sun had already set. The mist was growing heavier in the forest,

226

although the gilded clouds were still brilliant with the last rays of the sun. "The Illuminator's wind" had grown gentler, and the leaves of the trees hardly stirred. The deep silence of the forest was occasionally broken by mournful cries.

Night drew near. In the darkness, bitter enemies, awaken more easily. In the open air, lying on the ground, the naked, hungry people of Alashgerd, like a man startled by a frightful dream had only just begun to realize the misery of their condition. They had thought that they were rich, but now they were forced to live by begging. They had thought that they had houses and homes but now they lived under the open sky. They had thought that they had children, but now they were gone. Who took them? What has become of them? No one knows. All were lost in a confused and frightful disturbance when mother forgot son, when brother forgot sister, when husband forgot wife, when every person driven by the sword of the Turk and by fire, tried only to save himself. Everyone had incurable wounds in his heart, each had lost something which to him was the dearest thing in the world and which could not be replaced. This was the reason why all Vagharshabad echoed with the cries of the emigrants tonight. They were mourning and they could not be comforted.

At this time, a tall handsome young man passing among the trees of the forest, looked at the emigrants with attention, approached and spoke with them, and then resumed his journey. The sad distressed looks of this young man, the burning look of his face, his fearless and confident movements, drew one's attention to him in spite of oneself. He came out of the forest, passed the Vank of K... and stood near the cemetery. Labor had not ceased here yet — they still were burying the dead.

The sound of singing reached his ears.

"The nightingale is wearing shoes upon its feet He seeks the rose — his love, so sweet."

"Curse you," said the young man to himself as he continued his way. The sound of singing came from the depths of the forest where now the monks, after their enlivenment by reason of the rum, performed their nightly pilgrimages. The unknown young man approached the lake. Here also several monks were still enjoying themselves, looking like black specters. But one was seated alone, as if he was mourning alone, as though he found comfort in that position, where no one asked him anything and no one touched his wounded heart. Sun-burned, his dusky face and ragged clothing indicated that this monk must be a stranger. The brethren of the Vank, in their neat rich robes, did not come near him as though they feared they would be polluted by his garments although in that plain dress of a shepherd was concealed a body which bore within it noble traits.

227

The unknown young man, observed the strange monk in the obscurity, approaching him. "Ah, Holy Father John, is it you?"

"Ah, Vartan," cried the monk, embracing him.

The monk, John, was the head of the Vank of St. John and at the same time the bishop of Alashgerd, who had come with the emigrants to Russia, not wishing to be separated from his flock.

Vartan and the Bishop sat upon a stone which served as a seat beside the lake.

"When did you arrive?" inquired the Bishop.

"Today, this very hour," replied Vartan looking about him lest they should be overheard.

"Have you seen no one?"

"No one yet. Whom is it possible to find in all that crowd? I wished to see Melik-Mansoor especially. I bear that he also was among the emigrants."

"I saw him two days ago." replied the Bishop. "He must be in Erivan by now. I think he was obliged to see some men there who are planning to form a committee to look after the condition of the emigrants."

"There has been a committee formed at Tiflis, already. That at Erivan must be a branch of it."

"How are affairs here?"

"Very bad," replied the Bishop, mournfully. "I have been here a week. They have given me a corner in Ghazarabad. No one pays me any attention; no one has cared to inquire what circumstances brought us here. They promised to conduct me to the reception room of the Catholicos and question me there, but unfortunately I have passed these days in inaction. I was obliged to present the story of the unfortunate people in writing, and I hoped that after that they would call me and demand oral explanations. That attempt also bore no fruit. Is it possible to be so indifferent and so cruel? I observed how of 3,000 families, 1,500 have died, some of sickness, some of hunger. The remainder will die likewise if their condition continues like this."

Sad as these last statements were still they did not make a marked impression upon Vartan. He considered it only natural. He knew already

228

the loss entailed by such emigrations.

"Are all the emigrants located here at Vagharshabad?"

"No, they came from Iktir to Vagharshabad and they have scattered in all directions from here. Now, beginning with the province of Sourmali, the emigrants are scattered as far as New-Bayazid, and to Old-Nakhitchevan. You will find them everywhere in every village."

"How do the people of the place behave toward these emigrants?"

"The people have been very kind. They have given shelter, food and clothing and have not spared whatever they might give in aid. We must say that the people here are themselves in great poverty. Everything is expensive because of the war. But the emigrants need the aid of physicians especially, rather than bread. Many sicknesses have been destroying them mercilessly."

The shades of night had by this time entirely obscured the region around the Vank. The monks had retired to their cells. But the sound of singing was heard once more. "The nightingale, etc.."

"Where are you going now?" asked the Bishop of Vartan, rising.

"I don't know myself."

"Come with me."

"I did not wish to be seen here."

'No one will recognize you at the Vank now."

Chapter 39

The lodging of Holy Father John was situated in the upper story of Ghazarabad. Vartan felt cold chills run over him when he crossed the threshold of the Vank again. It was more than ten years since he had gone away from here. Now mournful circumstances had brought him here once more. Why did this monastery, separated from the world and this community, sworn to devote their lives to prayer and a hermit-life, produce such an unpleasant impression upon the young man?

He remembered his youth — that youth filled with folly and evil, which he had passed here. He remembered that dark past which now filled him with disgust and horror.

Holy Father John did not fail to notice Vartan's unwillingness and agitation, and he asked sympathetically, "What is it? Why are you so silent?"

"Nothing, sometimes I am subject to such agitation."

There was a small cot in the room where the father and his guest seated themselves. On the other side stood a common wooden table on which a candle burned and near it a small samovar with boiling water. The father prepared two cups of tea with his own hands. He gave one to Vartan and began to drink the other himself. The hot drink invigorated the young man's excited nerves. For a long time an irksome silence reigned. Conversation was not resumed until it turned to the object so near the heart of each.

"How do they regard the 'work' here?" asked Vartan.

"A short story will enable you to understand," replied the father. "A Vartabed Preceptor from Turkey had come here to be ordained Bishop. He is still here, you may possibly meet him. At first, when he had just come,

230

when speaking of the Armenians in Turkey, he pictured their condition in the most terrible colors. He told of the cruelties and barbarities of the Kurds; thousand and one proofs of the crimes perpetrated in Armenia. It was impossible not to believe him, for all that he said was verified by incontrovertible proofs. But since that man was interviewed by the superiors he has changed his tune. Since then he has begun to praise the humanity of the Turks, to defend their justice and to admire their magnanimity and nobility.

"What could the poor fellow do? If he had not changed his tune, if he had not justified them contrary to his convictions, although it was horrible and hateful to him, perhaps he would not have received the coveted Bishopric. Another example also: Another preceptor from Turkey, whose Vank was spoiled by Kurds, came here to beg for protection. This poor fellow related the story of his people's misery in still more moving terms, what sufferings they endured from the Government and the Kurdish outlaw chieftains. When his words reached the authorities, they not only paid no attention to the Vartabed's request for which he had come, but they ordered him driven out of the Vank. The wretch was obliged to change his tune and after that he was received with honor. He forgot his Vank, he forgot his flock and did not mention the oppression caused by the Kurds."

"I will add this. This Vartabed, in order to please them still more, drank to the health of the Sultan on a feast day, just at the time when the Turks were massacring the Armenians in Bayazid and Alashgerd. After all this, I think it is very clear how the 'work' is regarded here."

Vartan could not believe his ears. It seemed to him that he was dreaming this. He could not imagine such a degree of cruelty which amounted to a terrible conspiracy. In the critical crises of a nation when its life and its future hang on a thread which might break and cast it into an everlasting abyss — at such a crucial moment when the eyes of an entire people were turned toward the Ararat of salvation, it, the nation, met the indifference of its clergy and found them inclined toward their enemies and their murderers!

"Are all of the same mind?" asked Vartan much disturbed.

"No, only the superiors, they see everything as being just and right in the Turkish Government; and if Armenians have protested or evinced discontent that is all a lie and a slander."

"It is easy to understand. They are a kind of Thomas Effendi. The irregularities of the Turks are very profitable for Thomas Effendis. But let them at least consider the example of Nerses the Patriarch, the Khrimians and others — whoever wishes to leave an honorable name in Armenian

231

history."

"You speak very childishly, friend," replied the Father. "I assure you, if they could they would destroy all the works of Nerses today, and perhaps they have tried to do so. Here they have tried to have it believed that Nerses and his satellites are all charlatans, that they have deceived the people, that they have not considered the welfare of the Armenians, that they are the despicable tools of various European governments, who have worked for their personal profits, in order to load more sins on the neck of poor Turkey. Here they laugh about the fickle-mindedness of Nerses. Here they say that it would be wrong for the Armenians to demand what they need, and they are not worthy of more. If anything is lacking, they say, the Turk is so kind that he will kindly grant it, so what need is there of wearying the merciful Government?"

"Is the whole brotherhood of this opinion?" asked Vartan angrily.

The father did not answer immediately. He went out of the room, looked out into the dark, and returning to his seat said in a lowered voice, "We have been speaking too carelessly. Here the walls have ears. The head of the Vank occupies the next room and he has a scent as keen as the Devil's. If he heard anything, he will tell it tomorrow."

"I asked the position taken generally by the brotherhood," said Vartan without paying any attention to the father's last remarks.

"The Superiors are the only exception. Aside from them the whole brotherhood is not Turkophile. There are men among them of noble desires and perhaps they would be able to sacrifice everything to wipe the tears from the eyes of the Armenians in Turkey if — 'If the Superiors would permit'."

"Yes, what can the poor things do? They are bound so fast that they are not even allowed to speak, much less to act. There is one here named Mangooni, an actual monster who crushes and throttles all by his oppressive measures."

"Still I can not understand such infernal policy, which sees an entire people crushed under the oppression of Turkey to the point of annihilation, and still defends the destroyer."

"It is a puzzle to me also, neither can I understand it," replied the Father, at his wit's end.

"But how do they explain the emigration of the people from Alashgerd or the destruction of the Armenians at Bayazid? How do they explain the conflagration at Van?"

"They always have a set of phrases ready at the ends of their tongues with which to defend the Turks. They cast the blame on the Armenians saying that the Armenians are a restless, discontented and ungrateful people. They say, 'the wolf is not to blame when the lamb angers him'. And in the emigration from Alashgerd, they see not the sword of the Turk and Kurd that forced an entire people to leave its fatherland, but they try to show a secret and powerful hand which drew the wretched people away from their fatherland. How wrong this is you must understand better than anyone, Vartan, You, who have been engaged in the 'work' ever since the beginning."

"After all this, it is incomprehensible to me what hopes keep you here, Father. Tell me I beg, what protection or what help can be found from them?"

"None, I myself am persuaded that there is none. But what can I do, to whom can I appeal? Where can I go? I am puzzled."

"Appeal to the common people."

The Father made no reply, and after a momentary reflection, be said, as though speaking to himself: "It is hard to make it all clear now, but a day will come when time will reveal the shameful facts." It was as though these words sprang from the heart of the unfortunate monk like a gush of blood. He was so discouraged, so indignant, that he was unable to restrain himself ' and what need was there of concealment with Vartan. Vartan was no stranger to him. He had worked with Vartan. He had shared many confidences with Vartan.

The conversation turned once more to the emigrants. The Bishop of the Alashgerd people told of the wretchedness of the exiled people. He depicted the sufferings they bore. He proposed means for preserving them from entire destruction and annihilation.

"It is astonishing to me that there is such an immense number of sick among the emigrants," interrupted the guest. "According to that estimate more than half are sick. How did that happen?"

"If you were to hear the frightful details of the emigrants, you would be astonished that the emigrants have been able to live until the present. That is the miracle — an actual miracle. But I have not power sufficient nor a tongue able to relate it all to you. I will give you only a few special instances.

233

"After the siege of Bayazid, the details of which you know, General Lord Lucasoff was forced to withdraw the Russian Army. In that interval, he performed two great acts of gallantry. On the one hand he was obliged to fight the immense Turkish Army with his small number of troops. On the other hand it was necessary to rescue the inhabitants of the province of Alashgerd and Bayazid from the slaughter of the Turks. Both of these required great military strategy in which the General exhibited his skill. He was able to stem the frightful tide of the Turkish troops long enough to enable the Armenians to emigrate before their arrival.

"But the time was very short and the people totally unprepared to emigrate. Word was given suddenly that the Russian Army must leave the country, 'Emigrants flee from the country — if you remain, the Turks will massacre you'. That news traveled like lightning through all the provinces. Terror and confusion reigned. The enemy stood at their doors. It was impossible to vacillate or delay. It was necessary to leave their loved fatherland. It is hard for me to depict that frightful sight, when the people were torn from their own firesides. Frightful confusion and disorder reigned over the crowds. They were obliged to emigrate in the night.

"Most of the cattle remained in the fields. The men did not have time to bring them along. Father did not wait for son, absent from home. Brother forgot brother. The household utensils and furniture were left in their places or set fire to by their owners. Mothers took their children on their backs while the fathers, loaded with a few necessary articles, took their sons by the hand and set out. Very few families had carts, for the carts had been taken to transport the provisions of war. There was no time to wait, for the enemy was upon their heels. Those who were left were sacrificed to the barbarities of the Turks. Those who came away, thought they escaped, but here they met new difficulties more cruel than the Kurds or Turks, famine and sickness. And these sicknesses are the result of the privations which the people endured in their emigration. They had to travel a distance requiring some weeks, in a few days, without resting or stopping.

"Women, girls, children, old and young, all came afoot. Very few had beasts to ride. Many fainted, weakened, and remained by the wayside. Who paid attention to relative, friend, or even beloved child? General confusion reigned. Every man had lost heart and feeling. Add to this hunger, thirst, the climate of a new country, and you find sickness very natural. In order not to meet the enemy, they led us over infernal roads that were very difficult for the women and children. And this is the reason why a quarter of the emigrants remained on the way and were lost. In short, the story of the Armenian slaves carried off by Shah Abas to Ispahan, which is depicted in such horrid colors in our literature, must be reckoned a very ordinary affair compared with this emigration."

During this sad narrative, Vartan's mind was occupied with an entirely

234

different subject — he scarcely heard him. He was thinking of his beloved Lila. She should certainly be among those emigrants and she also must have been exposed to the same trials. Although Chavo had told him that Lila had been taken to Russian territory by means of the servants of Koorsit, the wife of the Kurdish Bey, her servants were not able to cross the Russian boundary, for they were Kurds and subjects of a hostile country. So they must have left Lila and Sara, her brother's wife, among the emigrants. But how could he find them? Were they alive? These questions began to torment the young man.

"Father, do you know anything about the family of old man Khacho?" he asked. "I think they must also have been among the emigrants. Where can they be found?"

"It will be rather hard for you to find them for the emigrants are scattered in various places. But their priests and landlords have come with them. I have commissioned the latter to prepare a census of their people, how many, and where they live, in order to be able to care for and relieve them. It will be easy to find from those lists in which group the family of old Khacho is found."

"When will they present the lists?"

"Perhaps tomorrow or the next day. I do not know exactly."

That "tomorrow or the next day" seemed an eternity to poor Vartan. For this reason he passed the night in insupportable agony.

235

Chapter 40

The sweet chimes of the Vank bell made known it was morning. The monks who were well off slept still in their comfortable rooms, but the more unfortunate monks hastened to the house of God to pray.

Father John awakened very early this morning and leaving Vartan asleep, he left his lodging and went out. He did not go to pray, but he was accustomed to visit the emigrants in Vagharshabad every morning to see what their condition was. This morning the wretchedness he saw was so heartbreaking that he had not the strength left to visit the remainder of the unfortunates. Everywhere he observed frightful scenes. Whole families sick, uncared for, living in dirty stables, not even one was well enough to care for the others.

In mournful despair, he returned toward the Vank, and he had determined by some means to penetrate the court and beg for speedy aid for the poor people so nearly dead. Just then a carriage passed him. The occupant, seeing the monk, ordered it to stop.

"Good news," he said approaching. "The Government of Erivan has appointed a committee to help the emigrants. Reliable persons were chosen. From Tiflis also the same good news has been received. The committee there has been very zealous. They promise to send money and physicians soon and remedies."

"That is cause for rejoicing," replied the monk.

"Here also they are thinking of writing orders to the leaders in spiritual affairs to collect offerings."

"Where will they be written?"

The monk pointed toward the Vank. The young man began to laugh. "That

236

can have no significance. What they collect will not feed the Alashgerd people." The newcomer was Melik-Mansoor.

"You made me happy with the news you brought," said the monk, "and I will make you happy in return."

"How?"

"Vartan is here, in my room."

"Really? Where has that devil come from now? I did not believe that people came back from the other world. Let us go."

They went together toward the Vank. On the way, Melik-Mansoor asked the monk, "Do you know Vartan well?"

"It is more than five years since I became acquainted with him. In our parts he is known as a fearless contrabandist, but for a long time I could not understand that his profession was not one engaged in for personal profit. He transported arms and often gave them freely to the villagers, and if he occasionally brought goods, it was only to cover the track of his actual merchandise. His motive was good, but unfortunate circumstances rendered them futile."

"I was able to meet him only a few times," replied Melik-Mansoor, "but till now I never met a man who won my sympathy so greatly as this zealous youth. I saw how brave and cruel he was in bloody work, and yet kind and faithful in friendship."

"Besides this, Vartan is remarkable for his astuteness. He has accomplished much in his life, as much as some would accomplish in a hundred years. Only he is very honest and always tries to minimize his achievements as nothing remarkable."

Vartan, upon awakening in the morning, found himself alone in the Father's room. The rays of the sun shone in through the narrow window of the cell, and lighted it up most brilliantly. But the heated air was suffocating. 'He stepped near one of the windows and opened it. A refreshing current of fresh, breezy air struck his heated f ace. But something seemed still to weigh upon him. He waited a short time for his host to return, but he delayed. Now Vartan became impatient. He stepped out to breathe a little fresh air, and as he did not wish to be seen or recognized by any at the Vank, he left by the back gate which led toward the lake. Then he found an old bishop whom he recognized immediately. He was one of the noted antiquities of the Vank.

237

"Good-day, Father." The entire brotherhood called him Babi. Babi was sitting in the hot sunlight warming his frozen limbs. He resembled the Hindu fakirs, who do not bathe, nor comb themselves, nor cut their fingernails, nor wear decent clothing, for they think those things sinful.

Hearing the voice of the young man, he placed his hand on his forehead to shield his eyes from the sun, and looking up, said, "I recognize your voice, but my eyes do not see well. Who are you, my son?"

"I am Vartan."

"Well, well, my son. Come, let me embrace you. How you have grown, my son!"

Vartan allowed himself to be embraced.

"Sit down son, here, beside me. There, that is fine. What a fine fellow you have become, son! Do you remember how you slipped into my cell like a cat and stole fruit? Then you were small, very small."

"Do you remember, Father," replied Vartan grinning, "that it was here I learned to steal?"

"Who hasn't stolen? They all steal now. Righteousness is as scarce as the milk of swallows; you can find it nowhere. Only two days ago, some cursed fellows stole several hundred rubles from my cell. I had kept it for my soul's salvation. How did they find it? I don't understand it. The devil couldn't have found it. I had put it behind the boards of the ceiling. The devils will have to take lessons from them. Ah, the accursed ones!"

It was such a common occurrence to have money stolen from Babi's cell that Vartan was not much interested. This man, nearly a hundred years old, never spent anything and would only collect and save whatever came into his hands. When his savings mounted up to the hundreds or thousands, suddenly some invisible hand would snatch it all away, and carry it off. But lately the frequent stealing had made Babi quite artful. He had hundreds of biding places in his room, and he kept a part of his money in each, so it never happened that he lost all his hoard at once, although he always used to swear that he had lost all.

Babi was a typical miser, and Vartan had known him from boyhood and his miserliness had attained legendary proportions in the brotherhood. Babi was considered one of the rich monks only with this difference, that others bad accumulated their wealth by shady means, but he only by great self-denial.

238

"You love money too much, Babi. What are you going to do with so much?"

"What my son! 'There is a fox which swallowed a camel but the wolf is blamed for it'. Now who doesn't love money? This is a money market and all work for money." With his trembling hand he drew his snuffbox from his bosom, opened it and saw that it was empty. He may have opened it a hundred times that day, only to find each time that it was empty, but still he could not believe his eyes, and seemed to think that it might have been filled by some miracle.

"Curse that preceptor Simon! Do you know him? I gave him 20 kopecks and gave him my tin box to go and get me some snuff from the city. He went and kept both the money and the box. Haven't you some snuff, Vartan?"

"I don't use it, Babi."

A cigarette butt had been dropped not far from where Babi sat. He pounced upon it and tearing off the paper covering he crushed the burnt tobacco in his palm with his trembling fingers and inhaled the acrid powder into his nostrils.

"Is that the way they treat you Babi, so that you don't get even money enough for snuff ?"

"Ah, my son. The world has changed. Where are the days of His Beatitude Nerses? Then there was love, then there was brotherhood, then there were great and small. But now everything is topsy-turvy. Whoever can lie the best, whoever can cheat well, he gets ahead. Who cares for fools like me? Now we have new hens which lay iron eggs."

Babi was one of the most ardent worshippers of Nerses. The name of that Catholicos, worthy of everlasting remembrance, was sacred to him. When he saw corruption on every side, when his head was sore, be used always to speak of the times of Nerses which were to him the Golden Age of Echmiadzin.

Babi mentioned the Golden Age now with special satisfaction. He showed the beautiful lake, and explained for what object that great man had caused the lake to be made. He pointed to a ruin near the lake which was intended for a paper factory so that the monastery need not bring paper from abroad, but now the peasants who worked for the Vank tied their donkeys there.

He pointed to other ruins across the lake, which were to have been silk factories for which the Catholicos had caused an immense portion of the

239

forest planted, which consisted of mulberry trees. When he mentioned the forest, he was unable to restrain his tears, and he told Vartan that the Catholicos loved this forest as much, as a father loves his children. When he went to the forest, he always carried a small pruning knife and he would cut away the superfluous branches of the trees with his own hands. He knew each tree and knew how much each grew during the year, and he would rejoice over their growth as a father rejoices over the growth of his children.

Vartan, observing that the story was going to be very tedious, wished to leave him.

"Bring your head near me, Vartan", said Babi.

Vartan drew near and heard the following words, "Go away from here quickly son. They look with suspicion at you here."

"No one here has seen me yet, Babi."

"It is sufficient that one has seen you. I heard bad things about you."

"Your ears don't hear very well, Babi. How did you hear?"

"It is only when the conversation doesn't concern him that Babi's ears don't hear well, but he hears the important things easily."

Vartan laughed and left him. Babi called after him. "Listen, Vartan, if you go to the city, don't forget to send me a little snuff. Didn't you see that my box is empty?"

Just then Melik-Mansoor and Father John appeared.

"What were you talking about with this Babi," asked the latter.

"He is the only decent man here," replied Vartan and turning to Melik-Mansoor, he said "I should like to speak with you alone. Are you acquainted with any families here?"

"I am."

Vartan was not alarmed by Babi's words, but he tried generally to keep aloof from monasteries. Besides this he was uneasy about Lila. He must go to her. He must learn something about her. He begged Father John to inform him when he obtained any news whatsoever through the priests.

"I received word that the priests will bring their lists today, by noon", said the father. "I will inform you then."

"Do you know our place?" asked Melik-Mansoor.

"I do."

"Then let us go, Vartan."

Just then a small group appeared upon the plain, moving slowly toward the graveyard. A few Alashgerd people were carrying a bier. There was no priest for they would find a priest already on the grounds. He did not leave the spot, knowing that more biers might be coming at any moment. A woman supported by two other women, followed the bier. She did not weep, and there were no tears in her dry eyes. She was in a terrible state of confusion, which is peculiar to that state of mind when all feelings are overwhelmed by a heavy and unexpected blow. It seemed that this woman must be a near relative of the deceased. None of the Vank people had accompanied the bier except a well known physician, who stood out prominently in that half-naked group.

Vartan and Melik-Mansoor saw this sad procession from a distance, but paid no attention to it, and passed on. And who would pay any attention to it? Every day, every moment, such scenes were repeated and they had become mere every day occurrences.

Chapter 41

Vartan, upon seeing Melik-Mansoor, seemed temporarily to forget his sorrow which so wore his spirit. Besides this, the hope given by Father John of learning the whereabouts of old Khacho's family through the priests and landowners who came with the emigrants, that joyful hope, gave him great tranquility. He thought that that information would enable him to find Lila and that his love would lighten the sufferings of her exile.

The house where Melik-Mansoor took him was situated in one of the old streets of the Vank. Although the buildings were small and poor, still like most of the houses of Vagharshabad they had large courts shaded by fruit trees.

"You will not be much pleased," said Melik-Mansoor, "to know where I am taking you."

"It is all the same to me," said Vartan carelessly. "I only desire to gain a little information about Salman. There will be no one to disturb us there, I hope."

"No one."

They knocked at a small door and a woman opened it. They entered and the gate closed after them.

"Well Nani, I have brought you a new guest", said Melik-Mansoor.

The old woman, giving Vartan a shy glance, replied, "Upon my eyes!"

"Now quickly, Nani, a bottle of wine for us, for we are very thirsty," said Melik-Mansoor. And approaching the woman he added, "I will kill you if you let in any other person."

The old woman shook her head mysteriously and turned away. The two young men entered a small but neat room which was furnished in semi-European and semi-Asiatic taste, and they seated themselves opposite each other, beside a small table. After a few moments a young woman entered the room with noiseless steps and placed a bottle of wine upon the table with two glasses. Then she retired. The Armenian headdress upon her head completely concealed her face with the exception of two black eyes under arched brows. But the little that appeared was sufficient to give one an idea of her beauty.

Melik-Mansoor, filling the glasses, drank one himself and, giving the other to Vartan said, "I am glad that our Vanks are usually built far from the habitation of men, among mountain villages or in wildernesses. There are not so many rascals and villains anywhere else as there are in Vagharshabad. Nowhere are there so many loose women as there are here. See this fair woman who entered in so modest and bashful a manner, and immediately retired. She is the mistress of a monk. The Vank, I thought, would at least preserve religious zeal, but here men believe nothing. The conduct of the monks has occasioned scandal and lack of faith in the people. Protestantism has already begun to rise up here. Passing through the streets, you necessarily saw some fine houses. If you were to inquire who are their owners, you would learn that they belong, usually, to some near or distant relative of monks who were formerly poor, but who have become rich, thanks to the Vank.

"To tell the truth, I cannot bear it, when I see hundreds of thousands spent here when every kopeck is so needed by us. We have a thousand and one needs, and we need money for them all. The national treasury in Constantinople is empty. The Patriarch hasn't money to pay his necessary expenses. But he is not burdened with business, which if delayed, will be a great loss to the nation.

"Notwithstanding, I do not observe in the Patriarch at Constantinople or in the Armenians of the Northern See, a glimmer of hope. Mangooni lost 25,000 in the stock market and, as I have heard, 30,000 have been sent lately, the devil only knows for what infernal purpose. But the Armenian Patriarch, our one active representative, has no funds."

"This wine seems rather sour," interrupted Vartan.

"Didn't you hear me?" asked Melik-Mansoor in a grieved tone.

"I heard — the Patriarch has no funds."

"It isn't right to speak like that."

"To speak how? I only know this, that whatever nation places all its hopes on the clergy, the beginning of that people's destruction is near."

The young woman entered once more, approached the table noiselessly and placed upon it the breakfast, arranged on a tray. This time the veil over her face, which at first showed only her eyes and her eyebrows, was now drawn back considerably and her rose-red lips showed also.

"Another bottle of wine for us also," said Melik-Mansoor, "but not like this."

The woman retired as silently as before.

"I am surprised at your selecting such a lodging place yourself," said Vartan.

"If you wish to know a monk well, make friends with his sweetheart," replied Melik-Mansoor, laughing. "Besides this, a group gathers here every evening which furnishes me with considerably interesting news.

"Chiefly about the Vank, of course?" asked Vartan sneering. "But let us leave the Vank temporarily and speak of our work. I wished to learn from you the fate of Mr. Salman, and what events took place in my absence. I know nothing yet, although Father John gave me much information, but what I wanted to know, he, himself did not know."

Gloom seemed to cross Melik-Mansoor's jovial face, and his purple lips began to tremble when he suddenly remembered the sad past, which he had forgotten for a time. He raised his full glass and drank it off.

"I will tell you," he said in an agitated tone. "You must know all, although it will not give you any pleasure. The night Mr. Salman was imprisoned, I learned of it the following morning. The traitor had so concealed his plans, that not even the owner of the house (where he lodged that night) knew anything about it. One of the acquaintances of the young man, who had happened to see him taken away, informed me.

"My first concern was to collect a few horsemen of our intimates, and to fall upon the party. Perhaps we might have succeeded in saving him if we had met him on the road which we took. But they took him by another way, which we had not thought of. There were more than 20 mounted men with me who were ready for any kind of business. After long investigations, I was only able to find the town where the military vice-governor was then residing, to whom the poor young man had been taken. I learned that he had been hanged on his arrival there. I was unable to find the body of the unfortunate young man. With what barbarity they treated his corpse - only

244

wild beasts could equal them! That crime filled my heart with desire for vengeance and the blood of that innocent victim sealed the vow to which we are sworn.

"After Mr. Salman, as you know, old Khacho and his two sons Hairabed and Abo were imprisoned. They did not kill them immediately, but kept them in prison under strict surveillance. It seems that they had tried to get all the rich land owner's gold which he had hidden before killing him. But the poor creature was not able to endure the dreadful tortures long, and the three died in prison.

"After all this I learned what happened to the village of o.... and I went to Ismail Pasha to whom was entrusted the government of the soldiers of the region of Bayazid. He is quite an able man, and I believed that my visit would not be fruitless. I did not conceal from him the preparations which had been made by myself and my companions. I informed him that a large quantity of weapons had been distributed to the people. But I said that preparation was not made with the idea of revolt as he had wrongly been informed but for self-defense.

"I told him that the Mohammedan crowd at the time of that furious fanaticism which the spirit of Islam had worked in it, might cause them to massacre the entire Christian population if no means were furnished them for self-preservation. In regard to that necessity, I added, the Government itself should have taken precautions in advance, if it did not wish to have repeated here the sad events which had taken place in Bulgaria, which had placed the Government under heavy responsibilities. Therefore the Government should be much pleased that we have lightened its burdens, and have performed that which it was its duty to perform. We have furnished the Armenians with weapons in order to preserve them from the fanaticism of the Mohammedans."

"The wily Pasha expressed much sympathy, promised to use every means himself, not to have any harm come to the Armenians, promised to arrange for the protection of their lives and their property without delay. Just then the Russian soldiers were going back. And he heard that the Armenians wished to emigrate with the Russian Army. The Pasha commissioned me to persuade the people not to stir from their places. I agreed to it gladly.

"But after seeing me off, he gave secret orders to the Kurd, Fattah Bey, who headed a bloody incursion, set fire to the village of O...., burned it and massacred most of the inhabitants. This event struck horror into the whole province and caused the inhabitants to emigrate. The efforts of myself and my adherents were in vain to keep the terror-stricken people in their places. The example was before their eyes. After that, if they had heard that advice from an angel from heaven, they would not have believed that the fate of the village of o.... would not overtake the whole land.

"But the deceit of the wily Pasha persuaded me more firmly that the Turkish officials, directly or indirectly, intended to annihilate the Christian population and rid Armenia of Armenians. All the efforts of myself and my adherents were able to retain only a portion of the Armenians in their land — an insignificant portion. Then Ismail Pasha allowed the Turks to wreak their vengeance against the Armenians who had gone to the Russians and on the remaining Armenians. Thus the Kurds exercised all their cruelty, and terrible massacres began in various places.

"I still believe that if the people had not stirred from their place, they would have been protected. The regular Turkish soldiers, it is easy to understand, would not attack an obedient and peaceful people. The local Government would not have perpetrated such atrocious barbarity, especially as the region of Alashgerd and Bayazid was full of English agents and correspondents of European papers. The local Government would do that — whatever it did. That is, it incited the Kurds secretly against the Armenians and peeked between its fingers at the barbarities perpetrated. But it would not have been very difficult to be protected from the Kurds.

"A small but very significant event proves that my supposition is not wrong; I will tell it briefly. After the emigration, when the Russian Army had left Bayazid and the province of Alashgerd, i.e., when those places returned into the hands of the Turks, then, as I told you, the Kurds began to rob, massacre and torture the remaining Armenians. At that time a few hundred families left their homes and fortified themselves in the mountains.

"Now picture several thousand Kurds fighting for several weeks against those brave men who not only would not surrender but, making more successful attacks, were able to snatch rich booty from the enemy and military materiel also. My heart is filled with unbounded joy when I remember those never-to-be-forgotten days. Not only the young men fought, but the old men and the women. I am sure now a people which has inherited valor from its ancestors, will never submit to enslavement. Enslavement may crush and break the spirit of bravery temporarily, but can never destroy it. When fortune strikes the hour it walks again with its ancient strength, and with ever more power. I saw that with my own eyes. And the only cause for rejoicing which can comfort me, in these days of misery is this."

Vartan's gloomy face brightened a little and he raised his eyes as if in prayer, and praise to the Supreme Power.

"How did it end?" he asked.

"To defend ourselves long in inaccessible mountains, although difficult, was still possible if we had had only the Kurds to deal with. But soon the regular Army joined the Kurds against us. It was also possible to resist the latter. On our side we had an invincible power, the mountains of Armenia, which so nobly preserved their refugees. But there came lack of provisions and food, an enemy whom we were powerless to resist. Although some of us went down the mountain by night and attacked some of the neighboring Kurdish villages and brought back provisions that succeeded very seldom, because the Kurdish villages were deserted and people and cattle had gone to distant pastures.

"Naturally, our position was not tenable for a long period when not an Armenian village remained in our vicinity from which we might obtain assistance, or provisions, at least.

"But the enemy came steadily nearer. Then those of our party performed miracles of bravery. One night, breaking through the cordon of the enemy they passed through the immense camp of the enemy. Imagine, that there were not only fighting men who accomplished this bold feat, but they had with them whole families, wives, daughters and children."

"Then where did they go?" asked Vartan impatiently.

"They crossed the Turkish frontier into Persia. But they were obliged to contend with not a few difficulties on the way."

"Then you came here from Persia?"

"Yes from Persia."

"Now what do you intend to do here?" asked Vartan.

"My effort now will be this," replied Melik-Mansoor, "and I think you will agree with me," he said with a more animated look. "We must try to preserve the lives of the emigrants who came here that they may not be destroyed by famine and sickness. I believe that the Russians are collecting their forces and will again rule the land they have left. Then peace will reign there and then we must labor to get the people of Alashgerd and Bayazid to return to their fatherland. If not, it will be a great misfortune for Armenia if those two frontier provinces, Alashgerd and Bayazid are depopulated of Armenians and savage Kurds occupy their places."

"You think that these provinces will remain in the hands of the Russians?"

"What if after the war, when a treaty of peace is made those provinces again return to the Turk. Then I believe that under changed conditions these irregularities will not occur again. The beaten Turk will come to his senses. I have still another hope."

Just then the old woman entered and informed them that a priest wished to see them. Vartan, thinking that it might be one of the priests whom Father John had promised to send, told her to bring him in.

Then appeared Der Marook, the priest of the village of O.... .

Chapter 42

Breakfast was over and several bottles of wine had been emptied when the priest appeared. It was very hard for Vartan to be obliged to meet again this man who bad caused so much unpleasantness and concern to himself and his friend Salman in the village of O.... .But circumstances force one to be friends with one's enemy.

The priest's pitiable condition, his pale, worn appearance, and ragged clothing, caused him to look more like a beggar than like a minister of the temple of God. These wretched signs caused Vartan to forget his hostility. Besides this, he was the man from whose lips Vartan was to hear about the fate of the family in which he was so greatly interested.

"Did Father John send you?" asked Vartan addressing him and motioning him to a seat.

"Yes, Holy Father John," replied he and he settled himself before the small table on which a little wine still remained.

Vartan filled the glass and gave it to the priest who blessed him and drank it without delay. The spirit seemed to be a refreshing dew shed upon the verdure wilted by the beat. The priest's immobile features lightened a little. Melik-Mansoor noticed it and said, "Would you like to eat something?"

"I haven't eaten since last night," replied the priest, in such a mournful tone, that it was impossible not to pity him. He asked the woman to bring breakfast for him.

It was difficult for Vartan to start his inquiries. His condition was like that of an unfortunate man whose house was entered by robbers in his absence, and robbed of everything he possesses. Upon his return he finds his house stripped bare. But he had hidden his treasures in a certain place. He still hopes that the hand of the malefactors did not reach that spot. He approaches the secret store-room and his heart is in his mouth as he stands before the spot, but he does not open it and look in. At first, he is in terror. "What will I do if I find the safe empty?" Then he will be deprived of his last hope, his only comfort.

Vartan swayed and vacillated in an indecision like this. He still had hopes that he might find Lila and know his fate, and that good or ill depended on word from the lips of this priest. Had he the strength of heart to endure the priest's revelations? A fearful presentiment filled his soul and he was unable to ask anything although he so longed to make inquiry.

Melik-Mansoor did not know of Vartan's affection for Lila, neither was he acquainted with old Khacho's family, but observing his friend's uneasiness, he asked, "Did you wish to talk with the priest, perhaps I –"

"No, I have no secret from you," said Vartan and turning to the priest, "Father, did you present your list to Father John? I am also anxious to know whether there are any families from the village of o.... among the emigrants and where these live."

"Bless you, who are left of my flock, that I should prepare a list of them?" replied the priest in such a tone as he would use in speaking of barnyard fowl. "I can count on my fingers those who are left and where they wander now."

Vartan was seized with a fit of trembling, impossible to control. "Were they all massacred?" he asked blanching.

"If not all, still I may say not a man was left. What became of them, I don't know myself. God grant that no such scourge fall upon any Christian place such as fell upon O.... . It was for our sins doubtless. It seemed as though the fire and brimstone, like that which rained upon Sodom and Gomorra, fell upon and devoured everything. Those who escaped from the fire were either taken captives by the Kurds or massacred. All that occurred in one night. In the morning the entire village looked like a charred fireplace. I lost my fees. I lost my fees! There is no hope left of getting them. Thomas Effendi, may God enlighten your soul, promised to collect my fees, but the Evil One took him too. So I remained poor and needy. Do you see in what condition I am?" and he exhibited his tattered garments.

Tears began to flow from the poor priest's eyes and he sobbed bitterly. Did he remember his daughter-in-law, Zoulo and her angelic children who were also missing from among the emigrants? Did he bring to mind his son-in-law Simon and his wife who was his own daughter, who also disappeared in the general confusion? Was it the sufferings of the people which agonized the priest, whose shepherd he was, and whose loss he had

250

described with such indifference? Not one of these was the cause of the priest's sorrow! He only thought of his fees which he was to have received, but thought not of his flock! It was gone and the fees were lost. But Vartan knew nothing about these unfortunate fees which occasioned the priest so much concern, and so he paid it no particular attention.

He did not venture to continue his cross-questioning and he was relieved in a way that the priest had wandered from the main question, to talk of his fees. He drank the glass set before him trying to dissipate his sorrows in the dulling influence of wine. But the wine inflamed the agony of his burning heart still more, like oil which burned in the flames.

Melik-Mansoor rescued Vartan from his difficult position. He had heard much about the family of old Khacho. He had heard of the death of the head of that great family and of his two sons. But he knew nothing about the rest.

"Who has remained of that family?" he asked.

"No one," replied the priest icily. "The landlord and his two sons died in prison. You must know that. They massacred the others, and took the wives and daughter prisoner."

The priest, observing the young man's frightened face, now realized how careless his answer had been.

"Sara is here," he said, "with her two children and Lila."

Vartan's joy was inexpressible. Now he resembled a man who, after a frightful shipwreck, having been tossed about by the angry waves, has struggled against death and destiny. His strength is exhausted. He closes his eyes. He opens them in the abyss. Suddenly, he finds himself upon land. How did he reach there? He doesn't know. A violent upheaval of the billows tossed him there. "Lila is here? Sara is here? Then I will see them," exclaimed he, leaping to his feet. "Let us go, Father. You must know where they live. Let us go. You also, my friend," seizing Melik-Mansoor's hand.

The two young men went out with the priest. But Vartan's joy was short-lived. The priest did not know of the last misfortune which had occurred to those emigrants. If Vartan, that morning, after coming out of the Vank, had looked a little closer at that mournful procession which moved toward the cemetery, then the tragic truth would have been made clear to him. But destiny decreed that he should be punished still more severely, and that he should never see the girl he loved.

Sara and Lila had been ill when borne to the lodging which the kind head-doctor had prepared for them. The kind-hearted landlady to whose care the two patients were entrusted, treated them with great kindness. The more so when she learned that they belonged to a family in good circumstances until these calamitous events had brought them to dire distress.

Tormented in heart and mind, physically worn out, the girl was taken with a high fever the first night. The landlady informed the physician instantly, and he found her in a dangerous condition. He told the landlady, "There is no hope," and remaining by the patient the greater part of the night, tried to cause the sinking life to return. After midnight, she appeared somewhat easy, so the physician left her. She even spoke and told the landlady who sat near her, many things. But in the morning, when the physician came to see the patient, she was dead. Sara knew nothing of it although she lay in the same room. But when the sound of the carpenter's hammer was heard outside she understood what had happened. The poor woman was unable to shed a tear. Health is needed for tears. She seemed to rejoice, she seemed to have wished for just that; that Lila should die, that she might have rest, that she might be taken away from a world where no good days awaited her.

When the bier was borne out, she begged to be allowed to be present at the funeral. And disregarding the opposition of the head-doctor who told her that it would make her worse and cause her to lose the little strength she had, it was impossible to keep her back. That strange desire seemed to restore her wasted powers. She seemed to feel quite happy and had her wits about her. When they placed the bier in the grave, she said, "I wanted to be buried with you, my darling Lila." At that moment her eyes fell upon her two children and her voice was choked.

They bore Sara, entirely exhausted, home from the grave, and at the very moment when the physician was engaged in trying to restore her to consciousness, the knocker of the gate was heard. A servant opened the gate and saw two strange young men and a priest there.

"Whom do you wish?" inquired the servant.

"We heard that there are two people from Alashgerd here," said Vartan, "one a woman, the other a girl."

"Yes, they are here, but the girl -"

"What has become of her?"

"She died."

Vartan fell like a tree, struck by lightning, and fell into Melik-Mansoor's arms.

Chapter 43

It was a dark, cloudy night. The hot air of summer seemed to bear down upon man's heart with a heavy weight. Not a sound, not a whisper was heard in the stillness of the night. Only from one corner of the cemetery at the Vank was heard dull groans.

A young man had thrown himself down upon a fresh mound, and sobbed bitterly. Tears flowed in floods from his sad eyes and soaked the dry earth. By turns he would embrace the mound of earth and press his face against its damp surface. "Lila, unfortunate Lila," he would repeat over and over, and his heart, his very soul seemed to leave his body as he spoke these words and called this name.

It was Vartan. After long wanderings he had found only the grave of the girl he loved. What now remained for him? In the trials of life, struggling continually against difficulties and misfortunes, there was one bright and shining star on which he had fixed his gaze, which led him toward the haven of safety. But now that star also had set. Now, what else remained? There remained a wretched wounded heart in need of healing balm, one drop of which would cure all wounds. His loss was irreparable. Vartan had never loved before. The cold hard-hearted young man had experienced no tender feelings, but before Lila's love, like delicate candle light, the coarseness of his nature melted. Lila's love had transformed him. But where was that angel of comfort now? Under that mound of earth which he embraced, which he wet with his tears. And under that mound of earth was buried the heart of that young man.

He agonized there long, sunk in despair and regret, and found no comfort until a kind of stupor overcame him which was neither sleep nor consciousness. His hot head fell upon the grave, and his eyes closed.

In his imagination he now had confused and disturbing dreams. What did he see? Sometimes frightful scenes which filled him with consternation and terror; while at other times beautiful scenes enchanted him. Years seemed to have rolled forward several centuries, and he saw Armenia, the ruined and forsaken Armenia, now entirely transformed and renovated.

What a wonderful transformation had taken place! Had the Lost Paradise returned to earth? Had the Golden Age come once more when injustice and evil no longer polluted God's sin-free earth?

But no, it was not Eden that he saw, the Eden which Jehovah set down near the source of the four rivers of Armenia, where the first human beings dwelt in perfect innocence, possessed of no knowledge. It was not that Eden where man labored not and toiled not to raise food to eat, but lived on fruit, and was fed from the bounteous table of God, spread before him by lavish Nature.

It was a different Eden; an Eden which man had created for himself by his own industry, where in place of ignorance there was knowledge, and in place of the simple patriarchal life, there was advanced civilization. Now, at last, the meaning of the words "By the sweat of thy brow shalt thou eat thy bread," spoken by the Creator to the first human pair, was made plain, for now man not only worked, but he had made work easy and did not sweat over it to any great amount. He labored to become prosperous and his earnings were not snatched away by the hand of cruel oppressors.

Behold — Vartan saw a village! Was it possible this was the village of o.... in Alashgerd? The surroundings were familiar to him, the same mountains, hills, rivers and green embowered villages — all were the same. The passage of years had effaced nothing there. Those miserable huts, dug in the earth, which resembled the dens of wild beasts more than dwellings of men, were no longer to be seen. Now the houses were of stone, white as snow and surrounded by beautiful gardens. The wide, straight streets were shaded by trees near which flowed a crystal stream.

It was morning. Children were coming out of their homes in groups, happy and well clad. Boys and girls together, with their books hung over their shoulders, hastened to school. Vartan looked at them in astonishment. How well-cared for were those lovely children, how happy they were! School and teacher did not frighten them, it seemed. Was it possible that these were those half-naked, sickly children whom Vartan had seen before?

Vartan was standing alone in the street, looking around him in astonishment not knowing which way to go. A sweet sound reached his ears; the sound of the church-bell. The morning service had begun. From the day he left the monastery and fled from the brotherhood of Monks this was the first time that sound which called to the house of God, had sounded so sweet to his ears. His hardened heart was softened. He turned towards the church on whose threshold he had not set foot for ten years.

255

He was amazed. What a simple, unpretentious church! No platform, no altar, no decorations, no gilded pictures. It had none of the tawdry splendor of the Armenian church. No readers, deacons or choristers appeared. He saw only two pictures there, one of Jesus Christ, the other of Gregory the Illuminator, each in a plain dark frame.

The people were seated on long benches, men and women together, each holding a small hymnal. The priest stood at a pulpit with the Bible before him and read a sermon. His dress did not differ from that of ordinary people. His sermon was so simple, so clear that Vartan understood the whole of it. The word of God flowed from his lips like a stream gushing from a pure and living fountain. He explained the meaning of that scripture, "By the sweat of thy brow thou shalt eat bread." Vartan was astonished at the explanation given by the priest. Until that day Vartan had understood it to mean that it was a curse which God set upon the brow of the first human pair which embraced all their seed. But now he understood that it was counsel rather, which if followed, rescued man from idleness and preserved him in industrious independence.

The sermon ended. A common villager stood up in the midst and prayed an extemporary prayer having the same thought as the sermon. He begged God to grant them health, wisdom and strength, that they might be able to work to cultivate the earth He had created, which produces boundless blessings.

"What a prayer that is?" thought Vartan. "What seekers after gain these men are! They ask for nothing for the soul. Do they expect nothing on the other side of the grave and so ask only for what is needed by the body; what their temporal life demands?"

The prayer ended. The whole congregation, men and women, old and young, began to sing a hymn together. It was arranged like one of the Psalms of David.

"Again the same material purpose," thought Vartan. "Nothing spiritual. The laborer sings of the abundance of the earth which he cultivates with his hands, which God has granted to him. It is astonishing how these men have adapted the abstractions of religion to the demands of material life."

But what a beautiful hymn that was, accompanied by the sweet notes of the organ. How sweet! How wonderfully it rose from the lips of hundreds of persons in unison. It seemed to Vartan as if the voices of men mingled with the melody of the cherubim's, was borne up to the Eternal Throne. It was the first time in his life be had heard such holy music.

The service ended. The congregation began to come out of the church.

Now, at the pulpit where the priest had stood, stood the teacher, and on the seats where the parents had sat and prayed, now the children were ranged. Girls and boys mingled in classes, began to listen to the exposition of the teacher. "Is this a school?" thought Vartan. "Has the church joined with the school? Ah, what miserly people these are that they do not erect a separate building for a school!" Again their materialism!

But the face of the teacher looked familiar to Vartan. Was he not Der Marook? His features, height and even his voice were very like his. It was he indeed, the priest clad in civilian garments. Vartan could hardly believe his eyes. Was he the man who was such an enemy of schools, who had occasioned Mr. Salman so much anxiety and trouble, but now he himself conducted a regular school. Was he the same priest who had sold the sacraments of the church for money and was constantly thinking of his fees? This doubt assailed Vartan so fiercely that he was unable to restrain his curiosity and approaching, he asked, "Holy Father, what did you do about your fees?"

The priest, thinking the strange man must be a lunatic, looked at him very sternly and made no reply only to say that the bell would ring soon and the class would end. His class was in Natural History. This also astonished Vartan not a little. A priest, a theologian and a naturalist at the same time — that was strange indeed!

Vartan did not wait for the close of the lesson, and left the church or rather the school. He saw no graves there as was the custom in the yards surrounding Armenian churches. It was ornamented with rare trees and flowers. He stood for a long time admiring the beauty of the terrace, until one of the villagers, noticing that he was a stranger, invited him to his house for breakfast.

His house was one of those neat buildings which although small, contained ample comfort. It was out of sight hidden in a grove of trees. There were only a few rooms necessary to the various uses of life, all simple, neat and furnished in good taste.

The young daughter of the mistress, humming a tune, ran joyously to meet her father. Sadness, sorrow, the disappointments of life seemed never to have touched the heart of this beautiful creature. Without the modesty peculiar to Armenian women, she was not afraid nor did she hide from the stranger, but spoke with Vartan graciously, and laughed and talked as though he were an old friend. But how much she resembled Lila! The wonderful likeness filled Vartan with such ecstasy that he longed to embrace her and say, "At last, I have found thee."

The meal was already set on the table. The hostess filled cups of coffee for them, adding thick cream and set them before the guest and her husband, while the young girl laid the morning newspaper on the table, and with a complacent smile called their attention to an article.

"Oh, your article has been published, has it, Lila?" asked the father putting on his glasses and looking at the paper.

"Lila!" exclaimed Vartan with agitation he could not conceal.

"This name is very frequent in our family," the host replied.

Vartan was little relieved, but still be was unable to reconcile it with the thought that she was not Lila. If she was not Lila, it must be her heavenly body come to earth. Necessarily people are changed after their resurrection. They have different attitudes and character, while keeping their individual likenesses.

Both the beautiful girl and the peaceful atmosphere of the home charmed Vartan. At first he had thought that these people took no rest, day or night, that they worked incessantly. But now he saw that they had their homes for rest and pleasure also, and that they had their modest way of life — full of contentment.

"The happiness of village dwellers," said the host, "is not so much in constant and unremitting toil as in knowing how to work and the means of making it easy. There are many forces in nature which God has given to aid us, but we must become acquainted with them and in that way secure their aid."

"That is true," replied Vartan, "but if the Kurds had left the villagers their earnings, I think they would always have been successful and prosperous."

"What Kurds?" asked the host in astonishment.

"The Kurds who rob you every day."

"Ah, the Kurds," replied the host, as if recalling the name of a tribe long-since forgotten. "In the history of our Iron Age I have read much about the Kurds, it is true. They robbed and even massacred our ancestors. But where are those barbarians now? They have vanished, there are none left. Such a tribe was unable to exist in the light of civilization, and they disintegrated and their characteristics changed. At the beginning of the last century they accepted our religion, began to come to our schools, and mingling with us, disappeared as a separate race.

Vartan, when he heard these words, could not believe his ears. It seemed like a dream to him, and indeed he did see and dream all this.

The host continued, "In our family records there are many papers concerning the Kurds that seem to be written in blood. Our ancestor from which the families now living descended, was called Khacho. He was once the landlord of this village. He and two of his sons died in prison. His oldest son Hairabed left just one male child-"

"Who, at the time of the emigration of the people from Alashgerd was taken to Vagharshabad with his mother Sara," interrupted Vartan.

"Yes. From that child our race descended." To which Vartan added, "His name was Hovagim; he had a sister Nazloo. The latter died with her mother and the orphan Hovagim was brought up by a physician."

"Where did you read that?" asked the host astonished that the details of the history of their family were known to the guest.

"I did not read it but I saw it with my own eyes," replied Vartan. "All that occurred when the Kurds destroyed this village and the whole province of Alashgerd."

"But that was nearly two hundred years ago, while you seem quite a young man still. You are not so old as Methuselah are you, so that you should be able to see it with your own eyes," replied the host with a kindly smile.

Vartan could make no reply. It seemed to him also as though ages had passed since those events. From the windows of the room where Vartan was sitting surrounded by the joyous family of his host, appeared verdant valleys beyond which stood beautiful hills. The mountains were covered with dense forests and the branches of the great trees etched against the clear blue of the sky formed a wonderful, beautiful picture. The morning sun shed its beams upon it and with its light showed numerous streams like silver serpents, winding, shining, as they crossed the level meadows.

Vartan was unable to turn his eyes from this wonderful view. Wild, uncultivated nature by the industrious hands of man had received such a beautiful form, such as a piece of canvas does under the painter's brush.

"You spoke of the sad times when Turks and Kurds were found," continued the man in an animated tone, "but there have been many changes since then. You see that splendid mountain? A century and a half ago it was entirely bare. Not even a small bush remained upon its hillsides. In those days the bands of the barbarians destroyed the trees ruthlessly, as they did men. It was all gone. People used cow's dung for fuel. There was no wood

259

for buildings so they were obliged to live in caves dug in the earth. But when peace was restored the ruined villages were filled with multitudes of inhabitants, and our mountains were covered with forests.

"All this was planted by the industrious hands of village people. Do you see that verdant meadow? Formerly it was a dry plain. It had only a small stream which became entirely dry in the heat of summer. When the forests grew up our valley had an abundance of water. It is now one of the most fruitful and fertile spots in our land.

"Yes, many things have changed. Formerly there were no roads there, but now you see smooth roads, everywhere which join our land to others, and cars travel on them not drawn by animals but by steam. We sell the produce of our land a thousand miles from here; we obtain in exchange whatever we need."

Vartan heard all this in astonishment, but when his eye fell upon beautiful Lila it occurred to him to ask where she had studied.

"Just a week ago she was graduated from the Seminary at Nor Vagharshagerd, and now she is preparing to study medicine at the University. She is not very strong and I wished her, to spend a few months at home, but we cannot persuade her to give up the idea."

"And how many sons have you?"

"There are always large families in our race. The family of our ancestor, Khacho was composed of over fifty souls, but I have only five children. Lila is my only daughter, the other four are boys."

"What business do they engage in?"

"One is a forester in one of these forests you see, and one is a Professor in the University at Garin. The third is an officer in the regiment at Van while the fourth is a teacher in the village school, at New Pakrevantz."

Vartan was not familiar with the names, and he said, "I don't recollect any such town by that name."

"That is old Bayazid. It bears this name now. Many of our cities, towns and provinces have changed their names. A few have taken their former historical names, while others have taken new names." The host took up his newspaper again and read a paragraph which seemed to disturb him greatly.

Vartan asked with interest, "What news is there ?"

"Nothing in particular. Soon a general meeting of representatives is to assemble in our town. Certain disputed questions are to be considered. I don't know what will be the result. It appears that the party is much exercised over them.

"You will be there also?"

"I must not be absent."

It appeared from the conversation that Vartan's host was the chosen representative from that village. The meal was over. Vartan arose and after expressing his thanks, intended to depart.

"If you would like to see a few of the institutions of our town" said the host, "I will be pleased to conduct you to them."

"I thank you, sir," replied Vartan.

"If you should happen to pass through our town again, you will always find our doors open to receive you," said the lady of the house.

"I thank you, madam," replied Vartan with a bow.

"If being in our house does not bore you," added the beautiful girl with a pleasant smile.

"I thank you, miss," said Vartan, bowing lower still. After leaving the house Vartan began to realize his strained attitude toward this family. He felt as though he was a boor who disgraces himself in a more civilized community. And he thought, 'why have I remained ignorant and coarse and why am I not able to speak, act and behave like these people'? What a marvel this was. The descendants of Goodman Khacho during the passage of ages had been culled, purified and improved, and a new and nobler race had been created.

Vartan and his host walked together through the streets of the town. Women passed them wearing neat simple peasant costumes, each with her knitting in her hands, and their husbands in workmen's clothes. No one was idle. Each had his own occupation. Vartan was surprised to see how life had changed and what attractive forms it now presented. Their former plebeian coarseness did not appear any longer. Everywhere the spirit of education breathed its invigorating strength. One thing remained unchanged, that was the Armenian language.

But how polished, how refined was that language, and with what beautiful expressions it was embellished! Vartan and his host had now reached the outskirts of the town. On all sides, wherever Vartan looked, he saw rich fields, beautiful vineyards, well cultivated fields and luxuriant meadows.

They passed by a mill where logs were sawed. This mill supplied the surrounding cities with lumber of various lengths and thicknesses.

"To whom does this belong?" asked Vartan.

"To our town. Whatever mill or factory we have is not the property of any single individual," replied his host. They belong to the community. Each villager has a share in them. The logs are obtained from the neighboring forests, which also are the property of the townspeople." They passed beyond the saw-mill.

"Look at this immense structure," said his host to Vartan, "this is a cheese factory. The finest cheese in our province is manufactured here. This also belongs to the townspeople. Each villager keeps a record of the milk he brings and at the time of the division of the proceeds, he receives his proportion, either in cheese or in cash payment."

Now they were in the fields. The ripe grain had been gathered, but was harvested, not with the sickle or scythe, but with machinery, one machine did the work of a hundred men. This is what was meant by making labor easy. Vartan understood now.

They passed by another great building. It was a mill, here also labor was made easy, and instead of water, steam power was used. The wheat of many villages was ground here and the flour, as white as snow, was sent to foreign lands. This also belonged to the entire community. But one thing which surprised Vartan more was that whenever they met any of the village workmen, they had looked up at them boldly as though their equals in independence. They seemed to have been born and brought up in perfect freedom. They seemed never to have suffered the sword of the Turk and had never feared the spear of the Kurd. He saw that this multitude of workmen was capable when necessary, of laying down the spade and plow and to take up arms instead and use them with equal skill.

"In time of war, these men become our soldiers," said Vartan's host. "Work ceases for the most part, and for this reason war has always brought disastrous results in our land, although that has its advantages also."

Crossing the fields they approached the village again. A new building stood before them. It resembled one of those buildings which are built on model farms. "This is our village industrial school," said Vartan's host. "That which you saw this morning was the elementary school."

What sort of school was this? Vartan had never seen such a one although he had been a teacher once upon a time. It embraced in it all the branches which pertain to village economy. To this great institution was added an extensive farm, which was cultivated by the students themselves. There were specimens of almost all the plants of the land. Here books and dead matter no longer engrossed the pupils. They learned everything from the wonderful book of nature. Here at stated hours the pupils had gymnastic exercises and training in handling firearms.

"Surely such schools must produce good laborers and good soldiers." thought Vartan.

Vartan, after expressing his thanks to his host, now left him. Where should he go now? He did not know. He saw a sort of an omnibus with people riding on it. He took a seat there when he learned that it ran to the railway station.

At the station he found a great crowd awaiting the departure of the train. Suddenly a familiar voice was heard saying, "Vartan." Vartan looked back. There stood Salman. The two old friends embraced.

"See this, my friend," said Salman not releasing Vartan's hand. "We see one another again after two hundred years, a good long interval. You have remained the same, Vartan, you have not changed at all. But these two hundred years have brought great changes to our country. Do you remember, Vartan, once I said that Armenia is the cradle of the infancy of mankind. In the age of innocence it was Eden, but some day it will reach its maturity, and the Eden of its age of progress. Now this has been accomplished. Now the livelihood of Armenians is safe; pleasant and peaceful on their native soil. But if you had known how we worked till we brought it to this condition — we worked hard — we passed through a thousand vicissitudes. We bought our ease with much blood and sweat."

"Where are you going now?" asked Vartan.

"To the city. The meeting of the representatives is going to convene, and I am the delegate from our province. Let us go together, Vartan. I am going to speak. Our debates may interest you."

The last whistle sounded. They entered the railway carriage. It was night. Before dawn, they reached the city. The beautiful noisy city was still asleep. Only workmen were to be seen on the streets, hastening to their respective factories.

263

"To the Dove of Noah," Salman said to the driver. The cab rolled along straight smooth streets. Magnificent buildings lined the way. It seemed to Vartan that he was passing a row of palaces. Salman pointed out the various imposing buildings.

"This is the University, and that the Academy of Science. That is an old palace now used as a museum, the next, one of the finest theatres of the city, and that a Hospital. Those are the statues of heroes who became famous in the last revolution. This is a newspaper office which has a daily circulation of 150,000 copies. That...."

"Are there no barracks?" interrupted Vartan

"There are none. Here every citizen is a soldier."

"A beautiful city, a wonderful city," exclaimed Vartan with great delight.

The cab stopped before the Hotel Dove of Noah, Salman and Vartan entered a small private room adjoining the lobby. 'Here Thomas Effendi was arguing with Melik-Mansoor.

"That would be the martyrdom of asses," Thomas Effendi was saying. "In my opinion that is the best course to take to reach the desired goal," replied Melik-Mansoor warmly.

"That course would take us far from the desired goal and we might reach it by the asses Easter-time," said Thomas Effendi laughing.

"Here is Salman. Let us hear his opinion," they said pausing in their debate.

Great was their surprise when they saw Vartan who, it seemed to them, arose out of the ground.

"Where did you come from?" asked Thomas Effendi with his peculiar smile.

"My surprise is equal to yours," replied Vartan pressing his hand. "I found your mutilated corpse at the foot of the mountains of Alashgerd and afterwards I buried it in the Kurdish graveyard - and now"—

"Now I have risen again," he replied laughing. "Don't you believe in the transmigration of souls. My wretched soul passed through the bodies of the vilest of animals. It remained in the bodies of wolves for several decades. I ravaged, I lived on my prey. For another period I lodged in the

264

bodies of dogs. I made the rounds of those persons who fed me. For other decades I twisted and writhed in the bodies of snakes. I crept on the ground and bit as occasion arose. For several years I brayed in the bodies of asses. They pulled me about by the ears so much that I had no wits left. Finally my wretched soul entered the body of a lion. There I became considerably purified. This round was accomplished in about 200 years. The Egyptian mummies have remained for thousands of years in the pyramids, impatiently awaiting the return of their souls but my soul performed its circuit sooner."

"And I have the good fortune to behold the transformed Thomas Effendi." interrupted Vartan.

"Yes. The Thomas Effendi you saw before was the legitimate child of his age, but time has changed him. Now he is one of the good representatives of his age. But the present race has made great progress, Vartan. Do you remember how Melik-Mansoor called 'good needles' formerly, as he wandered through the streets of Alashgerd, and now he is the commander of a private company of soldiers."

Vartan turned to Melik-Mansoor and shook hands with respect.

"Gentlemen, we are delaying. The meeting is about ready to begin," said Salman hastily.

"He is the leader of the free-thinkers of our party," Thomas Effendi whispered in Vartan's ear, pointing to Salman. "He has prepared a great speech for the meeting today. Ah, what a fine speaker he is!"

"Take me too, gentlemen. I wish to hear his speech also," cried Vartan gladly.

"Let us go," said a strange voice near him.

Vartan opened his eyes and found that it was all a dream. The shades of night still surrounded him and he lay on unfortunate Lila's grave.

But what strange voice was that which had awakened him, and had said, "Let us go!"

Suddenly four strong hands seized him and everything was blotted in darkness.

**

265

www.ingramcontent.com/pod-product-compliance
Lightning Source LLC
Chambersburg PA
CBHW031535260326
41914CB00032B/1816/J